D1714379

John Dryden is a natural subject for a revisionist study of influence. His pioneering criticism, his influential translations, his drama, and his "succession" poems reveal his close engagement with a host of other writers (classical, English, and continental), and an unprecedented theorizing of that relationship. The five new essays comprising this book treat a number of complementary aspects of Dryden's literary relations, from his responses to predecessors and contemporaries, to his reception by successors.

Earl Miner's introduction addresses the issues of authorial transmission and reception. Jennifer Brady examines the nature of Dryden's attachments to his Renaissance precursors – notably Ben Jonson – and his handing over of that valued legacy to Congreve. David Kramer focuses on the imperialist strain in Dryden's appropriations from seventeenth-century French drama. Earl Miner's study of Dryden's translations of Ovid looks at *Fables Ancient and Modern* in the context of epic tradition, Milton, and Ovid's *Metamorphoses*. Greg Clingham reveals the ways in which Johnson's "Life of Dryden" illuminates continuities between Dryden's and Johnson's careers, as well as showing their distinct, individual geniuses.

The book will be of value not only to scholars of Dryden, his predecessors, contemporaries, and successors, but also as a contribution to the growing body of work on the nature of reception, influence, and intertextuality.

CAMBRIDGE STUDIES IN EIGHTEENTH-CENTURY
ENGLISH LITERATURE AND THOUGHT 17

Literary transmission and authority

CAMBRIDGE STUDIES IN EIGHTEENTH-CENTURY
ENGLISH LITERATURE AND THOUGHT

General Editors
Dr HOWARD ERSKINE-HILL, Litt. D., FBA, *Pembroke College, Cambridge*
and Professor JOHN RICHETTI, *University of Pennsylvania*

Editorial Board

Literary transmission and authority

Dryden and other writers

JENNIFER BRADY, GREG CLINGHAM,
DAVID KRAMER, and EARL MINER

EDITED BY

Earl Miner

Townsend Martin, Class of 1917,
Professor of English and Comparative literature,
Princeton University,

AND

Jennifer Brady

Charles R. Glover Chair of English Studies
Rhodes College

CAMBRIDGE
UNIVERSITY PRESS

Published by the Press Syndicate of the University of Cambridge
The Pitt Building, Trumpington Street, Cambridge CB2 1RP
40 West 20th Street, New York, NY 10011–4211, USA
10 Stamford Road, Oakleigh, Melbourne 3166, Australia

© Cambridge University Press 1993

First published 1993

Printed in Great Britain at the University Press, Cambridge

A catalogue record for this book is
available from the British Library

Library of Congress cataloguing in publication data

Literary transmission and authority: Dryden and other writers / by
Jennifer Brady ... [et al.]; edited by Earl Miner and Jennifer Brady
p.   cm. – (Cambridge studies in eighteenth-century English literature and thought)
Includes index.
ISBN 0–521–44111–0
1. Dryden, John, 1631–1700 – Criticism and interpretation – History.
2. Dryden, John, 1631–1700 – Knowledge – Literature. 3. Influence
(Literary, artistic, etc.) 4. Dryden, John, 1631–1700 – Influence.
5. English poetry – Roman influences. 6. Authority in literature.
7. Rome in literature. 8. Authorship – History. 9. Intertextuality.
I. Brady, Jennifer, 1952–   . II. Miner, Earl Roy. III. Series.
PR3424.L58 1993
821′.4 – dc20   92–29788 CIP

ISBN 0 521 44111 0 (hardback)

Contents

Contributing authors

JENNIFER BRADY holds the Charles R. Glover Chair of English Studies at Rhodes College, where she teaches Renaissance and Restoration literature. She is the co-editor, with W. H. Herendeen, of *Ben Jonson's 1616 Folio* (University of Delaware Press, 1991) and has published several essays on Ben Jonson's poetry. She is a graduate of the University of Toronto and received her doctorate from Princeton University.

GREG CLINGHAM has published on Dryden, Boswell, and Johnson in British, American, and French journals. He is the author of *James Boswell: "The Life of Johnson"* (Cambridge University Press, 1992) and has edited *New Light on Boswell: Critical and Historical Essays on the Occasion of the Bicentenary of Boswell's "Life of Johnson"* (Cambridge University Press, 1991). He has recently completed a critical study of Johnson's literary biography entitled *Writing Memory: The Integrity and Paradox of Johnson's "Lives of the Poets,"* and he is North American Editor of the new annual, *Translation and Literature.* Dr. Clingham has taught English at Cambridge, New York, and Fordham Universities, and he is an affiliate of Clare Hall, Cambridge.

DAVID KRAMER, an Assistant Professor at the University of Arkansas, has recently completed a second book on Dryden, *"What More I Shall Desire": Eros and Textuality in Dryden's Comic Drama.* A previous book, related to his chapter here, is entitled *The Imperial Dryden: The Poetics of Appropriation in Seventeenth-Century France and England,* and is forthcoming at The University of Georgia Press.

EARL MINER is Townsend Martin, Class of 1917, Professor of English and Comparative Literature at Princeton University. His interests include seventeenth-century English literature, Japanese literature, and comparative poetics.

Preface

Of all English authors, Dryden has special claims for attention in a study of literary authority and transmission. He is the first English critic to reflect at length on the acts of his own poetic creation; the first to theorize about translation; the first to posit the existence of literary ages or periods; and the first to seek to arrange poets in an order from those originating a literary culture to his own day. He followed Ben Jonson in giving close attention, not only to poets who were his contemporaries, but also to readers, seeking to inform and shape their responses by prefaces and epistles dedicatory to publications of his works. In his lifetime two momentous, related ideas about literature were emerging: that of literary originality (as also borrowing, plagiarism, seizure of rights held by others) and that of literary property. Without the growth of these ideas, the first English copyright act would not have come into being in 1709.

In trying to account for Dryden as authority and transmitter, we undertake a familiar, but by no means resolved, subject. Its outlines are clear: who does not know of Dryden on his predecessors in *An Essay of Dramatick Poesie* or of his full *Virgil* of 1697? But the former has raised new questions for recent readers, and the latter is mostly unstudied in important matters. There have been studies of Dryden and Shakespeare, centering on *All for Love*, or the remarks about Shakespeare, Jonson, and Beaumont and Fletcher in *An Essay of Dramatick Poesie*. There has not yet been a full study of that relationship that takes in the Roman (or classical) plays of both, the handling of comedy, tragicomedy, and tragedy, or numerous borrowings. If that is true of Dryden *vis-à-vis* the greatest English writer, it is all the truer of similar subjects involving other writers. On the other hand, as this study shows, there has been a rising interest in particular features of Dryden's relations with other authors, an interest fortified by James A. Winn's excellent biography of Dryden.

Subjects – fashions, some may say – in literary study arise in recognition of features of particular authors and their times. In English studies, the subject of influence revived naturally enough as part of the rehabilitation of Romanticism, with its expressive theory as a central principle. The expressivism led to preoccupation with originality as a major problem that was in part solved, if that is the word, by writing movingly about the problem itself. In writing about the difficulty of writing at all, poets often left highly ambitious works that were, at least seemingly, incomplete. Dryden writes often enough about his problems in writing, but these commonly involve financial support or protection. The common became acute late in his life by illness and the problems of his holding steadfastly both to a religion whose believers were penalized in England and to a political, sentimental Jacobitism he shared with that fellow steadfast "Yorkist," Samuel Pepys, and other constitutionalists like the nonjuring divines early in the reign òf William and Mary. In their poetry at least, the Romantic writers seem to have been less pressed financially, but they bore more heavily than their seventeenth-century predecessors the burdens of theoretical expressivism and principled originality.

Or did they? One of the central aims of this study is to explore, from differing vantage points, the nature of Dryden's authority in the very act of translating, or otherwise engaging with, other authors "ancient and modern."

In exploring such subjects, we do well to understand that English studies do not color the whole world pink, as maps of the British Empire once seemed to do. Study of interrelations between authors and nations has been a staple of comparative study from the beginning. The model currently most familiar in English studies is the Freudian one in which influence induces anxiety and repression. That model is congenial to portions of bourgeois western society, but it cannot be assumed for earlier western, or non-western, cultures. The central Indian preoccupation is the ceaseless retelling of a few immense works. In east Asia, literary language is, by definition, precedented language, and if there is anxiety it may be more properly termed the anxiety of not being influenced. Of course the English Romantics' compulsion to be original, which intensified whatever anxiety exercised a given poet, does not conceal their common literary inheritances, subjects, and treatments. (How many Romantic poems *are* there about fallings-off, dead poetic geniuses, and skylarks?) Similarly, for all their veneration of that past which defined them as writers, east Asian poets could not go on saying the same things in the same words. In east Asia, one could innovate by that Protestant urge (or dodge) of going back to the pristine. What was once exceptional might be made a normative precedent in China. A new Confucianism could redefine Korean interests. An innovative Japanese poet could plead the spirit of the first great poetic collection, the *Man'yōshū*. An innovating

Islamic poet could find justification in yet another saying by the Prophet in the Qu'rān.

These remarks imply not only that Dryden is a particularly fit subject for study of a complex of related issues, but also that assumptions devised to explain later English literature need not be accepted uncritically. It is also true, however, that the rehabilitation of "influence study" by Claudio Guillén and Harold Bloom has become a presence in the minds of students, of other authors, and even in the minds of those who have not read the works of the two named. The four authors of this book examine quite different portions of, and outlooks on, Dryden's remarkably varied literary career. As a result, we proceed from presumptions that are not at all identical.

In what we have written we do not pretend to exhaust the subject of Dryden and others, much less the theoretical and historical issues. But enough ground has been covered to make it seem desirable to sort out various issues from three perspectives: seventeenth-century English litera-ture, comparative evidence, and the literary and historical principles ("theory") involved. That purpose has prompted my introduction. Those who feel no need to consider such perspectives may proceed to the four main chapters. (It is editorial graciousness to grant what readers will do in any event, from looking for their own names in the index to casual sortes.) In all this, we hope that we have given a four-dimensional Dryden – not a Cubist poet descending the stairs, but a real poet credible as one in his time, a century later, and today.

Acknowledgments

Each of the contributors to this volume would like to thank John Richetti and Howard Erskine-Hill, the editors of Cambridge Studies in Eighteenth-Century Literature and Thought, for their welcoming of this project, and Cedric D. Reverand II for his meticulous reading of our chapters. His suggestions, clarifying objections, and questions have assisted us greatly, as did those of the press' first reader. Kevin Taylor, Josie Dixon, and the jacket designer worked closely with us at the production stage and their labors deserve special acknowledgment. Earl Miner and I also join in expressing out gratitude to Gillian Maude. In copyediting the manuscript, she combined an intelligent eye with a hand that moved her pencil when necessary and not otherwise.

As a close friend of mine is fond of remarking, gratitude may be one of the weaker of human emotions. It gives me particular pleasure, then, to thank Robert Entzminger, Sara van den Berg, Karen Robertson, and C. Anderson Silber for their support, their editorial instincts, and, in Andy's case, his nurturing of my interest in Dryden over many years. Rhodes College has been, as ever, generous with funding. Harmon C. Dunathan enabled the completion of this book through grants and encouraged the project from the outset. Judith Runyan and Gail Stroud helped; so too did Charles C. Wilkinson, who worked assiduously with me in preparing the index.

Jennifer Brady

Introduction: borrowed plumage, varied umbrage

EARL MINER

One of the rewards of reading Dryden's literary and critical writings – and one of the problems in teaching them – is the rich sense one obtains of his engagement with those who have mattered, and have continued to matter, in western culture. In a rapid survey of the index to George Watson's two-volume Everyman selection of Dryden's critical writings, one discovers about 130 references to English writers, almost a hundred to Graeco-Roman writers, some eighty-five to postclassical European writers, and a couple of dozen to non-literary artists. There is no precedent for such engagement, and who among us can name half the Graeco-Roman writers or half the British writers before Dryden whom he not only names but engages with? The surprising thing about the subject of Dryden's claim as authority and transmitter is that it has not been made, long ago, the explicit object of critical attention, much less a model of how writers conduct themselves in engaging with predecessors and contemporaries.

If not explicit or the basis of a model, the subject has necessarily arisen for nearly every critic of Dryden in some more or less tacit or practical fashion. The interfusion of literature, religion, politics, social organization, and economics in the century made proper authority a revolutionary issue of the state of letters as well as politics. Transmission was not play, but engagement with predecessors and contemporaries inevitable to any serious writer. In one mood, Donne could make "one little room an everywhere," but even for his awakening lovers the interest lay in finding the macrocosm in the human microcosm, the world in the bed – if not tossed in Robert Burton's blanket.

Wars and rumors of them preceded and accompanied Dryden's career. The sanguinary struggles that stained England's green and pleasant land

1

more often sounded in words from diverse sources like Samuel Butler's drum ecclesiastic, the pulpit. The parliamentary and Protectorate causes sought to restore England to a blest state supposed to exist before "the Norman yoke" was imposed. In that, and other, respects, major groups in the English Protestant Church Militant were deeply concerned with recovering the pristine truth of the Bible (altar, church discipline, windows not idolatrous) before it had been corrupted by that bugaboo, the Whore of Babylon, papacy. In reaching back to the ancient to remove what was untrue, the Puritans (that undefinable but conceptually indispensable group) discovered something of prime importance for a Dryden born into a Puritan family: one's own age is as historical as King David's or Augustus Caesar's. And if the good of the past can be recovered while ridding it of the evil, human progress is possible. As this example germane to Dryden shows, the engagement of one's present needs with rivals and with the past may produce unexpected results, unintended results often ultimately more important than what was sought to begin with.

The aim of the following chapters is to address what it means for a Dryden to engage with predecessors and contemporaries, and for a later critic – Samuel Johnson – to engage with a Dryden. This is a subject susceptible to definitions various in breadth and in nature. On a gradation of solely literary encounter (and let it be said again that the subject is by no means solely literary), there is at one extreme dark ignorance. It would have meant something if Butler, Milton, and Dryden had known the Indian or Middle High German epics.[1] But of course they did not. At a lesser extreme there are those works that are known, but that simply do not seem to matter – examples include Ausonius' *Mosella* and Frascatorius' *Syphilis*. From there we might consider the opposite extreme, downright plagiarism.[2] Between the extremes there exist complex congeries of practices, attitudes, and issues, only a few of which claim critical fashion at a given time. To the extent that we are unacquainted with fashions at other times and in other cultures, we think our own the sole natural ones and, what is worse, think temporarily reigning concerns the inevitable ones. Yet what is perhaps still worse is the ignoring of the historical and cultural developments that make the presence of a given constellation of issues understandable. And what is probably worst of all is the assumption of a single explanation. Neither this introduction nor the ensuing chapters will cover all the grounds that ought, in conscience, to be traversed: none of us has systematically or theoretically concentrated on religion, economics, politics, gender, and certain other matters crucial to seventeenth-century English experience. But what we do provide will underscore the belief of four people in the importance of the general topic of literary relations and in the necessity for differing approaches.

That general topic is extensive enough. It involves the ways writers use other writers, the ways critics use writers and other critics, and the ways in which readers use writers and critics. In fact, those "literary relations" constitute but a part of the topic. There are also the state and commercial producers; there are those who may be designated the police. There are also the often unspoken rules of the game, the silent as well as noisy ideologies – the systems of values often contradictory but far more often mutually reinforcing. And there are differences, if not conflicts, between various social groups, as well as national efforts to exert power or prestige, and consequently efforts by other nations to wield or to resist dominance. In short, there is too much even to enumerate at decent length in an introduction to a single book.

It is necessary, therefore, to clarify a few issues that affected Dryden, before moving on to more theoretical concerns with authorial inter-relationships. Since it is to Dryden that England owes its very concept of a literary period and of literary succession, it will not be amiss to begin with a series of symbolic historical moments relating to the general subject of this study.[3] After that brief review, we can inquire into the general issues of what relations between, or among, authors imply. We may close with application of these matters to Dryden.

The first symbolic moment is that of Plato and his student Aristotle in the Greek Academy. Plato conceived of three rivals for intellectual allegiance: philosophy, poetry, and rhetoric (*Republic*, 10; *Phaedrus*). Aristotle conceived of a far wider range of subjects, including not only those mentioned but ethics, various sciences, and metaphysics. Aristotle's *Poetics*, although apparently incomplete as we have it, makes clear that he also thought in terms of intellectual rivalry: poets are, he said, superior to historians. (He probably also thought them superior to rhetoricians, but definitely not to philosophers.) Together, Plato and Aristotle show that one necessary condition for literary study had been reached: the positing of literature as an autonomous branch of human knowledge.[4] A second symbolic moment is reached with Alexandrian scholarship and writing. The scholarship involved collections of earlier writers, so that the plays of Euripides were brought together in intelligible fashion and, it is even sometimes hesitatingly suggested, the Homeric poems were first divided into 24 units based on the letters of the Greek alphabet. The first great library in the west was founded. Literature had not only been separated, but institutionalized.

Horace benefitted from the Alexandrian achievement and its imitations

and, like numerous other Romans, studied in Greece. His achievement
was a dual one. For one thing, his concept of *imitatio* redefined imitation
from the Aristotelian technical sense of the cognitive literary act to
emulation of the Greeks. Along with that, out of his own writing of lyrics
and satires he posited literary affect as a differentia and "end" of literature
that had not been feasible in the Greek Academy.[5] The two achievements
are at one in his lyrics, where affect and adaptation of Greek prosodic
measures are indistinguishable.

The sense of literature as a separable human activity weakened in the
earlier Middle Ages, as the anonymity of poets (with other evidence)
testifies. By the later Middle Ages, however, authorship is again known
because again assumed to be important. Around 1200 we observe the
potentiality for literary rivalry among the Minnesinger, and the fact itself
between two highly gifted narrative poets, Wolfram von Eschenbach and
Gottfried von Strassburg. Gottfried went so far as to distinguish the
important narrative and lyric poets in German.[6]

The Renaissance is hardly a moment, and is too close to Dryden
(presuming he was not part of it) to specify with confidence or describe
with clarity features that he and we would recognize with equal force. But
a few may be hazarded. One is the new institutionalizing of literature,
with the French Academy as the dominant model.[7] As an "original
member" (who apparently did not pay his dues) of the Royal Academy
chartered by Charles II, and as a participant in the unfulfilled attempts by
Roscommon to establish a committee–academy on the English language,
Dryden was clearly interested in literary institutionalizing.[8] He also benefitted from appointments as poet laureate and historiographer royal (benefitted in prestige at least, and sometimes he was paid his promised
money). The ever uncertain combination of monies from such sources,
along with others from plays, from prologues and epilogues to plays by
others, from translations, and from patronage made Dryden the first of
that institution we can, with some show of truth, term the professional
poet, the "independent" man of letters. (Aphra Behn followed shortly as
the first woman of letters and the second person in England.) He was also
familiar with that Renaissance innovation, the literary quarrel. Although
the Italians produced a number of lively versions of it, the ones over
Guarini's *Pastor Fido* and over Corneille's *Cid* were particularly hard
fought. Dryden was well aware of French quarrels. Even if he had not
been, his sense of literary history and of period would necessarily have led
him to consider his relation to poets of the distant past, the more recent
past, and the present. He was perpetually discovering that his soul was like
whatever poet of old he was engaged with. And, like other writers, he

heats up the closer he gets to his own time, being much more *complexly* involved with the poets of "the last age" or century, meaning roughly to 1625, than with earlier writers. And, as "Mac Flecknoe" and the poem to Congreve suggest, working out relations with his contemporaries required great care and on occasion major adjustment.

By the eighteenth century, the developing sense that writers should be entitled to the works they had written had become a fully fledged (if not yet fully soaring) conception of literary property. Moreover, the ideal of literature in something like its restricted modern sense of *belles-lettres* had been formed. The burden of originality was developing more or less in course with that of authorial property, and both became crucial with the Romantics. It would be possible to follow these developments further, but the rest is more or less our modern possession, even if we are barely aware, for example, of how very recent is the institutionalizing of study of vernacular literature.

The phrase, "authorial interrelations," may not be especially canorous, and is but one among many important issues. The problem lies in finding a sufficiently neutral term. It becomes acute when the authorial is taken from the standpoint of but one of the human agencies involved, for instance the "transmitter" or, alternatively, the "appropriator," terms that feature some, and ignore others, of the crucial issues.[9] Transmittal inescapably implies a deliberate sending agency, and appropriation a seizing one. Neither is a necessary presumption. Homer had no idea of his transmitting anything to a Joyce for *Ulysses*, and few members of the Tribe of Ben were likely to lay rude hands on Father Ben's goods. If for "transmittal" we substitute "imposition" or "making available," we obviously have two possibilities differing more from each other even than from the concept of transmission. Similarly, if for "appropriation" we substitute "reflection" or "colonized," we imply quite different processes. Although, as we say, we often give voice to words thoughtlessly, we mean without due thought, carelessly. For there are no indeterminate terms (that would be a contradiction), and there are none innocent of bearing some past and present freight. None the less, we require not only names but specifiable meanings if we are to achieve clarity in our own minds and offer that clarity to others. A corollary holds that we depend on the clarity of those who attend to us, and that certainly is true of what follows.

Clarity is needed by one who seeks to reorder some thoughts about authorial relations by redefining three familiar terms: rivalry, influence, and reception. When the question arose of what title to give my first little book, it was clearly necessary to avoid at all costs the then disreputable, even pedantic word, "influence."[10] Rehabilitation of that term came first with Claudio Guillén's revival of it in the first two chapters of his "Essays Toward the Theory of Literary History."[11] Since then Harold Bloom has made a massive subject of it with a series of studies featuring chiefly Milton, Romantic, and selected modern poets.[12] It is clear that critics such as Guillén and Bloom have enjoyed close attention, and have altered ideas about authorial interrelations. It is not clear that their models are valid for all periods, genres, and literary cultures.

For that matter, although the etymological meaning of "influence" is as innocent a word as could be hoped for, basic presumptions of influence – especially the idea of transmittal – have not been acceptable to all. In his own series of studies, Dionýz Ďurišin has argued that what is called influence is better considered reception, since no matter what a given literature has to offer others, in practice what is important depends on the receivers' choices and, it may be added, commonly on their misunderstandings.[13] Although for some reason (the rather wooden English translations?), Ďurišin's work has been unjustly neglected, it has been unwittingly confirmed and enlarged upon by reception theory, whether as Rezeptionsästhetik, as affective stylistics, or under other labels.

The major differences between those who stress the transmitter and those the receiver are clear enough, as are the differences between critics who look on authorial interrelations as benign or neutral, and others, Bloom in particular, who conceive of the relation in agonistic terms. One unavoidable difficulty posed by *puissant* Bloom to a comparatist is that he works on the evidence of a single language and focuses on a relatively restricted period of poetic history. "Modernist" and "postmodernist" writers use their predecessors in ways differently from those described by Bloom.[14] It is certainly true that Bloom's Freudianism is the product of late nineteenth-century bourgeois European culture and, as such, has little, if any, applicability to other times and places. Catherine Belsey amusingly makes this point in regard to the Davenant–Dryden revision of *The Tempest*. Of the doubling of Miranda with another sister and the description of both as women who have never seen a man, Belsey comments on what a pre-Freudian era it is when a father does not constitute a man.[15] In other cultures such as the east Asian, the centuries of Confucianism (not to mention other acculturations of human sexuality) led to such veneration of precursors as to make Freud irrelevant. To Chinese, Korean, and Japanese poets, there was a language of poetry, and that language was defined as precedented language. Their burden was not to be original, but to be faithful. There is another problem with Bloom's model. He seems to imply that his "Theory of Poetry" applies to all kinds of writing, but his subtitle and his evidence weigh in a scale of verse. If his account had validity, it would apply as much to novelists, dramatists, essayists and, for that matter, writers not considered literary in usual categories.

Bloom's and other recent conceptions of authorial interrelations in English literature might be explored for further utility. But the conceptions have been too readily presumed universal in applicability, when in fact they are limited chronologically, culturally, and in terms of their range of pertinence. The last especially concerns me. By restricting ourselves to poetry or even to literature, we have excluded much else that is important. Literature does not exist in the historical or cultural vacuum to which too many of our studies seem to have consigned it. The point is obvious, before our noses, which has not assisted its being taken in, anymore than has the contradicting evidence from other literary cultures.

Another important matter requires attention. Any account of the relations between one writer and others – say, Dryden and Shakespeare, Jonson, or Racine – requires assurance that the writers involved have been sufficiently defined and understood, if an account of their relations is to carry conviction. There must be historical and logical bases for connection or comparison to be valid.

The tenor of my preceding remarks is sufficiently clear – but negative. What follows therefore turns to positive argument that will involve Dryden among other examples. Because Harold Bloom has figured as an actual and heuristic presence in the preceding pages, we may begin with rivalry.[16] And, having rejected his central view of the matter, we must seek an alternative. Rivalry such as Bloom posits under the title of influence should be considered chiefly, although not solely, to involve writers who are contemporaries. Anyone personally acquainted with writers – whether poets or novelists, historians, or philosophers – knows that, although a writer may have a quarrel with Vida or Vico, the vital concern is with living Jacks and Janes. As it happens, there is plain testimony to the fact from the very field – English Romantic poetry – that Bloom has chosen as his agonistic arena. William Hazlitt says it well in his essay, "On the Living Poets."

I cannot say that I ever learnt much about Shakespeare or Milton, Spenser or Chaucer, from these professed guides [i.e., "the most popular poets of the day"]; for I never heard them say much about them. They were always talking of themselves and one another. Nor am I certain that this sort of personal intercourse with living authors, while it takes away all relish or freedom of opinion with regard to their contemporaries, really enhances our respect for themselves.[17]

Hazlitt's remarks have confirmation from other periods, cultures, and kinds of writing. They apply not only to the English Romantic poets, but to Pindar and his competitors in writing odes, to Chinese poets vying for office by the implications of their poems, and to modern mouth-watering over Nobel prizes. The subject is susceptible to comparative treatment. Hazlitt's remarks could be extensively examined by comparative study, for example by an examination of resemblances and differences between Athenian competitions in the writing of plays and Japanese competitions in poetry matches.

Examples nearer Dryden will better serve our immediate interests, however. For the second edition of *Paradise Lost*, Milton included a notice, "The Verse," at the bookseller's urging. The bookseller introduced the matter of Milton's prosody by saying that the lack of rhyme had "stumbled" many readers. Let us hear Milton out.

> The Measure is *English* Heroic Verse without Rime, as that of *Homer* in Greek, and of *Virgil* in *Latin*; Rime being no necessary Adjunct or true Ornament of Poem or good Verse, in longer Works especially, but the Invention of a barbarous Age, to set off wretched matter and lame Meeter; grac't indeed since by the use of some famous modern Poets, carried away by Custom, but much to thir own vexation, hindrance, and constraint to express many things otherwise, and for the most part worse than else they would have exprest them. Not without cause therefore some both *Italian* and *Spanish* Poets of prime note have rejected Rime both in longer and shorter Works, as have also long since our best *English* Tragedies, as a thing of it self, to all judicious ears, triveal and of no true musical delight; which consists onely in apt Numbers, fit quantity of Syllables, and the sense variously drawn out from one Verse into another, not in the jingling sounds of like endings, a fault avoyded by the learned Ancients both in Poetry and all good Oratory. This neglect then of Rime so little is to be taken for a defect, though it may seem so perhaps to vulgar Readers, that it rather is to be esteem'd an example set, the first in *English*, of ancient liberty recover'd to Heroic Poem from the troublesom and modern bondage of Rimeing.[18]

This is sometimes thought to be aimed at Dryden. If so, it has to do more with plays than with heroic poems. (And "vulgar Readers" seems a strange designation for a single contemporary.) For, as Milton comes to admit, *Paradise Lost* is "the first" epic written in English (since the Old English poetry he did not know of) that does not rhyme. More recently, in rhymed verse of varying kind, there had been Cowley's *Davideis*, Davenant's *Gondibert*, Chamberlayne's *Pharonnida*, Butler's *Hudibras*, and Dryden's *Annus Mirabilis*. Spenser and the Italian poets (who are the Spanish non-rimers he has in mind?) "of prime note" wrote in rhymed verse. Milton's complaint applies to contemporaries and all but a few lesser epic or similar poets he could have known of in vernacular languages. He professes to have thrown off not only "the Norman yoke," but also the whole "modern," or postclassical "bondage of Rimeing." Here is an example both of the anxiety of not being influenced and of Milton's radical Protestant pride in going back to a pristine, classical standard. It is no accident that *Paradise Lost* and later *Paradise Regained* are the first vernacular poems in English set forth like Homer and Virgil and Ovid in Renaissance editions: with marginal numbering of lines.

In 1678, that bludgeoning critic, Thomas Rymer, closed his *Tragedies of the Last Age* with something between a promise and a threat: "I shall also send you some reflections on that *Paradise lost* of Milton's, which some are pleas'd to call a poem; and assert Rime against the slender Sophistry wherewith he attacques it."[19] Both firm and hearsay evidence shows that Dryden admired Milton, probably in the older sense of feeling awe and wonder as well as respect. His most stringent remarks appeared in that gallimaufry of criticism that was prefixed to his *Satires* (1693).

As for Mr. *Milton*, whom we all admire with so much Justice, his Subject is not that of an Heroique Poem; properly so call'd: His Design is the Losing of our Happiness; his Event [outcome] is not prosperous, like that of all other Epique Works: His Heavenly Machines [God, the Son, the angels] are many, and his Humane Persons are but two. But I will not take Mr. *Rymer*'s Work out of his Hands. He has promis'd the World a Critique on that Author; wherein, tho' he will not allow his Poem for Heroick, I hope he will grant us, that his Thoughts are elevated, his Words Sounding, and that no Man has so happily Copy'd the Manner of *Homer*; or so copiously translated his *Grecisms*, and the *Latin* Elegancies of *Virgil*. 'Tis true, he runs into a flat of Thought, sometimes for a Hundred Lines together, but 'tis when he is got into a Track of Scripture ... Neither will I Justifie *Milton* for his Blank Verse, tho' I may excuse him, by the Example of *Hannibal Caro*, and other *Italians*, who have us'd it: For whatever Causes he alledges for the abolishing of Rhyme (which I have not now the leisure to examine) his own particular Reason is plainly this, that Rhyme was not his Talent; he had neither the Ease of doing it, nor the Graces of it; which is manifest in his *Juvenilia*, or Verses written in his Youth [no doubt the reprinted, augmented 1645 *Poems*]: Where his Rhyme is always constrain'd and forc'd, and comes hardly from him.

(*Works*, 4: 14–15)

Many thing may be said of this passage.[20] One of them is that Milton's haughty condescension to rhyme, with its distortions, is repaid by Dryden, with his distortions.

Dryden paid heed to other rivals, or contemporaries, besides Milton. There was George Villiers, second Duke of Buckingham, who played the major role in *The Rehearsal*, that satire of contemporary dramatists, and especially Dryden. As is well known, Dryden repaid the favor of hostile attention in devising the "character" of Zimri in *Absalom and Achitophel*, which concludes:

> Begger'd by Fools, whom still he found too late:
> He had his Jest, and they had his Estate.
> He laught himself from Court, then sought Relief
> By forming Parties, but coud ne're be Chief:
> For, spight of him, the weight of Business fell
> On *Absalom* and wise *Achitophel*:
> Thus, wicked but in will, of means bereft,
> He left not Faction, but of that was left.   (2: 561–68)

In the same meandering disquisition where he discusses Milton, Dryden takes satisfaction in his Zimri: "''Tis not bloody, but 'tis ridiculous enough. And he for whom it was intended, was too witty to resent it as an injury." He adds, "I avoided the mention of great Crimes ... It succeeded as I wish'd; the Jest went round, and he was laught at in his turn who began the Frolick" (*Works*, 4:71). That was far from the way Buckingham saw it, as a poem, "To Dryden," in his commonplace book shows:

> As witches images of man invent
> To torture those they're bid to represent.
> And as that true live substance does decay
> Whilst that slight idol melts in flames away,
> Such and no lesser witchcraft wounds my name,
> So thy ill-made resemblance wastes my fame.[21]

Buckingham could do no more. Dryden truly held over the ducal head the omission of "great crimes." If Buckingham tried public words, Dryden could remind the world of certain private deeds. The mercurial lord had infatuated the "sweet Maria," Marvell's name for Mary, daughter of Thomas, Lord Fairfax, who broke her engagement (after banns had been read twice) to the Earl of Chesterfield to marry Buckingham – who subsequently entered into open double adultery with the Duchess of Shrewsbury, whose husband he mortally wounded in a duel.[22]

We could consider other contemporaries such as Edward Hyde, Lord Clarendon, Anne Killigrew, Sir Godfrey Kneller or that complex matter – more in the Buckingham vein – of John Wilmot, Earl of Rochester.[23] What emerges is no less important for being simple. Dryden's response to potentially rival contemporaries varies greatly from individual to individual. It has been all too common for theorists of authorial interrelations to presume that they must be of the same kind and intensity. Evidence as well as common sense indicates that Dryden responds differently to Milton and to Shadwell as also, for that matter, to Oldham and to Congreve, all of whom were in some sense his rivals. Moreover, each of them responded differently to him. Any monolithic explanation does not bear serious consideration.

Rivalry extends much farther, crossing national borders as readily as a hot wind. Dryden's early dramatic criticism is marked by a rivalry with French and Spanish dramatists that sometimes leads him to new insights and at other times to vapidity: "of late years *Moliere*, the younger [i.e., Thomas] *Corneille*, *Quinault*, and some others, have been imitating afar off the quick turns and graces of the *English* Stage" (*Works*, 17:45). An emptier statement about contemporary French drama would be hard to devise. To be sure, Dryden's groundless patriotism is of a piece with the insular chauvinism running from Sidney to F. R. Leavis, which is to say through much of the best English criticism.

There is another tradition of rivalry that goes back to the Greeks but that is heightened in English criticism. Sidney held poets superior not only to historians (as Aristotle had) but also to philosophers. Dryden takes pains to show poetry superior as well to painting and science.[24] Neither critic goes to such detailed lengths to discredit other arts and "sciences" as Davenant does in his preface to *Gondibert*. Once again, we observe that a relevant category is not uniform, but varied.

As with the subject of rivalry, much the same holds for our second kind of authorial or literary relation, influence, which will also benefit from a clearer construal. In modern English, a person or institution with influence is one enjoying a certain sway, whether because of power, reputation, or trust. When influence is resisted, rivalry enters to a varying degree. Influence (as defined here) therefore presumes a fundamental inequality, which may beget a weaker rivalry and, as we shall see, varying reception as well.

Once again, *An Essay of Dramatick Poesie* provides useful evidence with its openly debated (and some more concealed) rival values. Three issues are debated: the relative merits of the ancients and the moderns, of contemporary French and English drama, and of rhymed versus unrhymed verse in "serious" plays. Dryden presumes that an intelligent case can be made for each alternative, as also that a given position may be more complex than it appears. For example, Crites, who largely loses in arguing on behalf of ancient drama, is himself a modern in "philosophy" or science.[25] And although Lisideius seems to lose his argument that current French drama is greater than English, Dryden gives him some hilarious and astute things to say about the absurdities of English theatrical conventions. Dryden does come down, with whatever qualifications, on the side of the moderns, the English, and rhymed verse. The opposition to the achievement of contemporary French drama deserves special examination.[26]

In 1664, Samuel Sorbière's *Relation d'un Voyage en Angleterre* chastised the English stage for its lack of rhyme (recall Milton!) and failure to observe the unities. Thomas Sprat replied in the following year and, slightly later, Dryden composed his *Essay*. These facts obscure the far more important conditions of the situation. French critics otherwise were almost entirely indifferent to English drama (until Voltaire), presuming, as influencing powers do, that only what is written on their terms – in French by French writers for French production – was worthy of consideration. Charles II had spent most of his "travels" in France. (Perhaps his subsequent sojourn in Spain helps explain Dryden's additional concern with "Spanish plots" in his *Essay*, where English drama is implied to be a golden mean between French rules and Spanish heterogeneity.) With their Sun King, for whom Dryden rarely had a good word, with their Academy, and with their aggressive foreign policy, the French were the obvious cultural imperialists, the influencers of the time. Of course Dryden was well aware of English commercial rivalry with the Netherlands and said grumpy, ungracious things about the "Dutch commentators" in editions of the classics that he none the less drew on. But Holland did not set up as a literary power. Even today, the French seek to maintain a cultural sway through what may be described as gestures of *la gloire*.[27]

Influence so conceived always has its positive and negative sides: what is to be followed and what avoided. Thus, a positive model like French classicism may be imperialistically decreed as the model for any country presuming to consider itself civilized. Of course the negative features involve either explicit or tacit rejection of what does not fit the positive canons. Tacit rejection is often harder to discern, because it commonly wears the mask of acceptance, or openly accepts one thing while silently rejecting others. That can be shown by a striking example from a different kind of literature in another literary age: the novel during the past century.

As is well known, Pound and Yeats were highly receptive to nō, following Pound's Vorticist enthusiasm for "hokku." Hearn and others sought to integrate Buddhism with western thought; Pound used Confucianism with enthusiasm; and I. A. Richards drew on Mencius. Japanese lacquerware ("japan"), prints, and pottery also show how features of Asian culture could enter European social and artistic practice; but kinds of literary prose narrative were denied visas by western literary consuls. Neither the *monogatari*, so superlatively handled in *The Tale of Genji* and *The Tale of the Heike*, nor the popular "modern Japanese novel" (*shōsetsu*), nor the "six great classical Chinese novels [*xiaoshuo*]" have been drawn on by our writers. Japanese, Chinese, Indian, and other traditions of literary prose narrative have not been judged much better than exotica by western novelists. The reason is obvious: Asian versions offered too serious alternatives to the novel, which has been traditionally taken to define ordinary reality. To that idea of how things are and should be, alien forms of prose narrative were denied access.[28]

As a single individual, Dryden could not exercise true cultural hegemony. In fact, he not only criticized (Spanish) exploitation of the New World (*The Indian Queen*, *The Indian Emperour*); he also worked with Davenant in redesigning *The Tempest* along the lines of post-Shakespearean dramatic treatments of sea voyages to feature the founding of a new state. Moreover, it was this conservative who introduced into English, perhaps after the example of his "honest Montaigne," the phrase, "the noble savage."[29] It is striking that a writer who innovated so much did not write even a proto-novel; the nearest he approached it was in his dialogue of *dramatic* poesy. He resisted lowering the heroic except for satire – which classically was written in the hexameters of epic and by Dryden in the couplets *cum* triplets of his heroic literary medium, his medium of verse – except in some tragedies, in songs, and in odes.

In smaller, but by no means negligible, matters Dryden resisted influence, although he might seize and make his own what others had devised, as David Kramer argues. To choose examples of avoidance and hegemonic seizure of other kinds, we can begin with his rejection of the Spenserian and Miltonic language of art in favor of an idiom far closer to what the people of his day actually spoke. Take this from *Absalom and Achitophel*:

> During his Office, Treason was no Crime;
> The Sons of *Belial* had a glorious Time:
> For *Shimei*, though not prodigal of pelf,
> Yet lov'd his wicked Neighbour as himself.   (597–600)

We seem meant to recall:

> In Courts and Palaces he also Reigns
> And in luxurious Cities, where the noyse
> Of riot ascends above their loftiest Towrs,
> And injury and outrage: And when Night
> Darkens the Streets, then wander forth the Sons
> Of *Belial*, flown with insolence and wine.
>
> (*Paradise Lost*, 1: 497–502)

(Dryden also seems to pun on "Balliol," the college where the Whigs caucused for the Oxford Parliament.) How much more natural is Dryden's "The Sons of *Belial* had a glorious Time," and how deliciously the stress falls on "glorious." That stress in turn anticipates Dryden's next couplet which, if it issued from Milton's pen, would no doubt have begun, "Of pelf not prodigal ..." Who remembers Milton for anything like the opening of the poem to Congreve: "Well then; the promis'd hour is come at last"? Milton aimed at grandeur, soaring above the sun, but proved a model of disastrous twilight for many a later, emulative Icarus. Dryden aimed at the natural terrestrial topography of English, and has proved a happy model for anyone with the wit to follow him.

In addition to such major decisions on the kind of subject suitable and the language to express what suited, Dryden made innumerable decisions that seem small today. A favorite exercise of seventeenth-century poets was providing a new version of Horace's Satire 1: 9 on being accosted by a bore in the Via Sacra. Donne, Jonson, and Marvell are no less original – or rather individual, since originality is a concept that concerned Dryden more than them – but Dryden's avoidance of the model says something. Similarly his avoidance of other standard topics: advice to a painter, Adam's fall, the Passion, the blazon, the "persuasion to enjoy," the imperfect enjoyment, the ramble, etc.[30]

On the other hand, what he does do is equally striking in its claim. With Milton, he continues lyricism for its last great moment until the Romantics. As Milton made the sonnet a trumpet in his hand (so Wordsworth said), Dryden claimed the human voice for the sopranos and tenors of his songs in plays, and the instrumental ensemble along with voices for cantatas like his St. Cecilia Day odes and his semi-operas.

In some of the things we identify as specifically Drydenian, he seems to have been the originator, and in others the latest to receive the letter patent. His major technical achievement is unquestionably the devising of a new, more natural language for poetry. It is not fashionable to say so, but his achievements in prose *outside the plays* are often strangely old-fashioned set beside Hobbes – or even Sidney, the author of the *Defence*, not of the two versions of the *Arcadia*.[31] He perpetually seems to be about to discover the modern paragraph only to lose it. His diction includes various old words (or meanings) alongside words he appears to have introduced into English. Anyone who has had to edit Dryden knows that the *Oxford English Dictionary* frequently cites his usage as the first or the last. For example as first: *biography*, *character* (person in a literary work), and *hero* (the chief male character in a literary work). And at times one discovers a usage by him that antedates the first *Dictionary* reference: one example is *heroine* (*De Arte Graphica, Works*, 20: 53, as opposed to *OED*, 1715). Other novelties include that sprightly comic invention, "the gay couple."[32]

Often, however, what seems so importantly Dryden's involves gold refined by others that he stamps with his own features as sovereign. With this appropriation we are required to recognize, if we have not done so already, the crossing of the issues of reception, influence, and originality.

The simplest instance is obvious: his translations. But another is afforded by his incomparable prologues and epilogues. In no wise his actual invention, they might yet make a difference – when written for plays by others – whether or not an author received third night's profits. There are two further dramatic examples. Although in more than one respect Dryden's heroic plays are not understood, it is clear that predecessors like Orrery deserve credit for the English invention, and that French models were crucial.[33] Because he made the case for heroic drama so strongly, Dryden seems to be granted title as inventor; and perhaps he did come to believe that he had first glimpsed its possibilities. There is also the last issue debated in *An Essay of Dramatick Poesie*: the proper medium for plays. The rhymed couplet was originally an acquired enthusiasm, a new development in Dryden's dramatic career, and it was followed in due course by a shift to dominant blank verse far rougher in cadence than that he had used early or in mid-career. Since the difference is visible after his collaboration with Nathaniel Lee on *Oedipus*, it seems natural to attribute the difference in Dryden's blank verse between, say, *All for Love* and *Don Sebastian* to what he discovered from Lee.

The examples given vary greatly in nature, and once again the variety must be held a matter of major importance. Whether from his own devising or from his adapting the devisings of others, Dryden shows little sense of strain in laying implicit or explicit claim to diverse kinds of literary practice. Although, paradoxically, the explicit *practice* or instituting of critical prose discussion of literature in prefaces and epistles dedicatory is actually more original than many of the causes argued for, the fact that Dryden was the copious *author* of criticism gave him the power to exercise great influence on others. A novelty, a programmatic hope shared with others but articulated by him, became his property to the minds of those who read his criticism then, and of those who read it now. The most long-lasting influence of his criticism was his instituting of critical discourse; for contemporaries, the influence involved propagation of ideas, argument, and emulation. Both then and now he often seems to claim, and frequently to be granted, full rights and title. He did not need to say that he created the heroic play or prologues and epilogues any more than that he had invented the "Pindaric ode" (which in fact Jonson or Cowley could better claim to have invented). Conspicuous practice, with or without conspicuous justification, gave him claim, just as Shakespeare's *Hamlet* and *The Tempest* seem definitive for the potentialities respectively of the revenge play and the theatrical romance.

Once again, emphasis must fall on the *variety* of kinds of influence Dryden exerted – large and small, trumpeted or silent. For that matter, there is as much variety in the degree of hegemonic claim or apparent claim as there is in the adequacy of the claim.

The assumption of authority that is central to influence relates contemporaneously to financial benefit and reputation, as ultimately to fame. In Dryden's development as a dramatic writer, that authority may shift its grounds and be treated in the sober sentences, and few are more sober, of an Allardyce Nicoll's account of theatrical "development." Alternatively, one could summon indignation for the authoritarianism of Dryden's "higher mimesis" in the instance of what he made of Shadwell in "Mac Flecknoe" by comparison to what he made of Oldham in "To the Memory of Mr. Oldham." As with rivalry, then, so with influence: a single term includes a multiplicity of phenomena. No doubt danger lies in the failure to see the ground common to the various kinds of influence. Distortion is far more likely to come, however, from assuming that all things given a name are the same in quality and importance, or are alike from one author to the next.

Influence cannot be separated more than theoretically, however, from reception. In fact, we may often define reception, with Ďurišin, as what often passes for influence. Perhaps it requires saying that reception is the use in given practice of that which is chronologically prior; similarly, reception depends on the identifiable existence of an element shared by authors and yet subordinate to the inevitable differences between authors. That is, what goes from A to B is determined by the receiver B instead of the supposed "donor" A.

The centrality of the act of authorial reception testifies to a further principle: the later, receiving writer can only draw on the earlier by means of an interpretation of the earlier. A new understanding – full or partial, hostile or friendly – is necessarily involved, because the ends of the receiving writer are not those of the writer received.

Of course Byronism would not have become the European phenomenon it did without a Byron. But that does not explain why Byron was chosen rather than Shelley – or Goethe. We more or less confidently distinguish (European) Medievalism, the Renaissance, the Baroque, Neoclassicism, and Romanticism as discrete periods. Yet they could all be judged alike, in contrast to Chinese literary periods, in that they all involve receptive choice of dominant models from Greek and, more particularly, Latin authors. During most of the lengthy duration of European literary history, Islamic, Asian, and east Asian authors were unknown, and probably would not have been "received" even if they were. African art has had an important reception by modern western artists. Why has not Islamic or central American? The simple and obvious (if not complete) answer is that, although they were in principle knowable, the desire to know was lacking.

A corollary is that what is eagerly received differs, in varying degree, from what is there to be borrowed. All interpretations are not equally valid – or, although this is a different issue, equally interesting – especially when the interpreters are enthusiasts who do not command the language of the original. So-called haiku offers one example, and Chinese poetry another. Poets often prove poor students but good friends of the predecessors they draw on. As has been remarked with great happiness, Pound's "Asianisms" offer "felicitous howlers."[34] Attention to reception also enables us to appreciate the importance of intermediaries, whether the prized Ernest Fenollosa to Pound or derided Dutch commentators to Dryden. It also explains what Dryden surely understood as well as anyone, the growing importance of literary translations.

We have been seeing how interrelated are influence, originality, and reception – whether in terms familiar to Dryden, to the Romantics, or to ourselves. To raise one of these issues is inevitably to raise another, and, precisely because Dryden reflected on his activity as no English author had before and as few have since, the issues will often command attention even when one is concerned with what seems another matter entirely. There is, for example, that side of Dryden perhaps least known of his major achievements: the stage. No other poet has written so many poems as Dryden about matters of theater. Putting aside all his prologues and epilogues along with his stand-in composition to "Gentle" George Etherege, we are left with poems to, or about, several dramatists: Granville, Lee, Motteux, and Southerne. Of course there are two more, "Mac Flecknoe," which *deals* with Shadwell, and "To my Dear Friend Mr. Congreve." These two last are uncannily alike.[35] In both we find a monologue by the abdicating prince of drama to the successor most like him except in the successor's not uttering a word. The fusion of the artistic with the monarchic is remarkable in both poems, although what is comic bathos in the one is dignified pathos in the other, as both Jennifer Brady's and Greg Clingham's chapters in this volume show. One major element in "Mac Flecknoe," however, is missing from the poem to Congreve: religion. What Dryden could locate and validate ironically in the satire was a topic off limits in the panegyric. The times had changed, but not Dryden with them.

The distinction between monarchy and religion as fields of value is essentially ideological.[36] The poem on Shadwell and the poem to Congreve are so similar in other than religious respects that Dryden could only have been aware that he was seriously parodying his own earlier poem.

The principle involved is one that we have seen with rivalry and influence. No matter how similar the situation or the treatment, it is variety, difference, that rules.

Of course there are some constants. As stressed at the outset, Dryden had – as a poet, for his poetry – unusually close engagement with his contemporaries. His major known rivalries have been mentioned. Yet the evidence of his poetry is confirmed from other sources: he got on well with most of his contemporaries whom we continue to regard highly.[37] The public events that underlie his "higher mimesis" testify to much the same thing. The tensions and temper of the whole century were sorely tried by the need to keep choosing one's side as events overtook one decision after another. We in a safer day are apt to think biographically of these matters as tests of character. So they may be. But they are something more that is central to Dryden's reception of his time and his contemporaries. He looked upon choice as a moral act of the will (*Works*, 20: 60). But, prior to the choice, the nature of the situation and its possibilities required understanding.

The same holds true of reception of writings by earlier figures as well. Interpretation is a necessity, and interpretation necessarily involves ideology.[38] Dryden's social ideology was as conservative as his literary was liberal, with the opposite holding for Milton. (I know of no effort to plumb these profound matters.) His interpretation of the authors he "received" was in general as hospitable as can be found in the age, or perhaps in other ages as well. For a contrast, one need only think of Milton's attitude towards his own age: disfavor heightened at times to hysteria. Without examining the wild flailing of *Eikonoklastes*, there is that paragraph on the verse of *Paradise Lost*.

How confident my judgment sounds! Yet the remarks involve the double nature of the account of a writer's reception: how can we know what a Milton or a Dryden knows? The "hermeneutics of trust" leads to ends different from the "hermeneutics of suspicion," and often to different evidence being used to validate an interpretation. We four authors of this book possess no miracle enabling us to step out of our personalities; like others, in writing of "the same author," we write unwittingly of ourselves. For that matter, we four hardly think completely alike – about what Dryden understood of what previous writers understood.

Nowhere in this study is the interpretive problem more acute than in my chapter, since Ovid's *Metamorphoses* has been notoriously the most difficult of classical poems to interpret rationally. The true answer as to how we can understand Dryden's understanding of Ovid is, "Imperfectly," as with all else important whose nature and meaning we seek to know. With the addition of tact, taste, luck, and other unlegislatable factors, it remains true that one requires historical evidence concerning Ovid, Dryden, and what may be termed Dryden's Ovid. The best evidence itself requires a critical understanding that is never a given of evidence alone.

Previous studies of rivalry, influence, and reception have ended at such a point: interpretation of whatever is taken to be Dryden's greatest or most revealing writing. We have chosen to go a step further to exemplify the issues posed by our study. We have chosen to include examination of how Dryden was understood by a major later author. Several choices for that later author are appealing, largely because Dryden did not have the baneful effect that was worked on later writers by Miltonism (so distinguishing a phenomenon from the greatest English poet's works themselves). Pope presents a valuable opportunity, partly because he found so much to emulate in Dryden that Dryden-and-Pope is an indistinguishable entity to many people who think themselves well read. Pope's generous remarks about Dryden refute the notion that one strong poet must seek to slay the strong predecessor. Or one might take a far more complex instance, that of T. S. Eliot, whose career was modelled on Dryden's (a Catholic in religion, a monarchist in politics, a classicist in literature; an attempt to be a playwright; an attempt at a dialogue on drama). "The Wasteland" is one of the descendants of "Mac Flecknoe," but out of its first great descendant, Pope's *Dunciad*.

Two matters are involved in Dryden's literary and critical wake: critical principle and choice of critical example. Our critical principle holds that to understand an artist's place in a complex of reception and influence – in authorial interrelations – it is necessary to consider succession as well as precedence. This principle has led to a host of studies of various kinds – the allusions to Chaucer, the adaptations of Shakespeare, the influence of Milton – but it has not been applied deliberately in the fashion of this book. That fashion involves the assumption that interrelations between authors require examination of an author's relation to three kinds of others: predecessors, contemporaries, and successors. Our critical example of the successor is, seemingly inevitably, Samuel Johnson.

The Great Cham seems to readers of Dryden today to have got a number of things wrong, and some of his historical information was in error. His strong emphasis on biography is not today's ruling passion in criticism. But what a mighty understanding Johnson possessed! He surveyed English poetry from the Metaphysicals to his own time, and his very insistence on the personality or character of the poet in lieu of textuality and intertextuality guarantees that he was responding to, involved in the reception of, Dryden as fully as was humanly possible.

In fact, it is clear that Dryden – limitations, warts, and all – was Johnson's idea of the modern poet. So many and such different poets have succeeded Dryden and Johnson that it requires an act of historical imagination to appreciate the place our poet held in Johnson's account of English poetry. Yet this so to speak unobserved Johnsonian assessment of Dryden as the modern poet affects us in ways we are unaware of. We are well used to the idea that our reception of a poet is influenced by previous, intervening criticism. But we have not honored the familiar concept in critical practice by considering that our approach to Dryden's reception of earlier writers may *require* inquiry into subsequent reception of him and his reception.

The principle is a crucial one, and it is illustrated, honored by Johnson's special treatment of Dryden (as also by Greg Clingham's chapter here). Only reconsideration of Dryden enters in a major fashion into the life and works of another poet. That instance occurs in the famous comparison of the two poets in the "Life of Pope." The attempt to maintain a balance is so scrupulous that the concluding confession of a preference for Dryden over Pope comes as a surprise with my every reading of the passage.[39]

There is, however, another passage that seems to have been ignored. In reviewing Johnson's *Lives of the English Poets*, James Boswell has a fascinating paragraph dealing with Dryden:

> In drawing Dryden's character, Johnson has given, though I suppose unintentionally, some touches of his own. Thus: – 'The power that predominated in his intellectual operations was rather strong reason than quick sensibility. Upon all occasions that were presented, he studied rather than felt; and produced sentiments not such as Nature enforces, but meditation supplies. With the simple and elemental passions as they spring separate in the mind, he seems not much acquainted. He is, therefore, with all his variety of excellence, not often pathetick; and had so little sensibility of the power of effusions purely natural, that he did not esteem them in others.' It may indeed be observed, that in all the numerous writings of Johnson, whether in prose or verse, and even in his Tragedy, of which the subject is the distress of an unfortunate Princess, there is not a single passage that ever drew a tear.[40]

Boswell's shrewd insight implies an important principle about responses to major writers: a response tells as much about the one responding as about the one responded to. Setting aside what the passage tells us of the passionate Boswell, we see that Johnson's discussion of a deficiency he found in Dryden was a way of dealing with highly similar features of his own possibility. It is all too easy to simplify Boswell's principle: for example, by considering solely negative features or by presuming that a strong point can be turned on its maker simply by reversal of direction.

Such matters granted, the important principle remains. What is important in a major writer brings out comparable features in the critic (including a later poet or a modern theorist), which is also to say that a given strong response reflects in kind on its maker. Like every other principle of criticism, this may be misapplied, but its force can be appreciated by rereading Dryden on earlier writers as well as later readers (including poets) on him. Two further examples will serve: Thomas Rymer as a critic of Shakespeare and of Milton; ourselves and our contemporaries in our response to individual earlier writers. *Caveat lector.*

Greg Clingham examines Johnson's Dryden in detail, and the lens of Johnson's personality turns out to be not surprisingly strong. It is difficult to say why "influence studies" should not have made this move a necessary one. In a sense there is only the difference of English genitives between "Dryden's reception," "Dryden's rivalries," and "Dryden's influence" and, on the other hand, "the reception of Dryden," "the rivalries of Dryden," and "the influence of Dryden." In fact, the three items in each set are themselves inconsistent in their possible meanings. Words apart, it simply is not possible for us to form our understandings and misunderstandings of a Dryden without attention to the explicit reception of him by readers between him and us. And the history of that reception is clarified for us by his notable successors from "cousin Swift" to our contemporaries. Greg Clingham's "Another and the same: Johnson's Dryden" is an integral part of the subject of authorial interrelations.

We have been seeing that it is possible to draw certain distinctions and infer certain conclusions involving the subject most generally known as influence by distinguishing what may usefully be designated rivalry, influence, and reception. Nothing that has been said suggests that any one of the three need exist alone. Influence is simply infeasible without reception (with or without rivalry). We have seen repeatedly that each of these cannot be accounted for by a single explanation, since each varies historically and indeed cross-culturally. As usual, the fallacy of the single explanation is evident without any special effort of discovery. We have also found it necessary to conclude that study of the subjects implied by Dryden and other writers requires a double act of interpretation, involving our own of Dryden's. And, by extending the subject of "influence" to include subsequent reception of a Dryden by a Johnson, we reach a tripled act of interpretation even before getting to ourselves as interpreters or welcoming our readers to an additional stage.

Of Dryden we may aptly say that his versatility and his activity as a translator along with his "higher mimesis" make him a particularly suitable candidate for "influence study." And of our readers we may say that, after all, they are not reduced to being mere meta- or fifth-stage versions in this account. That is because they, like each of the four of us, can and will respond vigorously to Dryden himself. He is a very rare example of a writer who engenders for himself the kind of study that he devoted to many a dozen predecessors and contemporaries. If it was left to Johnson to write the lives of the poets, Dryden may be said to have discovered a new art: the poetry of historical lives.

Literary authority and transmission become a continuing episode in the epic of English literary history and in ideas about England, literature, history – and human nature itself. Like oral epic, this one is open to countless retellings in order to account for what are, in more than one sense, the interests of individuals. By the act of reading Dryden and his earlier readers like Johnson, we do not cease to be ourselves. Our selves are freshly defined with new experience and new ideas about England, literature, and history by that act of encounter. It holds equally true, however, that Dryden is an unusually strong source for this kind of study. Because, that is, students of this greatly various writer discover that the tides of *influence* flow not only into Dryden from them, but also self-definingly into them from their understanding of him. Because also we inescapably repeat his efforts to define the bounds of our authority and lines of transmission to and from ourselves. Because finally in writing of him we write wittingly or unwittingly of ourselves. By the same token, we invite our readers to assess what we transmit, to define the grounds and bounds of *their* authority.

Notes

1 At the same dark edge of ignorance is our own ignorance about so much concerning Dryden and his century. Moreover, my efforts to explain Dryden by attention to Ovid use evidence even less clear than that we possess about Dryden. What I at least attempt here is very much open to question, and, if I do not follow fashion and make Dryden a skeptic appropriate to his century, it is because I am skeptical about my own powers and those of my contemporaries to be so certain of the limits to the knowledge held by all but ourselves.

2 Surveyed by Thomas Mallon, *Stolen Words* (New York: Ticknor and Fields, 1989). He emphasizes the variety of practices that have been included under that label, and includes a very useful bibliography.

3 Among the writings showing Dryden's concern with his age or period and others are: *Annus Mirabilis* (the passage on navigation), *An Essay of Dramatick Poesie*, and the poems to Roscommon, Congreve, and Kneller. The subject is explored in my "Dryden and the Issue of Human Progress," *Philological Quarterly*, 11 (1961), 120–29, which errs, however, for Dryden after 1688; he

kept to his conception of an age but no longer was optimistically progressive. Citations of Dryden that follow will be to the relevant volume in the California *Works of John Dryden*, ed. Edward Niles Hooker, H. T. Swedenberg, et al., 20 vols. (Berkeley: University of California Press, 1955–), cited as *Works*. There will also be reference to "Watson": John Dryden, *Of Dramatic Poesy and Other Critical Essays*, ed. George Watson, 2 vols. (London: Everyman, 1962).

4 The nearly contradictory phrase, "autonomous branch," is meant to imply by "branch" that literature does not exist in a cultural cordon sanitaire, and by "autonomous" that it can be known and studied on separable, integral terms. The importance of the latter is emphasized in my *Comparative Poetics* (Princeton: Princeton University Press, 1990), ch. 1.

5 *Ibid.*

6 See, most conveniently, A. T. Hatto's translation of (and introduction to) Gottfried's *Tristan* (London: Penguin, 1969), especially part seven, "Tristan's Investiture and Gottfried's Literary Excursus." Many versions of the original text omit the episode, for some reason. Features of the significance of the distinction between narrative "dyers" and lyric "nightingales" is suggested in *Comparative Poetics*, ch. 3.

7 David Kramer's forthcoming book will deal with Dryden's emulation and, turning on Corneille, of Corneille's own methods in insulating himself from restrictions the Academy sought to impose. This seems an appropriate point at which to observe that although *An Essay of Dramatick Poesie* has often been printed, there have been only two, and incomplete, collections of Dryden's critical writings: W. P. Ker, *Essays of John Dryden* (Oxford: Clarendon Press, 1926), and Watson's (cited above), which is not only easier to use, but better annotated. Stranger still, there is only one book accounting for Dryden's criticism, Robert D. Hume, *Dryden's Criticism* (Ithaca: Cornell University Press, 1970). James A. Winn, however, has published a study of Dryden's criticism of literature, painting, and music, *When beauty fires the blood: love and the arts in the age of Dryden* (Ann Arbor: Michigan, 1992).

8 On Dryden as an "original" member, see Charles E. Ward, *The Life of John Dryden* (Chapel Hill: University of North Carolina Press, 1961), p. 31. Of course the academy developed in stages out of its center at Wadham College, Oxford, so that the only really important point is that Dryden was interested enough for his friend Dr. Walter Charleton to nominate him to the growing group.

9 What follows draws on my "Possible Canons of Literary Transmittal and Appropriation," *Yearbook of Comparative and General Literature*, 37 (1990 for 1988), 109–12.

10 I should satirize myself. Short books may have long titles: so my *Japanese Tradition in British and American Literature* (Princeton: Princeton University Press, 1958). In a couple of decades (because of over-familiarity with Eliot's "Tradition and the Individual Talent"?) it would have been necessary to devise yet another title.

11 I have quoted the subtitle of *Literature as System* (Princeton: Princeton University Press, 1971), an admirable book.

12 Beginning with *The Anxiety of Influence: A Theory of Poetry* (New York: Oxford University Press, 1973). In this and sequent books, Bloom develops a vocabulary to describe various phenomena he finds operative, but his central argument and brilliance as a formalist critic have carried most weight.

13 Ďurišin, *Sources and Systematics of Comparative Literature* (Bratislava: Univerzita Komenského, 1974). In later work, his theories have been modified and rendered more complex. See *Theory of Literary Comparatistics* (Bratislava: Slovak Academy of Sciences, 1984) and especially *Theory of Interliterary Process* (Bratislava: Slovak Academy of Sciences, 1989), with the account of his work on pp. 163–68.

14 Judging by lectures he has recently given, Douwe W. Fokkema will posit modernist and postmodernist "codes" as inclusive of heavy use of predecessors, culminating in what may be termed a using-up.

15 Belsey, *The Subject of Tragedy: Identity and Difference in Renaissance Drama* (London and New York: Methuen, 1985), pp. 81–82.

16 Nothing so extreme as a complete dismissal of Bloom is intended here. As will be seen in the first chapter, Jennifer Brady is able to make sensitive use of his concepts. And, in addition to a prodigious memory (the Muse of his theory?), Bloom has great critical powers.

17 *Complete Works of William Hazlitt*, ed. P. P. Howe, 21 vols. (London and Toronto: J. M. Dent, 1931–34), V: p. 146. Jonathan Arac first directed my attention to Hazlitt's remarks.

18 *The Works of John Milton*, ed. Frank Allen Patterson et al., 20 vols. (New York: Columbia University Press, 1931–40), II (Pt. 1): p. 6; roman and italic usage reversed.

19 *The Critical Works of Thomas Rymer*, ed. Curt A. Zimansky (London: Oxford University Press, 1956), p. 76.

20 In "Dryden's Admired Acquaintance, Mr. Milton," *Milton Studies* 11 (1978), 3–27, I reviewed Dryden's transactions with Milton and Rymer, concluding that here his aim (contrary to what he says) is precisely to "take Mr. *Rymer's* Work out of his Hands" by entering reasonable criticisms and so forestalling Rymer, who never did follow through with his threat. That hardly exhausts this passage, as we next see.

21 The poem was recovered and printed by George deF. Lord, "Introduction," *Poems on Affairs of State*, I (New Haven: Yale University Press, 1963), p. liii.

22 Dryden is the more apt to have had these matters on his mind, as I have been reminded, because his own wife-to-be, Lady Elizabeth Howard, had been romantically associated with Chesterfield shortly before he wooed Mary Fairfax.

23 There is an account of passages between Dryden and Rochester in my *Restoration Mode from Milton to Dryden* (Princeton: Princeton University Press, 1984), pp. 415–18.

24 On poetry and painting, see "To Sir Godfrey Kneller," lines 89–96, 164–73. On science ("the enquiry of a Philosopher"), see preface to *De Arte Graphica*, *Works*, XX: 60. Numerous passages suggest the superiority of poetry to music.

25 Crites asks, "Is it not evident, in these last hundred years ... that almost a new

Nature has been reveal'd to us?" (*Works*, XVII: 15). The question includes an echo of Sidney's *Defence* but is potentially more radical than anything else in the *Essay*. For, if the nature poets imitate is subject to change, full-scale historical relativism is implied. Significantly enough, Dryden never followed this through. Even his faith in the possibility of human progress – some of which survived 1688 – did not presume a changing reality.

26 See the second chapter in this volume, by David Kramer, including his notes 8 and 9.

27 At my last notice in Kyoto, the British Council building was in scenic, but remote, hills; the American Cultural Center was in an office in a business section downtown; and the Maison Franco-Japonaise stood as an imposing classical presence on a wide street directly across from Kyoto University. There is also a Claudel prize (Paul Claudel was ambassador to Japan) given for a translation of a book from French to Japanese. The recipient gets a month's free stay from the French government, which is willing to let the recipient travel anywhere in Europe (and let people know about the Claudel prize).

28 See Janet A. Walker, "On the Applicability of the Term 'Novel' to Modern Non-Western Long Fiction," *Yearbook of Comparative and General Literature*, 37 (1990 for 1988), 47–68.

29 New Historicist preoccupations with Europeans in the New World were anticipated – and with far more in the way of literary and historical evidence – by many of the chapters in *The Wild Man Within*, ed. Edward Dudley and Maximillian E. Novak (Pittsburgh: University of Pittsburgh Press, 1972).

30 This is not to say that there are no reminders of those conventions in his poetry. For example, in the opening lines of "The Medall" and in passages (e.g., 166–73) of "To Sir Godfrey Kneller," touches of the advice to a painter can be found. But Dryden was not content merely to retrace the steps of others, and is remarkable for versatile innovation.

31 Dryden appears more modern than he is because of the ability to express himself both intelligently and clearly. Also, he shares with Hobbes (whose prose style is far more modern than Dryden's) a care to define what he talks about.

32 John Harrington Smith, *The Gay Couple in Restoration Comedy* (Cambridge, MA: Harvard University Press, 1948). Dryden may not have invented the pair, but he is a most notable user of it from early plays to the comic subplot of his last tragedy, *Don Sebastian*.

33 Dryden made the cause of the heroic play his, both by writing them, and by writing a criticism to justify them or their important features. For example, the following criticism: epistle dedicatory (praising Orrery) to *The Rival Ladies*; *An Essay of Dramatick Poesie*; preface to *The Conquest of Granada*, Part 1; defence of the epilogue to *The Conquest of Granada*, Part 2 (all found in Watson, I). See also: Eugene M. Waith, *The Herculean Hero in Marlowe, Chapman, Shakespeare, and Dryden* (London: Chatto and Windus, 1962), and *Ideas of Greatness: Heroic Drama in English* (London: Routledge and Kegan Paul, 1971); also Arthur Kirsch, *Dryden's Heroic Drama* (Princeton: Princeton University Press, 1965), and the chapter by David Kramer, below.

34 The phrase is that (in a personal letter) by Qian Zhongshu, the leading Chinese
   man of letters in this century. Similarly Konishi Jin'ichi has described Pound's
   insights and limits in discovering imagistic unity in nō: see *A History of Japanese
   Literature*, III (Princeton: Princeton University Press, 1991), pp. 539–41.

35 My readers will find as the most familiar verbal echo that of "Mac Flecknoe,"
   11. 105–6: "The hoary Prince in Majesty appear'd, / High on a Throne of his
   own Labours rear'd"; and in the poem to Congreve, lines 51–53: "Thou shalt
   be seen, / (Tho' with some short Parenthesis between:) / High on the Throne of
   Wit." Both are founded on the opening of *Paradise Lost*, 2 – and both are
   recalled by Pope at the beginning of the *Dunciad*, 2. The metaphorical
   connection of poetic to royal succession provides a larger subject common to
   the two poems, and another of Dryden's insights into issues being discussed
   here.

36 To avoid misunderstanding, "ideological" is used descriptively here for every
   individual's complex of mutually reinforcing values, prejudices, interests, and
   ideals, even when contradictory.

37 The major exceptions are Hobbes, who frightened nearly everybody, and
   Bunyan. Before condemning Dryden for not appreciating Bunyan in those
   class-ridden times, we may recall that the "liberal" Milton and the Quaker Pen
   also failed to recognize the achievement of the Bedford tinker. Dryden studies
   have not been untouched by the "hermeneutics of suspicion," which would no
   doubt hold that Dryden's positive reception of most of his better contemporaries was a calculated effort not to make enemies. The Rose Alley affair and
   Dryden's political engagement suggest no such thing, however, and the close of
   the preface to *Fables* is marred by his dyspeptic remarks about Luke Milbourne
   and Sir Richard Blackmore.

38 I wish to posit interpretation descriptively, as with ideology earlier. That is,
   without going into the norms – even the adequacy or inadequacy of this or that
   hermeneutic procedure – there is the question Hans-Georg Gadamer poses
   from Kant: "How is understanding possible?" (Gadamer is quoted from the
   foreword to the second edition of *Truth and Method*, reprinted in *The Hermeneutic
   Tradition*, ed. Gayle L. Ormiston and Alan D. Schrift [Albany: State University of New York Press, 1990], p. 203.) Of course Gadamer is less descriptive in
   general tenor, as his very title implies. It should also be observed that, just as
   interpretation reflects the interpreter's ideology, we have no access to an
   ideology other than by interpretation. It is strange that this obvious second
   "hermeneutic circle" has gone unrecognized.

39 Jennifer Brady has reminded me that Johnson's comparison was no doubt
   inspired by Dryden's of Jonson and Shakespeare (in *An Essay of Dramatick Poesie*),
   which Dryden's contemporaries would have expected to end in a preference for
   Jonson. The observation shows how important subsequent reception of an
   author may be for understanding that author's own reception of predecessors.

40 *Boswell's Life of Johnson* (ed. Edmond Malone), introd. Chauncey Brewster
   Tinker, 2 vols. in 1 (New York: Oxford University Press, 1948), II: 364–65.

1

Dryden and negotiations of literary succession and precession

JENNIFER BRADY

Due Honours to those mighty Names we grant,
But Shrubs may live beneath the lofty Plant:
Sons may succeed their greater Parents gone;
Such is thy Lott; and such I wish my own.
                Dryden, "To Sir Godfrey Kneller" (1694)

The third requisite in our *Poet*, or Maker, is *Imitation*, to bee able to convert the substance, or Riches of an other *Poet*, to his owne use. To make choise of one excellent man above the rest, and so to follow him, till he grow very *Hee*: or, so like him, as the Copie may be mistaken for the Principall. Not, as a Creature, that swallowes, what it takes in, crude, raw, or indigested; but, that feedes with an Appetite, and hath a Stomacke to concoct, divide, and turne all into nourishment.
                Jonson, *Discoveries* (1640)

Dryden in "The Battle of the Books"

Jonathan Swift assigned John Dryden an eminent place among the deluded moderns who dispute the reputations awarded the ancients in his *Battle of the Books* (1704 [1697]). Swift's burlesque of poetic rivalries that pit the classical writers against their putative heirs proposes, in effect, a caustic, astringent version of Harold Bloom's psychoanalytic model of influence. The ragamuffin troops who comprise Swift's moderns – Tasso, Behn, Milton, Wither, Davenant, Camden, and others – share the desperation of Bloom's Romantic ephebes and their penchant for disingenuous vaunting. Swift's satiric portraits of Dryden and Cowley, however, envisage a noteworthy variation in the styles of oedipal mutiny practiced by his moderns. He depicts both writers as ambiguous foes to his ancients. Dryden's and Cowley's strategy for displacing their rivals takes the form of

27

an apparently friendly take-over; each writer claims kinship to the classical poet whose "Address, and Pace, and Career"[1] he would imitate, and thus appropriate. According to Swift's "severe poem,"[2] the modern poets who claim to emulate an august precursor seek less to idealize him than to infiltrate the enemy's ranks. Dryden emerges from this burlesque as an uneasy amalgam of Bloom's "strong" and "weak" poets. He is caricatured by Swift as a kind of passive–aggressive. In setting out to lampoon Dryden, Swift targets for a particularly sustained assault one of the most prominent features of Dryden's self-presentation as a poet, critic, and translator: his embrace of influence.

The encounter between Virgil and Dryden in St. James' Library, the battlefield where the trumped-up controversy is to be decided, pits the ancient's modesty against the modern's wily humility. Swift's Virgil is at first dismayed by the grotesque spectacle of a superannuated foe riding a "spent" sorrel gelding. He is further affronted when his antagonist sidles up to him, presuming an affinity between them when Virgil can plainly see the absurd discrepancies in their armor, steeds, and phrenologic capacities. Dryden has come not to fight but to parley, at tedious length:

> The two Cavaliers had now approached within the Throw of a Lance, when the Stranger desired a Parley, and lifting up the Vizard of his Helmet, a Face hardly appeared from within, which after a pause, was known for that of the renowned *Dryden*. The brave *Antient* suddenly started, as one possess'd with Surprize and Disappointment together: For, the Helmet was nine times too large for the Head, which appeared Situate far in the hinder Part . . . [and] the voice was suited to the Visage, sounding weak and remote. *Dryden* in a long Harangue soothed up the good *Antient*, called him *Father*, and by a large deduction of Genealogies, made it plainly appear, that they were nearly related. Then he humbly proposed an Exchange of Armor, as a lasting Mark of Hospitality between them.   (157–58)

Dryden inveigles the unassuming Virgil out of his gold armor, then his horse. His presumption in exchanging his gelding for Pegasus, however, occasions an egregious oedipal defeat: "when it came to the Trial, *Dryden* was afraid, and utterly unable to mount" (158). Virgil spares his English translator's life out of embarrassment or a warranted disdain for his shabby successor. In any case, the "Mettle and Vigour" (157) of Pegasus combine with Dryden's own timidity to decide the issue of lineal descent.

In *The Battle of the Books* Swift makes shrewd satiric capital out of Dryden's lifelong investment in discovering his affiliations to other eminent writers, both precursors and heirs. There is ample precedent in Dryden's criticism for Swift's caricature of him as an avid genealogist, and even for the specific discomforts of the imagined meeting with Virgil. Dryden's publicized ruptures with Shadwell and Rochester in the 1670s had played themselves out as disputes over bloodlines, with Dryden claiming for himself the superior pedigree. In "Mac Flecknoe" (1682 [?1678]), most notoriously, Dryden had wrested Ben Jonson's mantle from its other conspicuous claimant, Thomas Shadwell. Shadwell's title to the patrimony is impugned with these scoffing lines:

> Nor let false friends seduce thy mind to fame,
> By arrogating *Johnson*'s Hostile name.[3]

"Mac Flecknoe"'s sardonic celebration of an alternative, debased succession for Dryden's rival – Shadwell is enthusiastically claimed as his legitimate heir by the poetaster Richard Flecknoe ("Thou art my blood, where *Johnson* has no part;/ What share have we in Nature or in Art?" [II: 59, lines 175–76]) – transfers all rights in Jonson to Dryden. His hostility to Shadwell's pretensions carries on the satiric progenitor's well-documented antipathies to bad writers; Jonson's will presumably speaks through Dryden. The inverted genealogies of "Mac Flecknoe" thus establish him as the rightful heir, dispossessing Shadwell of his borrowed lineage.

In 1678, Dryden had publicly rebuked Rochester for "persecuting" Horace through writing "vile imitations" (XIII: 16) of his poetry. As with Shadwell's unsound title, Dryden explodes Rochester's claim of descent by providing him with a new pedigree. Rochester is the "Legitimate Son of *Sternhold*" (XIII: 17), whose enduring popularity Dryden attributed to the vileness of his verses. Once again, in his Preface to *All for Love*, Dryden speaks out, ostensibly on behalf of Horace, the poet Rochester has maligned:

But how would he [Horace] disdain to be Copied by such hands [as Rochester's]! I dare answer for him, he would be ... uneasie in their company ... With what scorn would he look down on such miserable Translators, who make Doggrel of his *Latine*, mistake his meaning, misapply his censures, and often contradict their own?   (XIII: 16)

Dryden's rash denigration of Rochester's aspirations to some portion of Horace's "Soul and Fire" (XIII: 16) includes an explicit, if largely parenthetic, assertion of his own stake in both Horace and Virgil. Swift has merely to borrow Dryden's premature claim of descent for his own burlesque, flesh out the scenario of the ancestral poet uneasy in the modern's company, and turn it back on the author. Dryden has been deftly skewered in *The Battle of the Books* by what are, in essence, recycled gibes.

Swift's hostile characterization of Dryden has enjoyed considerable

influence in Restoration studies. Dryden's encounter with the precursor in
The Battle of the Books has been proposed as the definitive exposé of his
"cultural and historical pretensions."[4] The implications of endorsing
Swift's own perspective on influence by default have been less clearly
understood. Swift commits himself to a satiric economy predicated on the
assumption of an absolute polarity between the ancients and their
degenerate modern offspring. For him, the only texts that warrant
"classic" status are classical. Swift needs his ancestors to be, in Bloom's
terms, "anonymous Splendors" (*The Anxiety of Influence*, p. 43), inaccessible yet more fully present than the living or the recently dead. According
to *The Battle of the Books*, the ancients' sanctity must be preserved from
modern encroachment. Swift is wholly engaged in promulgating the myth
of an irreparable divide between the classical past and the recent past. He
does so in the service of his own nostalgia.

In her elegant redaction of Freud's clinical study of melancholia, Susan
Stewart delineates precisely the kind of nostalgia Swift's text practices.
She writes in *On Longing*:

[In] nostalgic reconstruction the present is denied and the past takes on an
authenticity of being ... Hostile to history and its invisible origins, and yet longing
for an impossibly pure context of lived experience at a place of origin, nostalgia
wears a distinctly utopian face, a face that turns toward a future-past, a past that
has only ideological reality ... Nostalgia is [the desire for desire,] the repetition
that mourns the inauthenticity of all repetition and denies the repetition's capacity
to form identity.[5]

As Stewart argues, the nostalgic longing for unmediated access cannot
be satisfied. The melancholy satirist who "mourns the inauthenticity of all
repetition" is incapable of achieving individuation; instead, the past
"continually threatens to reproduce itself as a felt lack" (*On Longing*,
p. 23) in the present, the time of his own work. Swift's burlesque empties
the present of all generative potential. It is symptomatic of his nostalgia
that Swift situates his ancients in an "impossibly pure" past whose very
inaccessibility spurs the impossible desire for reunion. His moderns are
invariably represented as bereft of the creativity that is uniquely ascribed
to the ancestors. Freud remarks in his "Mourning and Melancholia"
(1917) that the melancholiac exhibits a wishful "clinging to the [lost]
object" of his longing even when a "substitute is already beckoning."[6] In
The Battle of the Books the substitute that beckons but which must be
rejected is modern capacity.

When Dryden translated Virgil's epic in and for the present, his assertion of both literary continuity and poetic affiliation threatened Swift's
myth of pure disparities. Swift regards the moderns – the Tassos, Miltons,

and Drydens – as having tampered with properties that he holds to be inalienably the ancients'. Virgil's modesty belongs to him alone, not to Dryden or the modern age. Swift cannot account for that trait, beyond asserting its authenticity. It is a divine attribute ("the Goddess *Diffidence* ... cast a Mist before his Eyes" [*The Battle of the Books*, p. 158]) and, as such, inexplicable. The ancients' voices, remote in time or even atemporal, are likewise imbued with a courtesy and a strength that their successors cannot emulate. In a satiric reversal prompted by nostalgic revisioning, Swift hears Dryden's voice as "weak and remote." A Bloomian reading would emphasize the oedipal competition being enacted in Swift's determination to deny Dryden an audible voice, but it is also the case that Swift's nostalgia leaves him no option. *The Battle of the Books*, then, registers not only Swift's anxious contempt for his renowned satiric precursor, but what Freud would characterize as a "lowering of the self-regarding feelings" (XIV: 244). However inadvertently, Swift has implicated himself in the creative enervation he identifies as modern.

If the history of poetic successions charts an overdetermined descent into bathos according to *The Battle of the Books*, Dryden presents influence as a paradox of fluid, discovered affinities. "For Mankind is ever the same, and nothing [necessarily] lost out of Nature, though every thing is alter'd,"[7] he asserts in his Preface to the *Fables* (1700). Its dedication to the youngest Duke of Ormond celebrates the transmission of the Ormond ancestors' virtues to successive generations. As with the illustrious Roman lines panegyrized by Livy, the Ormonds' history, witnessed by Dryden over three generations, exemplifies an ideal continuity in the values the family has professed:

The World is sensible that you worthily succeed, not only to the Honours of your Ancestors, but also to their Virtues. The long Chain of Magnanimity, Courage, easiness of Access, and desire of doing Good ... is so far from being broken in your Grace, that the precious Metal yet runs pure to the newest Link of it ...

'Tis observ'd by *Livy* and by others, That some of the noblest *Roman* Families retain'd a resemblance of their Ancestry, not only in their Shapes and Features, but also in their Manners, their Qualities, and the distinguishing Characters of their Minds.   (Kinsley, IV: 1439–40)

Poets likewise can be worthy emulators of their precursors. They have their "Lineal Descents and Clans, as well as other Families" (*ibid.*: 1445), Dryden argues, underscoring the analogy he is drawing between two kinds of nobility. The Preface to *Fables* likens the transmission of influence to transfusion, so recalling Dryden's pindaric ode to Anne Killigrew (1685) and his earlier "Mac Flecknoe." His panegyric on Killigrew attributes her

early promise as a poet to her literary genes, inherited from her family's
"inexhausted Vain":

> Thy Father was transfus'd into thy Blood:
> So wert thou born into the tuneful strain,
> (An early, rich, and inexhausted Vain.)   (lines 26–28)

Or in "Mac Flecknoe," where genealogies (and bloodlines) are mis-
matched and where poetasters confuse real and imagined influences,
Shadwell lifts freely from Etherege's plays only to discover the limits of
transmission: Etherege, transfused "whole," "always floats above" while
Shadwell's plays "sink below," "so transfus'd as Oyl on Waters flow"
(lines 184–86). Dryden's late preface returns to this biological and genealogical trope for influence. As he reminds his readers, Milton was the
self-professed "Poetical Son of *Spencer*," who himself "more than once
insinuates, that the Soul of *Chaucer* was transfus'd into his Body; and that
he was begotten by him Two hundred years after his Decease" – and
Chaucer in turn bears a strong familial resemblance to Ovid (Kinsley,
IV: 1445). The career of each of these master poets forms a link in the
historical chain of poetic influence.

Where Swift detects a steady accretion of impurities in the newer links,
and suspects the heirs of being cunning traducers of their ancestors' fames,
Dryden projects a more benign possibility: harmonious coexistence. He
simultaneously champions the moderns' cause and adopts a pacific attitude towards his elected fathers. "I found I had a Soul congenial to his"
(*ibid.*: 1457), he writes of Chaucer; throughout this preface Dryden affirms
his partiality to the neglected medieval poet.[8] Chaucer is claimed as his –
and Spenser's, and through him, Milton's – "Predecessor in the Laurel"
(*ibid.*: 1445). Such professions infuriated Swift. He reacted to the undenia-
ble dimension of arrogation in Dryden's layered genealogical affinities,
just as Dryden had protested what he regarded as Shadwell's encroachment on the Jonsonian legacy.

"'Every talent must unfold itself in fighting,'" Bloom writes of his
Nietzschean ephebes who "wrestle with their strong precursors, even to
the death" (*The Anxiety of Influence*, pp. 52, 5). He adds this Romantic stric-
ture: "to be judicious is to be weak, and to compare, exactly and fairly, is
to be not elect" (19). Bloom's ephebe must "deny ... obligation" (6) if he
is to believe in his own strength. Dryden's career suggests an alternative
response to inheriting a literary tradition. He respects, in many ways
venerates, his precursors' achievements. Emulation, for Dryden,
need not inhibit creativity; "the Poets['] ... work is imitation," as he
remarks in his "Defence of the Epilogue" (1672; *Works*, XI: 217), and in so

far as the heir eschews "a servile imitation of all they [Shakespeare, Fletcher, and Jonson] writ" (*ibid.*, 218), his assimilation of his literary forebears engages him in a productive enterprise whose ethos is quite distinct from the laws of scarcity economics that govern Bloom's protagonists. Despite Dryden's periodic anxieties about the value of his work or that of his generation when he measures their achievement against that of his eminent Renaissance precursors, he persists in regarding his influential fathers as allies and mentors.

Dryden advocates a model of poetic succession that identifies both fathers and sons as objects of longing, and that has as its aim the forging of an ideal continuity between past and present. He identified with the generation after the Civil War who sought to restore the father *through* the son. The recent history of a monarch's beheading was enough to instill a certain compunction in the sons. That compunction for Dryden incorporates literary fathers, most notably Jonson, Shakespeare, and Fletcher, the "Gyant Race, before the Flood" ("To my Dear Friend Mr. Congreve, On His Comedy, call'd, *The Double Dealer*," [1.5]). William Congreve's filial tribute to Dryden's authorial modesty speaks not only to his subject's penchant to mentor other, younger poets but to his diffidence, a trait that can be misconstrued (on Bloom's model) as a symptom of oedipal defeatism but which rewards a second look.

In 1717, as he was preparing a posthumous edition of Dryden's dramatic works, Congreve reflected on the writer and the man. His portrait is a model of unobtrusive tact. "I had the Happiness to be very Conversant, and as intimately acquainted with Mr. *Dryden*, as the great Disproportion in our Years could allow me to be," he writes.[9] Congreve recalls that Dryden had been "extream ready and gentle" in his responses to other writers like himself who "thought fit to consult him" – and "full as ready and patient" (*Letters and Documents*, p. 127) in admitting lapses in his own work. At no juncture does Congreve explicitly acknowledge Swift's caricature of Dryden. His sense of the occasion alone would have precluded a direct retort. Moreover, Congreve was on good terms with Swift, as he had been earlier with Dryden. By emphasizing Dryden's generosity to others and his modesty, however, Congreve does respond to the lampoon in *The Battle of the Books*. His summary remarks in the character he draws of Dryden are oblique yet pointed rebuttals of the censure Dryden had attracted:

He was of very easy, I may say of very pleasing Access: But something slow, and as it were diffident in his Advances to others. He had something in his Nature that abhorr'd Intrusion into any Society whatsoever. Indeed it is to be regretted, that he was rather blameable in the other Extream: For by that means, he was

Personally less known, and consequently his Character might become liable both
to Misapprehensions and Misrepresentations.

   To the best of my Knowledge and Observation, he was, of all the Men that ever
I knew, one of the most Modest, and the most Easily to be discountenanced, in his
Approaches, either to his Superiors, or his Equals.   (127–28)

   Congreve's carefully drafted testimonial provides a perceptive description of Dryden's stance before his precursors or those contemporaries he
regarded as his "Superiors, or his Equals." The brief memoir also
addresses the public relations' quandary the diffident writer negotiates.
Implicit in Congreve's tribute to Dryden is his pained, shrewd discern-
ment of the pitfalls of authorial modesty, its liability to mockery and to
misconstruction. Congreve intends his readers to understand his
restrained subjunctive ("might become liable") as having already been
realized in Dryden's case. Congreve has read Swift's burlesque of Dryden
attentively. His admission of the ease with which diffidence can slide into
compunction further anticipates Harold Bloom's thesis, without advocating Bloom's dire remedies for anxiety. Congreve elects to honor those very
qualities in Dryden that he identifies as most liable to misconstruction.
That his distinctly undramatic corrective reading has had less impact on
Dryden's reception than did Swift's is revealing. By emulating the stance
he ascribes to his subject, Congreve consigns his posthumous expression of
gratitude to an equivalently modest middle ground. While his sincerity
has never been questioned, Congreve's portrait of Dryden remains underread. Its perspective needs to be assimilated by modern readers as an
intelligent counterbalance to Swift's caricature of the temporizing translator in *The Battle of the Books*.

The diffident heir: Dryden and the Renaissance Titans

In the critical prose of the 1660s and the 1670s, Dryden tended to mitigate
the flaws he identified in his Renaissance precursors' works, either by
drawing conspicuous attention to similar lapses of his own or by recoiling
in disgust from the activity that he (following Scaliger) termed "hypercriticism." "'Tis malicious and unmanly to snarl at the little lapses of a pen,"
he insists in the preface to his opera, *The State of Innocence* (1677), adding
that the progenitors' "negligences" are "only marks of human frailty" no
author could escape.[10] At no point does Dryden endorse the accomplishments of his own age without qualifying contemporary claims to
superiority. In the early essays and prefaces, his most optimistic stances are
couched in conditionals and concessives. By the late 1670s, even these
tempered expressions of high self-regard undergo a significant retrench-

ment, when he confronts his fear that the fathers have not been restored in the sons. As Congreve hypothesized, Dryden's approach to his fathers typically veers between a mutually affirmative filial devotion and an abashed sense of their achieved greatness.

Dryden's respect for his Renaissance progenitors is affirmed by explicit acknowledgments of their abiding influence on his work. It is also confirmed by his reflexive distaste for his own occasional forays into detraction. When he "inquire[s] into the ... Errors" (XI: 203) of Jonson or Shakespeare in what begins as a defence of his ill-tempered Epilogue to The Second Part of *Conquest of Granada* in 1672, he retracts more than he justifies. The Epilogue had argued a simple proposition:

> Fame then was cheap, and the first commer sped;
> And they have kept it since, by being dead.
>
> (XI: 201, lines 11–12)

Neither playwright could pass scrutiny by contemporary audiences, "no not *Jonson*, in his height" (XI: 201, lines 15–16).

Dryden supports his defensive Epilogue with what amounts to a checklist of Jonson's faults of composition in *Catiline*. The enumeration of its flaws is twice interrupted, in one instance to comment on Jonson's habit of ending his sentences with prepositions: "a common fault with him, and [one] which I have but lately observ'd in my own writings" (XI: 208). The other aside ostensibly serves to implicate Shakespeare in lapses akin to Jonson's. Dryden takes a nervous sideswipe at *Macbeth*. In this instance, it is authorized by Jonson who "us'd to say," Dryden suddenly recalls, that some of *Macbeth* was unintelligible "bombast" (XI: 208). The works Dryden chooses to challenge Jonson's hegemony are telling, as are the specific passages he quotes. Both imply Dryden's compunction about the role he is assuming in relation to his literary father.

"The Defence of the Epilogue" has been proposed by modern scholars as evidence that Dryden was either a self-serving detractor of the great or that he "turned against and seriously undervalued the Elizabethans." Robert D. Hume and Hoyt Trowbridge have ably challenged this view of Dryden's attitude towards his Renaissance precursors in the 1670s.[11] On closer scrutiny, Dryden's essay demonstrates his discomfort with the project he has tackled, rather than a sustained urge to defame the achievements of his beloved fathers.

The critique of Jonson's dramatic work pursues a highly associative train of thought, and begins with an admission of Dryden's misgivings: "As for *Ben. Jonson*, I am loath to name him, because he is a most Judicious Writer" (XI: 207). In the next breath, Dryden proleptically begs his reader's pardon for taxing Jonson with any faults. He does so only in extenuation of his own failings, he explains. The imagined reader, addressed as "he," is transparently a screen for Father Ben himself, whose sanction Dryden needs for this enterprise. His detour into Jonson's scathing opinion of *Macbeth* offers the successor a bolstering precedent. Dryden's excursion into hypercriticism is licensed by Jonson's example; yet despite his self-protective ceding of ultimate judgment to the reader and of authorizing precedent to the precursor, he remains disconcerted, uneasy with the role he has assumed.

Dryden understands the son's exposure of his father's nakedness to public view as a shameful, even obscene, act.[12] "I cast my eyes but by chance on *Catiline*" (XI: 207), he says, at once fascinated and loath to look. There is, of course, nothing random in Dryden's choice of *Catiline*; he would not in this context select *Epicoene*, which had provided him with "the pattern of a perfect Play" (XVII: 55) in *An Essay of Dramatick Poesie* (1668). Dryden is drawn to *Catiline* by conflicting impulses: the tragedy is vulnerable to charges of uneven writing and, like *Macbeth*, it features parricidal displacement and treason. Rereading the opening pages of Jonson's study of corrupt ambition, Dryden detects more than another poet's errors of composition. He remembers Jonson condemning *Macbeth*'s overblown rhetoric, associates that act of hubris with the "deeds/ Ranker than horrour" that will spring from Catiline's ambition, and draws a disturbing parallel between his critical activity and Jonson's. The passages he excerpts offer a metacommentary on deeply competitive relationships. They also effect a subliminal and powerful check on the son's incipient rivalry with his dramatic predecessor.

Sylla's Ghost proposes treason to Catiline in the first passage from Jonson's tragedy that Dryden selects for close analysis:

> Let the long hid seeds
> Of treason, in thee, now shoot forth in deeds
> Ranker than horrour.   (XI: 208)

Dryden's response to *Catiline* is peculiarly intense. Rereading the first scene of *Catiline*, he fixes on the instant in which the urge towards treason hardens into conscious resolve. The horror that seems to confront Dryden here is his own conceivable implication in such "long hid" impulses: what he reads in Jonson's play are the urges prompting the treasonous text he is now in the process of writing.

"The Defence of the Epilogue" exhibits Dryden's mounting recoil from his own critical procedures. He is not able to maintain the testy challenge of his verse Epilogue in the prose defense; with or without Jonson's sanction, the successor cannot countenance his own tactics. A parenthetical aside clarifies why. "[If] our present Writers ... reach not some excellencies of *Ben. Jonson*; (which no Age, I am confident, ever shall)" (XI: 215), Dryden concedes, undermining his argument in a single stroke. He goes on to praise the superior gallantry of his own age, but it is an exercise largely in damage control. The laurels have been awarded to Jonson.

The analysis of *Catiline* has not, then, produced the essay Dryden envisioned when he began his defense of the moderns. He is soon moved to "close the Book" (XI: 210). Dryden confesses his veneration of Jonson and his "weariness [at pursuing] ... an argument which is so fruitful in so small a compass" (XI: 210). These rationales speak to key concerns of Dryden's criticism, his resolve to treat the precursors with scrupulous fairness, and his essential dislike of mean-spirited criticism. The essay ends on a subdued note: "let us render to our Predecessors what is their due, without confineing our selves to a servile imitation of all they writ: and, without assuming to our selves the Title of better Poets" (XI: 218). The son has been thoroughly chastened.

Dryden has, in fact, staked his entire career on his claim to the title of successor. His understanding of his place in literary history can perhaps best be represented through analogy. In his earlier *Essay of Dramatick Poesie*, published in 1668, Dryden's surrogate Neander defends English dramatic practice against Lisideius, who has argued in favor of French models. The debate centers, in part, on the variety in dramatic plots and the economic distribution of heroic qualities among a play's characters. Neander concedes to Lisideius that the hero of a well-constructed play "will have advantage of all the others," then adds:

But this hinders not that there may be more [that is, other] shining characters in the Play: many persons of a second magnitude, nay, some so very near, so almost equal to the first, that greatness may be oppos'd to greatness, and all the persons be made considerable.   (XVII: 49)

All but one of Neander's examples illustrating this generous ideal are taken from Jonson's comedies.[13] Neander's celebration of the multiplicity of his nation's dramatic plots voices not only Dryden's esteem for his Renaissance fathers but, on another level, his aspirations to inherit that legacy. As the putative successor to Jonson and the other Titans, he conceives of his part as complementary and enhancing. A career "of a second magnitude" may approach that accomplished by the precursors. The heroes retain the advantage of priority over the sons, but the heirs, considerable themselves, also achieve a kind of magnitude. Decades later,

Dryden returned to this analogy, making its application to his own career far more explicit. In "To Sir Godfrey Kneller" (1694), he contemplates (according to his marginal notes) "Shakespear's *Picture drawn by Sir* Godfrey Kneller, *and given to the Author*," and reflects:

> *Shakespear* thy Gift, I place before my sight;
> With awe, I ask his Blessing e're I write;
> With Reverence look on his Majestick Face;
> Proud to be less; but of his Godlike Race.   (lines 73–76)

Kneller is advised, through Dryden, to "be bold; with dauntless breast / Contemn the bad, and Emulate the best" (lines 79–80).

In a companion piece to *Dramatick Poesie*, also published in 1668, Dryden identified Aristotle, Horace, Corneille, and Jonson as his heroes. He uses a classical analogy to characterize his relation to these ancestors. Recalling the example of "little *Teucer*, who shot the *Trojans* from under the large Buckler of *Ajax Telamon*," he claims that he too fights "under the ... protection" of his eminent forebears ("A Defence of an Essay of Dramatique Poesie," [IX: 13]). The self-deprecating reference to his short stature and neophyte status provides another layer of protection that Pope, who was a quick student, would soon learn to exploit. In Samuel Johnson's memorable phrasing, Dryden was at this juncture in his career "but a timorous candidate for reputation," aware that if he had inherited Ben Jonson's capacious critical mind, he did not measure up to his legendary bulk.[14] The analogy argues Dryden's ironic appreciation of the task before him.

Dryden's self-portrait in the early criticism is essentially accurate and discerning. He seeks legitimation for his work and conservative values by citing his precursors' methods as his precedent. Jonson's plays and his *Discoveries* provide a key frame of reference for Dryden. While he acknowledges some phenotypic strains in the transmission of influence, the figure of Ben Jonson offers him a predecessor whose stable judgment secures and enables his own. Jonson's posthumous mentoring of "little Teucer" (and later John Dryden) spans several decades.

During the first period of intense influence, the precarious years of the 1660s, the would-be heir speaks through the father and, progressively, for the father. In both of his elected roles, Dryden aspires to being the "shining" son of the "second magnitude" (XVII: 49) in whom the progenitor would have been well pleased. This pattern of mutually affirming affiliation becomes particularly pronounced in the prose published between 1668 and 1671:

Ben. Johnson himself, after whom I may be proud to erre, has given me more than once the example of it.   (Preface to *An Evening's Love* [X: 208])

But for death, that it ought not to be represented, I have besides . . . the authority of *Ben. Johnson*, who has forborn it in his Tragedies; for both the death of *Sejanus* and *Catiline* are related.   (*An Essay of Dramatick Poesie*, [XVII: 50–51])

[T]he latter half of the *Hemistich* as commonly made up, or a second line subjoyn'd as a reply to the former; which any one leaf in *Johnson*'s Playes will [make] sufficiently clear to you.   (*An Essay of Dramatick Poesie*, [XVII: 76])

And this, though *Ben. Johnson* has not told us, yet 'tis manifestly his opinion: for you see that to his Comedies he allows generally but 24 hours . . .
          ("A Defence of an Essay of Dramatique Poesie," [IX: 20])

You see in *Catiline* and *Sejanus*, where the Argument is great, he sometimes ascends to Verse, which shews he thought it not unnatural in serious Plays: and had his Genius been as proper for Rhyme, as it was for Humour; or had the Age in which he liv'd, attain'd to as much knowledge in Verse, as ours, 'tis probable he would have adorn'd those Subjects with that kind of Writing.
          ("A Defence of an Essay of Dramatique Poesie," [IX: 7])

Jonson is a massive presence in these essays that do homage to him. Dryden remains engaged with his precursor throughout this formative decade. His talismanic invocations of the father's name and his speculations about the forms Jonson's genius might have taken in his own age are indices of his longing to be mentored. The heir's anxiety about individuation proves less pressing (before "Defence of the Epilogue" [1672]) than his desire to locate in the chosen precursor a past that can be reclaimed as his, that can inform and irradiate the present.

Dryden elevates Jonson, Shakespeare, Beaumont, and Fletcher to near-iconic figures in the prose of the 1660s. In Neander's words, these writers are "honour'd, and almost ador'd by us, as they deserve" (XVII: 72). By introducing the saving qualification, Neander articulates Dryden's awareness of the ease with which veneration of the dead can slide into the attitude of nostalgia. In *An Essay of Dramatick Poesie*, that nostalgia is given voice, but in a displaced form. The ultra-royalist character, Lisideius, offers a revisionary history of the great triumvirate that encapsulates the cavalier ideology at its most fanciful. In his fantasy, which centers on the deaths of Beaumont, Fletcher, and Jonson, the fathers' premonitions of the impending carnage spur them to a strategic withdrawal from the horror of the Civil War. The cavalier muses, who are similarly prescient, decamp with the prince to France. Reflecting on the last 40 years, Lisideius proposes this wistful view of their abandonment:

If the Question had been stated, replied *Lisideius*, who had writ best, the *French* or *English* forty years ago, I should have . . . adjudg'd the honour to our own Nation: but since that time, said he, (turning towards *Neander*) we have been so long

together bad *Englishmen*, that we had not leisure to be good Poets; *Beaumont*, *Fletcher*, and *Johnson* (who were onely capable of bringing us to that degree of perfection which we have) were just then leaving the world; as if in an Age of so much horror, wit and those milder studies of humanity, had no farther business among us. But the Muses, who ever follow Peace, went to plant in another Countrey.
                                                                          (XVII: 33–34)

Lisideius takes considerable liberties with the facts in his reconstruction. The dates of these writers' deaths, editors remind us, span the years 1616 through 1637. Only Fletcher's death, in 1625, comes close to falling within the time frame Lisideius designates as the nation's critical turning point. Lisideius has promoted a "pleasing" – because romanticizing and self-romanticizing – "Fallacy" (XVII: 36). He expects his audience to accept factual disparities as true because he expects them to subscribe to the ideological needs that have prompted them. It is Lisideius who champions classical writers who "dispense . . . with the severity of History" in order to exalt the fortunes of their heroes, even "when the event is past dispute" (XVII: 36). His is, then, a deliberate nostalgia that knowingly remakes the Renaissance precursors into cavalier forebears. Lisideius rewards his fathers with uncanny foresight, authorizing his revisionary history by appealing to "the privilege of a Poet" (XVII: 36). Jonson and Fletcher are transfigured in death, the end (or "design") of their lives invested with luminous significance. The fathers' pointed withdrawal from the world signals the imminence of its collapse. They have evidently preferred to die rather than live "in an Age of so much horror," a choice the cavalier son applauds. For Lisideius, the fathers' deaths foreclose the possibility of creative regeneration in their successors. Everything of value has gone with them, crushing the sons' prospects. Or, as Freud observes in his clinical study, the survivors' egos have "become poor and empty" ("Mourning and Melancholia," XIV: 246) in the state of melancholy Lisideius endorses. The strong precursors have abandoned their offspring to time – and to an impoverished present.

In one of the rare stage directions Dryden inserts into his essay, he has Lisideius turn to Neander to address him directly at the precise moment he begins to refashion history into royalist myth. The gesture of inclusion invites Neander to share Lisideius' nostalgia.[15] Neander is tempted. Lisideius has offered him an emotionally freighted vision of a lost Caroline past he might identify with.[16] Neander is drawn, on some level, to this defeatist fantasy; by contrast, the work of cultural and literary renewal he is embarking on commits him to a more difficult prospective struggle. But Dryden will not allow his deputy to be overwhelmed by the fatalism Lisideius embraces in *An Essay of Dramatick Poesie*. Neander replies optimistically: "Be it spoken to the honour of the *English*, our Nation can never want in any Age such who are able to dispute the Empire of Wit with any people in the Universe" (XVII: 63). He is willing to yield the highest honors to the previous age, but his concession is itself provisional. Even now, "we see reviv'd Poesie lifting up its head, & already shaking off the rubbish which lay so heavy on it" (XVII: 63).

Neander, of course, intends to lead that revival through the career of John Dryden. He fends off Lisideius' melancholy apprehensions of defeat, in essence postponing any resolution of the question of influence by leaving it open-ended. Neander identifies the paradox of succession in phrasing that reverberates throughout Dryden's career: "if we, I say, can be thus equal to our selves" (XVII: 64), he wonders aloud, uncertain of victory in a contest with the English precursors. By 1679, Dryden will be unable to parry the question his fictional surrogate so adroitly sidesteps in *Dramatick Poesie* any longer. When the fear comes back, as it does at the mid-point of Dryden's career, it returns in undisguised form, with Dryden speaking in his own voice.

During the turbulent months of the Exclusion Crisis, Dryden undertook a project that would try his claim to the Titans' estate. He rewrote *Troilus and Cressida* (1679), adding a preface on "The Grounds of Criticism in Tragedy." Reviving his metaphor of the previous decade, Dryden announces that his aim in altering Shakespeare has been "to remove that heap of Rubbish, under which many excellent thoughts lay wholly bury'd" (XIII: 226) in the predecessor's work. He insists by way of justification that Shakespeare's play is deficient in plotting, and that various of its characters are underdeveloped or extraneous.

A portion of the preface, however, is devoted to impugning his own achievements in heroic tragedy, the form he had developed to challenge the precursors' hegemony. "I think it no shame to retract my errors, and am well pleas'd to suffer in the cause, if the Art may be improv'd at my expence" (XIII: 229), he explains. His conscientious resolve is not over-stated. He treats his dramatic forebears with scrupulous respect throughout, reserving the epithet "unpardonable" for his own dramatic excesses, which are documented in sardonic detail. After remarking, apropos of dramatic propriety, that "no man is at leisure to make sentences and similes, when his soul is in an Agony," he proposes *The Indian Emperour* (1667) as what he will term, in the next paragraph, "the blown puffy stile":

this fault ... may serve to mind me of my former errors; neither will I spare my self, but give an example of this kind from my *Indian Emperor: Montezuma*, pursu'd by his enemies, and seeking Sanctuary, stands parlying without the Fort, and describing his danger to *Cydaria*, in a simile of six lines;

> *As on the sands the frighted Traveller*
> *Sees the high Seas come rowling from afar, &c.*

My *Indian* Potentate was well skill'd in the Sea for an Inland Prince, and well improv'd since the first Act, when he sent his son to discover it. The Image had not been amiss from another man, at another time: *Sed nunc non erat hisce locus*: he destroy'd the concernment which the Audience might otherwise have had for him; for they could not think the danger near, when he had the leisure to invent a Simile.   (XIII: 243–44)

Freud notes in his portrait of the melancholiac a "trait of insistent communicativeness which finds satisfaction in self-exposure [and] ... distressing self-denigration" (XIV: 247). Dryden's preface exhibits this impulse, especially in the closing pages where, in a striking about-face, he abases himself before the icon of Shakespeare.

This personal admission should not be taken as a measure of Dryden's worth. It is, rather, a gauge of his freshly irrupted anxieties over succession:

If *Shakespear* were stript of all the Bombast in his passions, and dress'd in the most vulgar words, we should find the beauties of his thoughts remaining; if his embroideries were burnt down, there would still be silver at the bottom of the melting-pot: but I fear (at least, let me fear it for myself) that we who Ape his sounding words, have nothing of his thought, but are all outside; there is not so much as a dwarf within our Giants cloaths.   (XIII: 247)

James Winn has suggested that Dryden's diminished self-confidence in the 1679 preface was precipitated by the Exclusion Crisis (Winn: *John Dryden and His World*, p. 323). Dryden's eroding authorial self-esteem when he compares himself to Shakespeare does, I think, speak to his melancholy premonitions of his own exclusion from the laureateship he valued as an external corroboration of his worth, and from the succession itself. He candidly admits his fears that his aspirations to the mantle of the Renaissance playwrights may have been deluded. He is no longer the cherished son, fighting under the protection of his fathers; "little Teucer" has transmogrified into a dwarf swamped by giants' clothes. When in his middle years he confronted his estrangement from the direction national politics was taking, his sense of crisis reactivated anxieties about his legitimacy. Dryden's grief over James' impending exclusion, and his own, spilled over to incorporate his Renaissance fathers: he experienced it as his abandonment by the fathers.

Swift's satiric wit would naturally seize on such instances of faltering self-regard in his eminent rival. Dryden suggests in a moment of despair that the Restoration sons "have nothing" of the Titans' "thought, but are all outside." Swift was to give him the benefit of this doubt. In *The Battle of the Books*, the modern's oversized visor lifts to reveal "a shrunken pea-head within."[17] Congreve, by contrast, tried to assuage his mentor's fears. His tribute to Dryden appropriates the conceits of the 1679 preface. Congreve commits what could be termed a *clinamen* on the precursor's essay, but his corrective misreading of Dryden amends his text to ends quite other than those projected by Bloom. Congreve's revision swerves from Dryden's harsh estimation of his own talent. He adopts the trope Dryden had used to transform Shakespeare into an icon, and applies the encomium instead to Dryden:

his Diction is ... so Sublimely, and so truly Poetical, that its Essence, like that of pure Gold, cannot be destroy'd. Take his Verses, and divest them of their Rhimes, disjoint them in their Numbers, [and] ... make what Arrangement and Disposition you please of his Words, yet shall there Eternally be Poetry, and something which will be found incapable of being resolv'd into absolute Prose: An incontestable Characteristick of a truly poetical Genius.

   I will say but one Word more in general of his Writings, which is, that what he has done in any one Species ... would have been sufficient to have acquir'd him a great Name. If he had written nothing but his Prefaces, or nothing but his Songs, or his Prologues, each of them would have intituled him to the Preference and Distinction of excelling in his Kind.   (*Letters and Documents*, 129)

Congreve counters Dryden's lowered confidence in himself during and after the Exclusion Crisis with expressions of unabated filial regard and support. He declares that Dryden "was an improving Writer to his last, even to near seventy Years of Age" (128). As Dryden had before him in his tributes to his Renaissance forefathers, Congreve elected to emulate his precursor's character in the generous, affirming tribute he offered to him some seventeen years after Dryden's death.

Father and son: Dryden's rediscovery of Jonson in his Epistle to Congreve

When Dryden rediscovered Jonson as a major influence in the last decade of his life, the Jonson he assimilated was the Caroline poet who wrote odes to himself in the years of his eclipse. Dryden had, early in his career, achieved the "intelligent saturation" in Jonson's work "as a whole" that T. S. Eliot would commend him for.[18] The prose of the 1660s and 1670s contains scattered, yet precise references to Jonson's poetry, but Dryden remains primarily invested over those decades in the drama and in *Discoveries*, which is repeatedly cited in *Dramatick Poesie* as the English precedent for his own criticism. The 1668 essay is also the locus for

Dryden's infamous dismissal of Jonson's late work. Neander's otherwise admiring character of Jonson opens with a brusque distinction; he prefers, Neander says, to "look upon" Jonson "while he was himself, (for his last Playes were but his dotages)" (XVII: 57). This somewhat facile separation of Jonson's canonical folio works from those Caroline productions Neander relegates to a parenthetic aside no longer holds for Dryden by 1693 and 1694. In his final years he draws creative sustenance – and a salutary caution – from rereading the poet who had apparently declined from himself. Now sixty-three years of age and in failing health, Dryden can learn from the struggles of men who are considered by their contemporaries "past their termes."[19] He had just completed *Love Triumphant*, the comedy he thought of as his "Valedictory Play"; as he predicted, it was a failure on stage, just as Jonson's *New Inne* had been.[20] Dryden had lost the post of laureate; his finances, as a result, were more than usually wobbly. Under these circumstances, which reinforced Dryden's growing conviction that he was not the future but already part of the past Congreve's genius was casting into the shadows, his identification with Ben Jonson regained its former intensity – and shifted in focus. Jonson had been for decades Dryden's authoritative mentor, in Eliot's terms his "master." Near the end of his career, when he brings himself to look upon Jonson, Dryden sees a frailer, more human Titan. He now absorbs the Jonson of *Under-wood*, a project he had inaugurated with the deft comic allusions of "Mac Flecknoe," released in 1682, but only completed with the Jonsonian interpolations in his 1693 translation of Juvenal's satires and the verse address, "To my Dear Friend Mr. Congreve, On His Comedy, call'd, *The Double Dealer*," published the following year.

Perhaps inevitably, Dryden rereads himself by rereading Jonson's autobiographical poems written at an analogous stage of his career. Dryden had subscribed to the conventional Caroline wisdom about Jonson's late works; to sneer at them as "dotages" in 1668 simply ratified the judgment Jonson's contemporaries had vigorously promulgated more than thirty years earlier. Jonson responded to his detractors with defiant odes of reproof. The two odes occasioned by the disastrous debut of *The New Inne* in 1629 are particularly notable. As Sara van den Berg has argued, these odes "craft ... a poetics of anger"; they are unabashedly personal and embittered, despite their professed stance of disdain.[21] Stung by the response his return to the stage had elicited, stung also by the snide witticisms being circulated by his contemporaries, whose jests about his paralytic strokes passed in some Caroline circles for literary criticism, Jonson wrote odes of self-vindication.

> Make not thy selfe a Page,
> To that strumpet the Stage,
> But sing high and aloofe ("An Ode. To himselfe."
>   [VIII: 175, lines 33–35]),

he resolves in one. The companion ode begins with an equally pointed injunction to himself to withdraw from the arena of his humiliation:

> Come leave the lothed stage,
> And the more lothsome age:
> Where pride, and impudence (in faction knit)
> Usurpe the chaire of wit!
>   ("Ode to himselfe," [VI: 492, lines 1–4])

Jonson's repudiations of "the lothed stage" strike a responsive chord of anger in Dryden by the early 1690s. His own autobiographical embellishments of Juvenal's third satire have, as James Winn has pointed out, "no basis at all in the Latin" (Winn: *John Dryden and His World*, p. 458); instead, Dryden's interpolated complaint in his translation of Juvenal derives from an intense resurgence of investment in Ben Jonson's poetry. The speaker in Dryden's transliteration of Jonson's late odes is Umbricius, whose mounting disgust and frustration with the diminishing rewards of public service in Rome prompt him to a solipsistic retreat. Umbricius exits, cursing:

> Since Noble Arts in *Rome* have no support,
> And ragged Virtue not a Friend at Court,
> No Profit rises from th'ungrateful Stage,
> My Poverty encreasing with my Age,
> 'Tis time to give my just Disdain a vent,
> And, Cursing, leave so base a Government.
>   (IV: 115, lines 39–44)

In these lines, Dryden emulates Jonson's risky assertions of aloofness – and his inability to detach from the circumstances that have occasioned his bitter resolve. Few of Jonson's Caroline readers were persuaded by his professed disdain; few readers of Dryden's third satire would be convinced of his. The solace Dryden claims to find in self-righteous repudiation has little persuasive power; it requires, after all, a readership capable of interiorizing the reproof of their judgments implied in his publicized gesture of withdrawal. The comfort Dryden can take from rereading Father Ben is more private. It inheres in the reassurance that his poetic father, his "Syre" (IV: 432, line 3) in the language of the Congreve epistle, continues to mentor him, even in misfortune.

Dryden will craft a subtler poetics of anger in "To my Dear Friend Mr. Congreve." He softens Jonson's "lothed Stage" to "th' ungrateful Stage" that he is "just abandoning," in part because he is "worn with Cares and Age" (IV: 434, lines 66–67), in part because his nostalgic works no longer please contemporary audiences. He jokes that he is "Unprofitably kept at Heav'ns expence," then modulates wit into earned pathos: "I live a Rent-charge on his Providence" (IV: 434, lines 68–69). The bitterness that is overt in the interpolated passage in Juvenal and in Jonson's precursor odes is masked in Dryden's address to Congreve: it centers on the ignominy of losing public office.

In Dryden's case, the throne of wit had been usurped twice over, by Thomas Shadwell, who succeeded Dryden as poet laureate after the Revolution, and most recently by Thomas Rymer, who became historiographer royal in 1692. When Dryden alludes, as he must, to his own exclusion from these offices, he adopts a posture that is for the most part as disdainful as the stance Jonson had wanted to take towards the impudent writers who were "usurp[ing his] ... chaire of wit." Dryden initially resorts to casual, perhaps too casual, contempt:

> But now, not I, but Poetry is curs'd;
> For *Tom* the Second reigns like *Tom* the first.
>
> (IV: 433, lines 47–48)

His humiliation at being stripped of the laureateship is nevertheless acute; it could only have been revived by Rymer's elevation to his other cherished post. He begins to negotiate the awkward task of stepping down in favor of Congreve, a maneuver made considerably more tense by another pressure: Dryden must confront the insulting fact that he has already been deposed. Hailing Congreve as his rightful heir, he protests:

> Oh that your Brows my Lawrel had sustain'd,
> Well had I been Depos'd, if You had reign'd!
> The Father had descended for the Son;
> For only You are lineal to the Throne.
> Thus when the State one *Edward* did depose;
> A Greater *Edward* in his room arose.   (IV: 433, lines 41–46)

The epistle invites Congreve to see himself as a type of Edward III, the more fortunate heir to the "Throne of Wit" (line 53) who will assuredly wrest his father's crown back from its ignoble usurpers, the Shadwells and the Rymers. Dryden's celebration of Congreve's future preeminence is nevertheless shadowed by his confession, however *sotto voce*, of his own residual pain and humiliation when he confronts his ouster from offices that had seemed to confirm his legitimacy as the heir apparent to the Titans.

Two parentheses are introduced into the poem at the juncture at which Dryden surveys his diminished prestige. The first, a self-conscious pun on the now obsolete use of "parenthesis" to denote a "hiatus" or "interval," interrupts Dryden's prediction of a spectacular rise for his protégé. Congreve's ascension to the pinnacle of his profession is inevitable, the proud mentor prophesies: "Thou shalt be seen, / ... High on the Throne of Wit." His confident boast is briefly suspended by an apparently stray interpolation: "(Tho' with some short Parenthesis between:)" (IV: 433, lines 51–53). The next digression disparages the estate he has to leave to Congreve: "Not mine (that's little) but thy Lawrel wear" (IV: 433, line 54). What is being exhibited here, and throughout Dryden's prose, is a more localized poetic influence. Dryden has learned more from Ben Jonson than the bad habit of ending his sentences with prepositions: Jonson's legacy, which Dryden had thoroughly assimilated, included "the extensive use of parentheses."[22]

To understand how the rhetorical figure of parenthesis functions in Dryden's poem, we need to attend to Puttenham's *Arte of English Poesie*, the popular sixteenth-century manual of style that Ben Jonson owned, annotated heavily, and drew on for his *English Grammar* and his creative work. Puttenham is the first English theorist who considers the parenthesis. He includes it in an equivocal category, under those figures of speech that work "by disorder."[23] Jonson follows suit by designating the parenthesis in his *Grammar* as one of the distinguishing marks of an "*imperfect* Sentence" (VIII: 551–52). Puttenham elaborates:

Your first figure of tollerable disorder is [*Parenthesis*] or by an English name the [*Insertour*] and is when ye will seeme for larger information or some other purpose, to peece or graffe in the middest of your tale an unnecessary parcell of speach, which nevertheless may be thence without any detriment to the rest. The figure is so common that it needeth none example ... [Puttenham then gives examples.] This insertion is ... [often] utterly impertinent to the principall matter, and makes a great gappe in the tale, nevertheless is no disgrace but rather a bewtie and to very good purpose, but you must not use such insertions often nor to[o] thick ... for it will breede great confusion to have the tale so much interrupted.

(*The Arte of English Poesie*, pp. 180–81)

According to Puttenham, parentheses introduce an element of "tollerable," because bounded, "disorder" into the sentence. The figure of parenthesis proposes itself as an unedited aside. It further insinuates that its interruptions, in essence, make nothing happen. These are "unnecessary parcell[s] of speach" which the writer cannot apparently bring himself to part with – the purely additive, even the "impertinent," in short, whatever is considered extraneous to the perfect hierarchical order-

ing of the sentence. Parentheses thus signal the incursion of the inconsequential into a text. The figure operates out of a necessary fiction, namely
that its rupturing of a syntactic sequence does not materially affect the
reception of that construction. As Puttenham says, it "may be thence
without any detriment to the rest." At the same time, the parenthesis does
create a hiatus or "gappe" in the sequence. It embarrasses the sentence's
ideal order or composure, both by disrupting the syntactic sequence and
by incorporating whichever elements cannot be integrated into a harmonized whole. The parenthesis, Jonson would add in his *English Grammar*,
"mark[s] off" (VIII: 551) incongruous elements, brackets them from the
rest in order to designate them peripheral. But they are not jettisoned.
Instead, the parenthesized material survives in the text as traces of a
counter-impulse – towards complication, or equivocation. Parentheses
mediate between what the writer deems "principall matter" and those
subsidiary, often contradictory, elements that have somehow resisted
erasure.

In encomiastic literature, parentheses often serve the writer's need to
admit reflexive thoughts of self into the work. Jonson's sonnet to William
Camden provides a prototype for the uses Dryden will make of this figure
in his epistle to Congreve. Published in *Epigrammes*, this sonnet pays a felt
tribute to Camden's scholarly contributions, and insists on the enormity of
Jonson's intellectual debt to his former headmaster at Westminster.
Jonson's praise of Camden is unconditional. He owes his mentor "All that
I am in arts, all that I know" (VIII: 31, line 2). This admission prompts a
sudden parenthetic doubt: "(How nothing's that?)" (line 3). Jonson then
resumes his enumeration of Camden's exemplary virtues. He speaks *as
though* no such interpolation has happened, even as though he has not
overheard his own question. The recoil from "all" that seems implied by
"nothing" is acknowledged, but only in a circumspect form, and only on
the illusory premise that what Jonson thinks to question – the impact on
him of an influence so massive and authoritative that it can be said to
define "all that I am" – is incidental to an understanding of his relation to
Camden.[24] Were it not for the saving parenthesis with its neatly demar-
cated boundaries, which preserve by separating, the thought would be
intolerable. The pressures generated by encomiastic tributes – to be
other-centered, not self-absorbed – tend to dictate that the indecorous ego
be relegated to the peripheries, the place reserved for the parenthesis.

In so far as Dryden's "To my Dear Friend Mr. Congreve" doubles as an
address to himself (and to the self he found in Jonson), the figure of the
parenthesis serves him well. Dryden understands its ambiguous position in
the hierarchy of the poetic line, as his deliberate manipulation of its

multiple meanings and associations underscores. His punning "(Tho' with some short Parenthesis between:)" draws attention to the arbitrary boundaries that separate the "principall matter" from what seems to be an incidental graft. The interval of the personal aside takes up an entire line; it separates Dryden's prediction of his protégé's ascension to the throne of wit from its certain realization. In effect, Dryden's parenthesis briefly postpones that moment. While his "short Parenthesis" may prove inconsequential, a detour as it were in literary history, it is not felt to be so by the speaker of the poem.

Dryden's last years surely constitute a remaining obstacle to Congreve's coming into his rightful inheritance. The father has acted responsibly in settling his estate during his lifetime on his son; still, Dryden cannot be altogether comfortable with the notion of emulating a Lear, or even his own Flecknoe. The intellectualism of Dryden's meta-parenthesis bears its own controlled, self-aware pathos. From the vantage point of 1694, his life's work may have appeared to him a mere parenthesis when he compared his own achievements with those of the Titans or with the early evidence of Congreve's dramatic genius. (The synoptic literary history that opens his epistle privileges his Renaissance progenitors and his designated successor over any of the dramatists of Dryden's own generation.) Or, to construe the matter more cautiously, when Dryden characterizes himself as a "Rent-charge" on Heaven's providence he had no way of knowing how productive his final years would be.

The uncommon successor: William Congreve

Throughout the epistle, Dryden appeals to Congreve's discerning decency: he knows to whom he writes. His compliment was not misplaced. Neither writer would renege on the bond he formed to the other over the decade of the 1690s. The longing to mentor and be mentored, shared by both men, was actualized in their friendship. Dryden's support, which extended to editorial advice on Congreve's early comedies, shared professional contacts and public expressions of his admiration, enabled an illustrious career in the theater for Congreve, who was nineteen years of age when they first met, twenty-three when Dryden handed over the succession to him. The gift of Congreve's esteem in turn did as much for Dryden, assuaging some of the chagrin he felt over having been deposed as laureate.

Congreve was the uncommon successor any writer invested in a poetic lineage would want. His comedies had already demonstrated that he valued nuanced admissions cast in the form of equivocal, epigrammatic asides. Dryden's preoccupation with thoughts of his own mortality and his place in literary history surface in the epistle, then, not only because they must be admitted in some form, but because he trusted Congreve to appreciate the wit, and the subtext of pain, in his eloquent abdication. Some twenty-five years later, Congreve would speak of the "very Elegant, tho' very partial Verses" (*Letters and Documents*, p. 126) Dryden had addressed to him. He recalls the epistle's closing lines:

> But You, whom ev'ry Muse and Grace adorn,
> Whom I foresee to better Fortune born,
> Be kind to my Remains; and oh defend,
> Against Your Judgment Your departed Friend!
> Let not the Insulting Foe my Fame pursue;
> But shade those Lawrels which descend to You:
> And take for Tribute what these Lines express:
> You merit more; nor cou'd my Love do less.   (lines 70–77)

The intensity of Dryden's appeal to Congreve and the candor of his tribute to the writer he believed to have been blessed with "ev'ry Muse and Grace" found their complement in Congreve's retrospective. He focuses on Dryden's plea that he "*be kind to his Remains*" (126; Congreve's emphasis). Congreve acknowledges that he has interiorized his mentor's request, felt it as an "Injunction laid upon me ... to do something answerable" (126) to the trust placed in him. But Congreve does more than discharge an obligation he feels to his "*departed Friend*" (126; Congreve's emphasis). In the 1717 preface to his edition of Dryden's dramatic works, he chooses to respond in kind to Dryden's emotional investment in him. "I was then, and have been ever since most sensibly touched with that Expression" (126), he writes: what moves Congreve is Dryden's vulnerability and his diffidence about the value of his work. These needs are honored in Congreve's portrait of Dryden. Answering the objections of those contemporary readers who would tax him with "Officiousness" for undertaking the project of commemorating Dryden's character and work, Congreve responds: "I have but one thing to say either to obviate, or to answer such an Objection, if it shall be made to me, which is, that I loved Mr. *Dryden*" (126). For readers accustomed to the habitual reticence of his correspondence, this is a rare moment of self-disclosure.

Dryden had forged affiliative ties to other writers throughout his career, including his Renaissance progenitors and other, living mentors. The legacy of the epistle to Congreve is anticipated, in the form of desire, as early as 1666. In dedicating *Annus Mirabilis* to Sir Robert Howard, Dryden begs "the greatest favor you can confer upon an absent person, since I repose upon your management what is dearest to me, my Fame and Reputation" (I: 59). With Congreve, that favor was granted. In the dynamic between these two writers there was a sustained mutual mentoring that interrogates the premises of either Swift's or Bloom's anatomies of intergenerational poetic rivalries. Neither Dryden nor Congreve was much drawn to the ethos of creative solipsism; they invested instead in the distinctly unBloomian ideal of affirming influence. Poetic affiliation, as practiced in these careers, can be construed as weakness, as evidence of oedipal defeat, but whether such knowingness does much beyond foreclosing the question of influence in favor of a single, totalizing explanation is debatable. The careers of these Restoration writers offer a challenge to the sufficiency of Bloom's model of poetic relationships. Their efforts to realize a cultural and literary paradox in their work, to privilege exchange and emulation over unmitigated competition with the precursors and each other, deserve a closer investigation, perhaps even a provisional suspension of critical disbelief on our parts answerable to theirs.

Notes

1 Jonathan Swift, "*The Battle of the Books,*" *A Tale of a Tub, With Other Early Works, 1696–1707,* ed. Herbert Davis (Oxford: Basil Blackwell, 1957), p. 158.

2 Harold Bloom, *The Anxiety of Influence: A Theory of Poetry* (London: Oxford University Press, 1973), p. 9.

3 John Dryden, "Mac Flecknoe," *The Works of John Dryden,* ed. Edward Niles Hooker, H. T. Swedenberg, et al., 20 vols. (Berkeley and Los Angeles: University of California Press, 1955–), II: 58, lines 171–72. Unless otherwise noted, all references to works by Dryden will be to the California edition, cited by volume and page number and, where appropriate, line number. For a defense of Shadwell's claim to Jonson's legacy of humorous comedy, see Brian Corman, "Thomas Shadwell and the Jonsonian Comedy of the Restoration," *From Renaissance to Restoration: Metamorphoses of the Drama,* ed. Robert Markley and Laurie Finke (Cleveland: Bellflower Press, 1984), pp. 127–52.

4 Nicholas Jose, *Ideas of the Restoration in English Literature, 1660–71* (Cambridge: Harvard University Press, 1984), pp. 172–73.

5 Susan Stewart, *On Longing: Narratives of the Miniature, the Gigantic, the Souvenir, the Collection* (Baltimore: Johns Hopkins University Press, 1984), p. 23.

6 Sigmund Freud, "Mourning and Melancholia," *The Standard Edition of the Complete Psychological Works of Sigmund Freud,* trans. James Strachey, 24 vols. (London: Hogarth Press, 1953–74), XIV: 244.

7 Dryden, Preface to *Fables, The Poems of John Dryden,* ed. James Kinsley, 4 vols. (London: Oxford University Press, 1958), IV: 1455; poetic passages hereafter cited by line number and prose by volume and page number from this edition when the work is not yet included in the California edition.

8 Dryden's account of his motives in translating selections of Chaucer in his *Fables* bears on this point. Finding Chaucer underread by contemporary readers because his Middle English is inaccessible to many of them, Dryden

sets out to promote a renewed interest in his works, to "perpetuate his
Memory, or at least refresh it, amongst my Countrymen" (Kinsley, IV: 1459).
His own translation is not designed to replace Chaucer's tales, but to make the
excellence of his precursor more generally known; those readers who understand Middle English are pointedly advised to "neglect my Version, because
they have no need of it" (*ibid.*). Dryden similarly authorizes other poets to
modernize his works when they in turn become inaccessible to subsequent
generations of readers.

9 William Congreve, "Congreve to Thomas Pelham-Holles, Duke of Newcastle,"
William Congreve: Letters and Documents, ed. John C. Hodges (New York:
Harcourt, 1964), p. 125.

10 Dryden, "The Author's Apology for Heroic Poetry and Poetic License, Prefixed to *The State of Innocence: An Opera*," *John Dryden: Selected Criticism*,
ed. James Kinsley and George Parfitt (Oxford: Clarendon Press, 1970),
p. 134. The ideal Dryden articulates in his "Apology" and elsewhere in his
criticism could be abrogated in practice; his feuds with Sir Robert Howard,
Elkanah Settle, and Shadwell all demonstrated his capacity for lethal nitpick-
ing. On occasion, Dryden's "naturally vindicative" (IV: 60) streak overrode
the self-restraint he held up to his contemporaries as a model of responsible
humanist criticism. It is also the case, however, that Dryden maintained a
dignified silence about many of the provocations he might have chosen to
respond to: "More Libels have been written against me, than almost any Man
now living . . . But let the World witness for me, that I have been often wanting
to my self in that particular; I have seldom answer'd any scurrilous Lampoon:
When it was in my power to have expos'd my Enemies: And being naturally
vindicative, have suffer'd in silence, and possess'd my Soul in quiet"
(IV: 59–60), he observes in his "Discourse of Satire" (1693).

11 Robert D. Hume, *Dryden's Criticism* (Ithaca: Cornell University Press, 1970),
p. 94. See further for Hume's succinct refutation of the still widespread
assumption that the "Defence of the Epilogue" maligns Dryden's Renaissance
precursors, pp. 94–96 and 165, where Hume points out that in this 1672 essay
Dryden rejects "unquestioned submission to the past." Hume also cites on this
debate, *contra* William E. Bohn and others, Hoyt Trowbridge, "Dryden's
'Essay on the Dramatic Poetry of the Last Age'," *Philological Quarterly* 22
(1943), 240–50. It is also worth remarking that, in arguing against a slavish
devotion to Jonson, Fletcher, or Shakespeare, Dryden is emulating Jonson's
precepts to his readers in *Discoveries* (1640), his critical prose fragment that
advocates both the humanist transmission of influence through imitation and
the need for an heir to that rich legacy, including classical writers, to retain a
measure of critical independence in assimilating his eminent precursors.

12 My metaphor is borrowed from Dryden's Preface to *Ovid's Epistles* (1680)
where he alludes to Noah's sons' embarrassment at discovering their father
naked in Genesis 9: 18–29. In his preface, Dryden applies the biblical episode
to the situation faced by Ovid's translators; like Shem and Japheth, Ovid's
heirs "blush at the nakedness of their Father" (I: 112) when they are confronted by imperfections in his writing: their first impulse is to cover up Ovid's

faults. See further James Anderson Winn's discussion of this allusion in his *John Dryden and His World* (New Haven: Yale University Press, 1987), p. 331.

13 Dryden's examples of the Jacobean dramas that achieve this feat include Beaumont and Fletcher's *The Maid's Tragedy*, and Jonson's *The Alchemist* and *Epicoene*. *Volpone* is proposed as a tentative candidate, but Neander decides that its labyrinthine plot arguably contains two distinct actions. See further *Works*, XVII: 49.

14 Samuel Johnson, "Life of Dryden," *Lives of the English Poets*, ed. G. Birkbeck Hill, 3 vols. (New York: Octagon Books, 1967), I: 412. See also Johnson's response to Congreve's portrait of Dryden, pp. 394–99. For an extended discussion of the trope of the body in late Jonson, see my " 'Noe fault, but Life': Jonson's Folio as Monument and Barrier," *Ben Jonson's 1616 Folio*, ed. Jennifer Brady and W. H. Herendeen (Newark: University of Delaware Press, 1991), pp. 192–216.

15 Winn has proposed an alternative reading of Lisideius' direct address of Neander in his monumental biography of Dryden. Winn emphasizes that Neander lacks "the protective nimbus of title and fortune that surround[s] ... his aristocratic acquaintances" and that he is further vulnerable because, as Dryden's stand-in, he bears "the stigma of his employment by the Protectorate" (p. 163). Lisideius' gesture, according to Winn, is a calculated dig at Dryden for his early association with Cromwell's Protectorate.

16 See further Robert Markley, *Two-Edg'd Weapons: Style and Ideology in the Comedies of Etherege, Wycherley, and Congreve* (Oxford: Clarendon Press, 1988). I am indebted to this provocative book, in particular to its analysis of cultural nostalgia in late Caroline and Restoration appreciations of Fletcher, and its timely research into Fletcher's centrality for Dryden and other Restoration playwrights. Markley argues persuasively that Dryden "constantly reassesses his predecessor's historical significance, the changing influences that Fletcher's example provides at different times. His comments on [Fletcher's] ... dramatic language, scattered over a thirty-year period ... might be taken as a limited and necessarily incomplete 'history' of Fletcher's influence after 1660" (p. 77). This pattern of continual reassessment of a precursor's work typifies Dryden's relation to his Jacobean forebears, including Jonson and Shakespeare.

17 Michael Seidel, *Satiric Inheritance, Rabelais to Sterne* (Princeton: Princeton University Press, 1979), p. 50.

18 T. S. Eliot, "Ben Jonson" and "John Dryden," *Selected Essays* (New York: Harcourt, 1932; reprinted 1964), pp. 127–39 and 264–74. See further Ian Donaldson's astute essay, "Fathers and Sons: Jonson, Dryden, and *Mac Flecknoe*," *Southern Review* 18 (1985): 314–27. Donaldson argues for Dryden's "exceptionally intimate knowledge of Jonson's work," a position he documents by studying Dryden's allusions, "both acknowledged and concealed," to Jonson's poetry and criticism.

19 Ben Jonson, "An Epistle to Master JOHN SELDEN," *Ben Jonson*, ed. C. H. Herford and Percy and Evelyn Simpson, 11 vols. (Oxford: Clarendon Press, 1925–52), VIII: 159, line 21. The phrase "past their termes" is invoked by Jonson to castigate himself for praising the undeserving. *Under-wood*'s focus on

Jonson's own experience of waning public acclaim, however, tends to interrogate the premises of such easily dismissive judgments. See also the discussion of Dryden's identification with Ovid's ignominious last years in Cedric D. Reverand II, *Dryden's Final Poetic Mode: The Fables* (Philadelphia: University of Pennsylvania Press, 1988), pp. 23–24; and, for an exemplary discussion of Dryden's complex, shifting sense of his relations to contemporary readers once he "had lost by his [religious] conversion the political centrality that derived from his alliance with a strong political party and that allowed him [before the Exclusion Crisis and James II's deposition] to represent his political views as the ideal of a whole people," see David Bywaters, *Dryden in Revolutionary England* (Berkeley and Los Angeles: University of California Press, 1991), p. 33.

20 On the reception of *Love Triumphant*, see Winn, *John Dryden and His World*, pp. 471–75, and on the failure of Jonson's *New Inne*, David Riggs, *Ben Jonson: A Life* (Cambridge: Harvard University Press, 1989), pp. 302–10.

21 Sara J. van den Berg, *The Action of Ben Jonson's Poetry* (Newark: University of Delaware Press, 1987), p. 173; see also Annabel Patterson, "Lyric and Society in Jonson's *Under-wood*," *Lyric Poetry: Beyond the New Criticism*, ed. Chaviva Hošek and Patricia Parker (Ithaca: Cornell University Press, 1985), pp. 148–63.

22 David Riggs, *Ben Jonson: A Life*, p. 276; for a more detailed study of Jonson's punctuation, see Kevin J. Donovan's "Jonson's Texts in the First Folio," *Ben Jonson's 1616 Folio*, pp. 23–37, especially pp. 27–29.

23 George Puttenham, *The Arte of English Poesie*, ed. Hilton Landry (Kent, OH: Kent State University Press, 1988), p. 180. For a facsimile of Jonson's annotated copy of Puttenham's treatise, see George Puttenham, *The Arte of English Poesie, 1598*, ed. R. C. Alston (Menston: Scolar Press, 1968); see also David McPherson, "Ben Jonson's Library and Marginalia," *Studies in Philology*, 71 (1974), 1–106.

24 On Jonson's sonnet to Camden, see further W. H. Herendeen's, "'Like a Circle Bounded in Itself': Jonson, Camden, and the Strategies of Praise," *Journal of Medieval and Renaissance Studies*, 11 (1981), 137–67. After long neglect, Jonson's *English Grammar* is receiving deserved attention. See: Timothy Murray, *Theatrical Legitimation: Allegories of Genius in Seventeenth-Century England and France* (New York: Oxford University Press, 1987), pp. 44–49; Martin Elsky, "Words, Things, and Names: Jonson's Poetry and Philosophical Grammar," *Classic and Cavalier: Essays on Jonson and the Sons of Ben*, ed. Claude J. Summers and Ted-Larry Pebworth (Pittsburgh: Pittsburgh University Press, 1982), pp. 91–104; Wyman H. Herendeen, "Ben Jonson and the Play of Words," *Craft and Tradition: Essays in Honour of William Blissett*, ed. H. B. DeGroot and A. Leggatt (Calgary: University of Calgary Press, 1990), pp. 123–36.

2

Onely victory in him: the imperial Dryden

DAVID B. KRAMER

Dryden remarked of Ben Jonson that "He invades Authours like a Monarch, and what would be theft in other Poets, is onely victory in him."[1] The comment distinguishes between simple plagiarism ("theft") and another kind of appropriation that is a kind of "victory." As practiced by Dryden upon such figures as Thomas Corneille, Quinault, Madeleine de Scudéry, and Molière, this aggressively public mode of poetic assimilation is the literary equivalent of invading weaker foreign realms and diverting their resources back to the conquering capital. Dryden vindicates this imperial practice with arguments similar to his justifications for national conquest. Although often charged with literary theft, Dryden regards literary imperialism – "victory" – differently from plagiarism; when in the imperial mode, Dryden publicly asserts his right to seize other poets' work and incorporate it into his own. Appropriating others' work without comment is plagiarism; glorying in such depredations is peculiar to the imperial poet.

Dryden's transactions with those he considers poetic equals and inferiors approximate the complicated dealings of an imperial power with its vassal states, ranging from brute conquest to the more subtle strategies of denigration and replacement of the invaded culture.[2] His treatment of those he does not fear is often Almanzor-like: arrogant, splendid, glorious – and ultimately quite far from the silent and surreptitious manipulations of the plagiarizing sneak-thief his critics wished to make him. As I shall show by examining how Dryden refashioned Thomas Corneille's *Le Feint Astrologue* (1650) into his own *Evening's Love, or The Mock Astrologer* (1668), plagiarism, the contemporary charge most leveled against Dryden with regard to his appropriation of dramatic plots, is inadequate to describe his manner of taking from other poets.

55

From the mid-1660s to 1688, Dryden was the imperial poet *par excellence*, but his interest in the forcible seizure of the wealth of others was not peculiar to himself. The appetitive traits of the imperial mode reflect larger political and economic concerns of Dryden's age and, as Margaret Anne Doody points out in *The Daring Muse*, signs of an aggressive imperial urge run through Restoration and early eighteenth-century poetry.[3] The shining vision of London that concludes *Annus Mirabilis* is but one of many visions of a world-dominating England:

> Now, like a Maiden Queen, she will behold,
>   From her high Turrets, hourly Sutors come:
> The East with Incense, and the West with Gold,
>   Will stand, like Suppliants, to receive her doom. (lines 1185–88)

In this marvelously prescient vision, not only of a rebuilt London, but of an empire at peace, its battles of conquest fought and won, the "mother city" commands the world's wealth by the power of her own beauty, no longer by dint of the force described so vividly earlier in the poem.[4]

As we read the Dryden of the 1660s and 1670s, we are constantly reminded of his reverence for England's military and poetic might. Indeed, English military and poetic greatness are often used to signify one another, and the myth of English poetic and military invincibility is articulated throughout his criticism, poetry, prologues, epilogues, and plays. At the end of his examen in the *Essay of Dramatick Poesie*, Neander says of English poets:

Be it spoken to the honour of the *English*, our Nation can never want in any Age such who are able to dispute the Empire of Wit with any people in the Universe.
(*Works*, XVII: 63)

And in the same essay, pens and swords, evoking one another, conflate into a statement by Eugenius of England's poetic and military invincibility:

I am at all times ready to defend the honour of my Countrey against the *French*, and to maintain, we are as well able to vanquish them with our Pens as our Ancestors have been with their swords.   (*Works*, XVII: 33)

Though he exaggerates the accomplishments of the modern English poets and the faults of all others, we see from the preceding passages that Dryden is keenly aware of the relative strengths both of countries and of writers. That he chooses this international arena in which to stage this series of proofs of English literary superiority shows his eagerness to consider English writers (himself chief among them, a fact he modestly declines to

bring to our attention) in contest with the continental – specifically
French – dramatic achievement.

Dryden is also acutely conscious of the means and forms by which
nations – and poets – measure their strength against one another. Fifteen
of his twenty-eight plays contain competitions between nations or cultures. From the earliest dramas of the 1660s through the final masterpieces
of the 1690s, this measuring of strength, expressed in the conquering of one
culture by another, is explored in substantial detail from myriad points of
view. Dryden's representations of the measuring of strength between rival
cultures, interesting as military and cultural means-to-power might be,
will be examined with the primary aim of understanding his own relations
with foreign contemporaries and predecessors. My method is based on the
premise that his views of national and poetic destiny are in many ways
related; he uses similar language to describe relations between nations and
poets. For example, in the *Prologue* to Tomkis' Albumazar (1668) Dryden
says of Ben Jonson's use of the work of predecessors:

> But *Ben* made nobly his, what he did mould,
> What was anothere's Lead, becomes his Gold;
> Like an unrighteous Conquerer he raigns,
> Yet rules that well, which he unjustly gains.   (*Works*, I: 141)

He uses the same imperial language (conquering, ruling unjustly appropriated territory, and improving the seized material beyond its original
quality) when referring to his own depredations upon the works of others.
Of obtaining plot material for *An Evening's Love*, he says of himself:

> [The poet] ... us'd the *French* like Enemies,
> And did not steal their Plots, but made 'em prize.
>   (*Epilogue, Works*, X: 313–14)

Plots are lawful booty in Dryden's imperial scheme, the rightful possession
of whoever has the poetic strength to take them. To the imperial poet the
works of others are to be made war upon, "made prize" (taken), and
"ruled well" (reworked). In his mythologies of poetic origin, inheritance,
and "strength," Dryden often recurs to such imperial language.

Dryden's representations of imperialism are cast in a series of three
cultural oppositions: himself vs. certain foreign poets, England vs. countries of the European continent, and Europe vs. the "pagan" cultures
(often associated with the Orient or Americas). Though each set of
oppositions can be ordered with respect to its distance from the actual
conditions of creation of his poetry, Dryden frequently uses terms of the
same side of the opposition (himself, England, Europe, or foreign poets,

Europe, "pagan" cultures) to signify each other. In other words, through
his representations of cultural alterity in plays that deal with neither
Englishmen nor poets, such as *The Indian Emperour* (1665), *Marriage
A-la-Mode* (1673), or *Amphitryon* (1690), we may often read Dryden's
attitude towards the works of foreign poets. The differences are to be read
in the border of exchange between what is familiar and powerful (Europe,
England, himself), and what is rich and strange (the Orient and
Americas, Europe, foreign poets).

Representations of cultural alterity in the drama, dramatized always in
a state of opposition to that which constitutes home to Dryden (Europe,
England, himself), are usually of a piece. Before 1688, the Europeans-
English-himself are victorious. After 1688, the side with which he associates himself (Europeans, English, himself) is always vanquished and
exiled in a strange land (or one's own land made strange, as in *Amphitryon*).
That the balance between the two clashing cultures should shift so
absolutely with the decline in his own fortunes suggests an intimate
relation between the plots of these hetero-cultural plays and the events of
his own life. When the English get the better of the Spaniards in Madrid,
as occurs in *An Evening's Love*, we might read the play, in part, as a
dramatization of his getting the better of Thomas Corneille, from whom
he seized the play. When Don Sebastian, guilty of a crime he innocently
committed, buries himself forever in a monastery in a strange land, we
might read that, too, as a reflection of Dryden's relationship with the new
order, in which his place is that of a defeated leader under a "foreign"
regime.

Dryden's widest-ranging representations of cultural conflict are stagings
of clashes between Europe and the East; his interest in this type of meeting
is lifelong, and recurs throughout his dramatic career. Such encounters
occur in *The Indian Emperour* (1665), *Tyrannick Love* (1669), *The Conquest of
Granada I & II* (1670–71), *All for Love* (1677), *Troilus and Cressida* (1679),
Don Sebastian (1689), and *Cleomenes* (1692) – nearly a third of his plays.
Moors (three plays), Egyptians (three plays), Aztecs and Trojans (one
apiece), constitute the represented Other that Europeans (Spaniards,
three; Romans, two; Greeks, two; and Portuguese, one) encounter and
defeat.

Dryden's next most common form of representing the imperial urge is
the depiction of England struggling with another country, either in the
comic or the heroic mode. Such encounters occur in *Annus Mirabilis*
(1666), the *Essay of Dramatick Poesie* (1668), *An Evening's Love* (1668),
Marriage A-la-Mode (1673), *Amboyna* (1673), and *King Arthur* (1691).[5] Five
of the six dramas depicting the English at war with other nations were

written during times of Anglo-Dutch conflict (1665–67, 1672–74), and the English encounter Dutch in three of the above six works. In the remaining three, the English encounter Spaniards, French (specifically their customs and language in *Marriage*), and heathen Saxons. The *Essay of Dramatick Poesie* has an especially contentious setting; a sea-battle against the Dutch frames three verbal battles fought between four disputants for the terms of contemporary dramatic writing, pitting the present-day English against the French, Spanish, Italians, Ancient Greeks, and Romans. The former are found to win every contest, reflecting the eventual outcome of the sea-battle which frames the debate. Replete as it is with so many different types of interrelated battle, the *Essay of Dramatick Poesie* contains one of the key formulations of an ideology advocating the forcible seizure of poetic property. Neander (the main speaker for Dryden's position) says of Ben Jonson:

> He was deeply conversant in the Ancients, both *Greeke* and *Latine*, and he borrow'd boldly from them: there is scarce a Poet or Historian among the *Roman* Authours of those times whom he has not translated in *Sejanus* and *Catiline*. But he has done his Robberies so openly, that one may see he fears not to be taxed by any Law. He invades Authours like a Monarch, and what would be theft in other Poets, is onely victory in him. (*Works*, XVII: 57)

Bold borrowing, disregard for the conventions of poetic property, regal invasion of others – all describe the imperial mode of taking from other poets. In that mode, theft, plagiarism, is transcended – at least, so the commentator claims – for a more public form of appropriation in which sources are acknowledged, poetic originators named, and the poetic material itself seized upon and re-fashioned. Dryden often takes the royal conqueror's route as he approaches the work of those he regards as poetic equals or inferiors, those whose fame or greatness does not threaten to define the way he wishes to write. Just as Almanzor conquers all "because he dares," so Dryden often follows Jonson down the high road of imperial conquest, "invading like a monarch."[6]

Dryden treats the works of his forebears and contemporaries with varying degrees of esteem, ranging from the most respectful quotation down to the contemptuous light-fingered swipe. His oft-stated cavils aside, he accords considerable respect to the work of his English "fathers," Shakespeare and Jonson. Nor could Dryden borrow contemptuously from Pierre Corneille, because of the great prestige Corneille enjoyed.[7] But from Molière (to Dryden, merely a prodigious *farceur*), Quinault, Thomas Corneille (Pierre's younger brother), Madeleine and Georges de Scudéry, La Calprenède, and a host of others, Dryden felt licensed by his nationality and poetic status to take what he needed without apology. That these writers were French merely served to justify Dryden's imperial attitude. Such invasion, mounted in daylight, is not an ignominious theft, but, according to him, a patriotic "victory."

Dryden's interest in the imaginative representation of victory over other nations and poets finds one of its fullest expressions in *An Evening's Love, or the Mock Astrologer* (1668, published 1671), a play less known than its merits deserve. Written in the same year that the *Essay of Dramatick Poesie* was published (the year of Dryden's accession to the laureateship), *An Evening's Love* succeeded on the stage, and was revived at irregular intervals until its last recorded performance in 1717.

Although much scholarly ink has been spilled in ascertaining the sources of individual sections of *An Evening's Love*, the origins of the main plot and the most salient scenes have long been known.[8] The main plot (as well as the subtitle of Dryden's version) is adapted directly from Thomas Corneille's *Le Feint Astrologue* (1650), which in turn is adapted from Calderón's *El Astrologo Fingido* (1648). Dryden made no secret of his debt to Corneille, admitting it in the *Epilogue* to the play. An English Monsieur is made to say:

> I am a rogue
> But he has quite spoil'd the *feint Astrologue*.
> [The poet] *neither swore nor storm'd as Poets do,*
> *But, most unlike an Author, vow'd 'twas true.*
>
> *Works*, X: 313, lines 15–16, 26–27)

Dryden here admits the larger borrowing from Thomas Corneille, but other important – though unacknowledged – scenes are translated from Molière's *Le Dépit Amoureux* (*c.* 1658) and that rich mine of Restoration and eighteenth-century English comedy, *Les Précieuses Ridicules* (1659). Dryden's sources were remarked upon at the time. Mrs. Pepys observed his debt to Madeleine de Scudéry, and the captious Gerard Langbaine retailed a list of sources, many correct, others dubious.[9]

Le Feint Astrologue takes place entirely within the city of Madrid (thus observing the unity of place as defined by Thomas' older brother, Pierre).[10] The comedy opens with the playboy Don Fernand complaining of Lucrèce's indifference. His servant, Phillipin, soon learns through Lucrèce's maid that Lucrèce loves the impoverished aristocrat Don Juan, who, pretending business in Flanders, actually hides at the house of his friend Don Lope, suitor to Lucrèce's cousin, Léonor. Although Don Juan visits Lucrèce's garden nightly, he has also courted Léonor (who believes him to be *en route* to Flanders).

Don Fernand hints to Lucrèce that he knows of her lover, leading Lucrèce to suspect her servant Beatrix of betraying her. To save Beatrix's job, Phillipin wildly asserts that his master learned of Don Juan's nightly visits through astrology, and soon all Madrid knows of Don Fernand's "powers." Léonor consults the now "great" astrologer, desiring the spiritual body of Don Juan to appear to her that night. The astrologer dictates the request for a rendezvous to Don Juan's spirit, and Phillipin delivers the letter to the horrified Don Juan. The scene changes (in the middle of the act, thus breaking the *liaison des scènes*) to Léonor and her waiting-maid awaiting the spirit of Léonor's lover. Calm as they await him, at his appearance Léonor hides in a closet, Jacinte under the table. Don Juan, understandably confused, leaves to keep his previous appointment with Lucrèce.

Act Four begins with Don Juan's meeting with Lucrèce in the street, where she gives him a diamond ring. Her father, Leonard, learning from the astrologer that Don Juan has the ring but believing he has stolen it from his daughter, requests the diamond back. Don Juan believes that Lucrèce has revealed their love to her father; he returns the jewel and asks for her hand. Leonard believes him mad. The misunderstanding is unresolved at the scene's end – Don Juan believes himself a favored son-in-law-to-be, Leonard thinks him a thief and madman.

The dénouement occurs at night in Leonard's garden. Leonard and Don Fernand arrive, Léonor accuses Lucrèce of loving Don Juan, and of meeting with and concealing him in the garden. Her father commands a search, Don Juan reveals himself, admits his love, and asks Leonard for his daughter. "The stars decree," says Don Fernand to Leonard, "that Lucrèce must marry Don Juan," and Leonard dutifully orders the nuptials.

As one might gather from the preceding summary, Corneille's *Feint Astrologue* is not a piece for the ages. The two women, Lucrèce and Léonor, are differentiated by no hint of character or individuality; the two-timing Don Juan is neither admirably clever nor more than mildly repugnant (and why this flawed and unattractive character is rewarded with Lucrèce and her father's money is not clear); Juan's friend Don Lope is only mildly faithful; and the mock astrologer, Don Fernand, is only mildly resourceful. The wily servant Phillipin is not above robbing and humiliating an old man, the industrious Beatrix not above betraying her mistress. The rather sour conclusion does not much please or displease, and one is relieved, not that the couples are paired off, but that the play is over.

Seventeenth-century formalist critics would have seen that *Le Feint Astrologue* contains serious structural flaws. The play observes neither the unity of time nor the *liaison des scènes*, for the action takes place over a period of two days and two nights, and the third, fourth, and fifth acts break into three, two, and two scenes. More seriously, unity of character is not maintained; Don Fernand, who throughout the play expresses only odium and scorn for Lucrèce, inexplicably helps her to marry the man she wants. Leonard, adamant that his daughter marry a rich man, consents without a murmur to her marrying a poor one. Don Juan, in hiding for days, appears for no reason in the street. The sense of poetic justice is wounded by allowing Don Juan to triumph; he who has so abused the trust of both women and has insulted Léonor to her face is rewarded with Lucrèce and her father's money.

We do not know what brought to Dryden's attention this lackluster product of a second-tier talent (perhaps it was the English translation which appeared in 1668), but the changes he wrought in the play show, in myriad ways, his interest in entering into the discourse of imperialism, both as an active imperialist in the realm of poetry, and as a representor of the larger struggle for monetary and poetic wealth between England and other cultures.

Dryden's version of Thomas Corneille's play shows interest in the drama of imperialism in two different but complementary ways. First, the stuff of the drama itself – characters, main plot outline, title – are all taken from Corneille in an act of poetic appropriation whose magnitude is not uncommon in Dryden's work.[11] Second, what was in the hands both of Thomas Corneille and Calderón a love intrigue between Spaniards set in their home-town of Madrid, becomes, in Dryden's play, a battle for women, money, and national glory between Spaniards and Englishmen. Moreover, as his interest in imperialism is shown on two planes, so his defense of this type of struggle is also dual; regarding the appropriation of the play itself, he mounts his most complete defense of poetic appropriation in the *Preface* (written in 1671, three years after completion of the play).[12] The defense of the struggle between nations *per se* is contained within the play itself.

Turning first to Dryden's staging of international struggle in the body of the play, we again note the most salient alteration from Corneille's original: Corneille's Spanish characters act and speak like Frenchmen; Corneille incorporates no Spanish element into the scenery or language. Dryden, on the other hand, recasts the plot as a struggle between Spaniards and Englishmen, with some attempt to suggest (if not actually to depict in detail) characteristic mores of each. Corneille's Madrid might have been Paris for all its lack of situational specificity; Dryden's Madrid is truly exotic, replete with Gypsies, Moors, Spanish food, Catholicism, street names, serenaders, and many words from the Spanish language itself. (Corneille's play contains none of these.)

The principal love affairs have increased from two to three; two Englishmen named Wildblood and Bellamy, attached to the English ambassador's entourage in Madrid, fall in love with two sisters, Jacinta and Theodosia. The two-timer of Corneille's play, now named Don Melchor, makes love both to Theodosia and the sisters' cousin, Aurelia. The wily servant Phillipin is replaced by the much wilier servant, Maskall, who is brilliantly inventive and unwaveringly cowardly. Characters have recognizable humours; Jacinta is bold and quick, forming half of an early "gay couple." The father, Don Alonzo, can let no one talk, interjecting "I know what you would say," then mis-completing his interlocutor's intended statement. Aurelia, whose humor of affected speech will be discussed further on, imports French words and phrases into her native tongue.

The act of appropriating the *Feint Astrologue* from Thomas Corneille is reinscribed in the plot itself, in which Englishmen defeat Spanish men in the battle for women, money, and national honor. This battle between nations (conducted on the very border between Englishness and Otherness) is contested at a number of sites. English language, religion, dramatic form, food, wit, swordsmanship, music, and especially standards of masculinity are all measured against their Spanish counterparts; in every case the Spanish counterpart is found inferior.

The theme of international war is carried into the plot and language of the love intrigue. And, in a scene which is itself the result of international poetic "strife," the languages of love and international strife conflate. While the scene depicts a joint lovers' quarrel in which master and man fall out with mistress and maid – couched in terms of international war – the scene itself is borrowed without acknowledgment from Molière's *Le Dépit Amoureux*.[13] The very terms of Dryden's "imperial" appropriation from Molière are reinscribed in the language of the scene:

Maskall. Courage, Sir; how goes the battel on your wing?
Wildblood. Just drawing off on both sides. Adieu *Spain*.
Jacinta. Farewel old *England*.
Beatrix. Come away in Triumph; the day's your own Madam.
Maskall. I'll bear you off upon my shoulders, Sir; we have broke their hearts.
Wildblood. Let her go first then; I'll stay, and keep the honor of the Field.
Jacinta. I'll not retreat, if you stay till midnight.   (*Works*, X: 292)

And as the couples begin to mend the quarrel, they modulate from the language of warfare to the language of diplomacy:

Maskall. Do you hear this, *Beatrix*? they are just upon the point of accommodation; we must make haste or they'll make a peace by themselves; and exclude us from the Treaty . . .

Jacinta. The prime Articles between *Spain* and *England* are seal'd; for the rest con-
     cerning a more strict alliance, if you please we'll dispute them in the Garden.
Wildblood. But in the first place let us agree on the Article of Navigation, I beseech
     you.
Beatrix. These Leagues offensive and defensive will be too strict for us, *Maskall*: a
     Treaty of commerce will serve our turn.   (*Works*, X: 293)

Structuring amorous interchange along the lines of national discourse
permits Dryden to mingle national (and martial) qualities into romantic
conversation, and the dialogue throughout is suffused with spirited references to all sorts of relations between nations and races; indeed, the word
"racy," used to denote "a distinctive quality of character or intellect;
lively, spirited, full of 'go' " (*OED*) receives its first recorded use in this play
in a context that reveals the word's roots in cultural alterity. In inviting his
intended to England, Wildblood drops the new word while defending the
stodginess of the English:

Faith, we live in a good honest Country, where we are content with our old vices,
partly because we want wit to invent more new. A Colonie of *Spaniards*, or spiritual
Italians planted among us would make us much more racy.   (*Works*, X: 232)

Unlike Corneille's *Feint Astrologue*, Dryden's *An Evening's Love* centers itself
firmly in the imaginative realm of the imagined Other by its use of Spanish
language, place names, and customs. *Alguazil, juego de cannas, Calle Major,
St. Jago, inamorado, borachos, Sennor Ingles, albricias, corigidore*, are some of the
Spanish words Dryden introduces into the play, vocabulary which
reminds us that these Englishmen face a foreign world which is truly different, where whatever they obtain will be by their wits.

   Nearly every measure of comparison between cultures in *An Evening's
Love* can be seen to have a corollary in the production, staging, and reception of English plays. For example, Spanish food is found wanting in
exactly the same terms in which foreign drama is found wanting in the
contemporaneous *Essay of Dramatick Poesie*, wherein Neander remarks on
the differences between English and French dramatic writing:

the barrenness of the French plots . . . the variety and copiousness of the *English* . . .
[English] variety, if well order'd, will afford a greater pleasure to the audience . . .
our own [plots] are fuller of variety.   (*Works*, XVII: 46–47, 53)

Foreign poetic productions, Dryden emphasizes again and again, are dull,
uniform, restrained, similar each to other. So, says one Englishman to the
other in *An Evening's Love*, is Spanish food:

Bellamy. I hope we had variety enough.
Wildblood. I, it look'd like variety, till we came to taste it; there were twenty several
     dishes to the eye, but in the pallat nothing but Spices. I had a mind to eat of a

Pheasant, and as soon as I got it into my mouth, I found I was chawing a
limb of Cinamon; then I went to cut a piece of Kid, and no sooner it had
touch'd my lips, but it turn'd to red Pepper: at last I began to think my self
another kind of *Midas*, that everything I touch'd should be turn'd to Spice.
Bellamy. And for my part, I imagin'd his Catholick Majesty had invited us to eat
his *Indies*.   (*Works*, X: 218)

The vocabulary is the same: "variety," that prime English desideratum of
both drama and cuisine, is missing from foreign productions of stage and
kitchen. Not only are Bellamy and Wildblood forced to eat dish after dish
which seem different yet turn out to be the same, but there is a sense of
tremendous wealth, unending copiousness (similar, down to the eastern
exoticism, to the language describing Holland/Carthage in *Annus Mirabilis*). Food and spices abound, as do foreign plays; what each lacks, in its
own sphere, is variety. And variety – even in this discussion of Spanish
food – is precisely what Dryden introduces into Corneille's stale version of
Calderón's play. This discussion of Spanish food, occurring in the first
scene, is the first of many instances in which the play's action and discourse
comment both on the play's origins in foreign alterity and on the process of
the play's transformation from one more boring item of foreign wealth to a
various, rich, and full product ready to please the English dramatic palate
with its taste for variety.

Even the quality of personal honor, an overabundance of which is often
ascribed to the Spanish character in Dryden's time, is introduced into this
English drama only to find it inefficient, as well as morally defective.
When the two-timing Don Melchor threatens to inform the father of
Jacinta and Theodosia as they elope with Bellamy and Wildblood, he
invokes his (deeply compromised) honor:

Melchor. No Sir, 'tis not for my honor, to be assisting to you: I'll to *Don Alonzo*, and
help to revenge the injury you are doing him.
Bellamy. Then we are lost, I can do nothing.
Wildblood. Nay, and you talk of honor, by your leave Sir.
[*Falls upon him & throws him down.*]
I hate your *Spanish* honor ever since it spoyl'd our *English* Playes, with faces
about and t'other side.   (*Works*, X: 299)

Spanish honor spoils English plays, just as Spanish honor is about to spoil
the "plot" of the Englishmen within this play.

In *An Evening's Love* sex is treated as an event of multiple import,
connoting pleasure indeed but, perhaps more importantly, serving as an
emblem for artistic and political concerns. Both in the *Prologue* and
Epilogue, Dryden explicitly likens writing and reading poetry to the male
aspect of sexual union; he conflates physical and poetic begetting into a

vision of the poet, a newly wedded groom, writing poetry with the pen of the body:

> WHEN first our Poet set himself to write,
> Like a young Bridegroom on his Wedding-night
> He layd about him, and did so bestir him,
> His Muse could never lye in quiet for him.
>
> (*Prologue, Works*, X: 214)

Dryden develops this equating of sex with poetry throughout the play as the irresistible Englishmen seize Spanish women sexually as Dryden seizes foreign plays with his pen. Here at the imaginatively reconstituted border of England's relations with the foreign world (literally – the protagonists are attached to the ambassador), the front line of imperial penetration is composed of these three men, seeking with ingenuity and ardor to possess the objects of their sexual desires. Writing, reading, and sex, rendered interchangeable by the *Prologue* and *Epilogue*, are the means to represent and understand the actions depicted in the play, and signs for one another. Winning women from foreigners, Dryden implies, is like taking plays from foreign poets. The martial vocabulary of forts and sieges, applied to foreign women, by extension applies equally well to foreign plays. For Englishmen, Dryden suggests, the wealth of the world is for the taking, be it another country's ships (*Annus Mirabilis*), another country's women (the plot of *An Evening's Love*), or another country's plays (the actual appropriation of *An Evening's Love*).

Dryden's notion of imperial power is enacted on yet another plane as these three sexually voracious Englishmen seek to appropriate the sexual and monetary goods of Spain. As portrayed in *An Evening's Love*, there is a natural rightness in the Englishman's spirit which makes his appetites charming, his lusts justified. Dashing and likeable, he is all but irresistible to the sex-starved women of Spain, and Spanish women leap to his arms as if no Spanish male had ever existed. Elopement with Englishmen is made to seem liberation in a sexual modulation of a myth that often accompanies the act of imperialism: that to be conquered and subjugated by the imperial power represents an enlargement from the slavery and misery of living outside imperial rule, and is thus instinctively welcomed by the new subjects of the empire. Since Dryden uses relations between Englishmen and Spanish women as a way to talk about English and foreign poetry, we might read the Spanish women's eagerness to be taken by the English as Dryden's imperial recognition that foreign plays require appropriation, use, and improvement at the hands of a capable, wily, and ardent English poet. In yet another way the plot of *An Evening's Love* recapitulates its origins in literary "rapture."

As we have seen, *An Evening's Love*'s metaphorical equation of writing with sex invites us to accord the play's use of sex other significations than that of mere sensual gratification. But, on the level of plot, brute sexual desire drives the events of the play; Wildblood in particular provides much of the comedy as he attempts to seduce Jacinta, principal object of his affections, each time she reappears disguised as another woman. Seeking indiscriminately to possess whatever woman is near him, Wildblood swears undying love to whoever wears a mask and skirts, be she even a servant or a Moor. As he turns from England outward towards female alterity, his omnivorous appetite makes him a sympathetic parody of the imperial urge; Dryden renders explicit the connection between seizing women and countries in the disguised Jacinta's bemused reprimand:

Heyday, You dispatch your Mistresses as fast, as if you meant to o're-run all Woman-kind: sure you aime at the Universal-Monarchy.   (*Works*, X: 272)

In this parody of insatiable desire for the foreign, the indefatigable sexual urge of the likeable young Englishman takes upon itself the desire to possess all of foreign womankind – an analogue, implied in the play's motif of literature as sex, of the poet's literary satyriasis toward the works of Molière, Quinault, Corneille, and the de Scudérys.

Certain classes of alterations effected by Dryden in Thomas Corneille's *Feint Astrologue* justify his poetic imperialism by demonstrating that the appropriated material is better "ruled" under the governance of its new master. A self-designated conqueror vis-à-vis the appropriation of *An Evening's Love* from Corneille ("he [Dryden] us'd the *French* like Enemies, / And did not steal their Plots, but made 'em prize," *Epilogue*, lines 28–29), Dryden demonstrates his determination that the poetic realms he rules, though "unrighteously conquered," be "ruled well" – like Jonson's poetic appropriations before him. To that end Dryden improves his conquered material, and from the nature of these improvements we learn something of his aims and anxieties regarding the French.

One such improvement is the compression of the incidents. The French theoretical ideal for dramatic extension in time was that the action represented in a play ought ideally to occur in the time taken to represent it. The complete coincidence of stage time with real time remained an infrequently attained absolute to the French; few plays actually achieved it, and few playwrights seemed to have tried. Thomas Corneille, in adapting Calderón's *El Astrologo Fingido*, only reduced the time from three days to two. Dryden, however, in adapting *Le Feint Astrologue*, shortened the time from two days to an evening, and, in case the public might have overlooked either the fact itself or the importance of this dramatic nicety, he called attention to this improvement, or "ruling well," by naming the play after the play's duration, relegating its former title to subtitle. And if, in spite of the title, the audience remained unaware of, or unimpressed by, his improvements, he mocked their unconcern in the person of a fop who mingles oaths with a brutish insensitivity to the fine points of seventeenth-century dramatic rules and decorums:

> Pox, *sayes another*; here's so great a stir
> With a son of a whore Farce that's regular,
> A rule where nothing must decorum shock!
> Dam' me 'ts as dull as dining by the clock.
> An Evening! why the devil should we be vext
> Whither he gets the Wench this night or next?
>
> (*Epilogue, Works*, X: 313)

Dryden underscores the importance he gives his own improvements by ascribing indifference to them to a contemptible fool seated among us. By means of the fool's dramatized insensitivity, Dryden indicates precisely to what he wishes us to be sensitive.

Another improvement of Dryden's (like the play's duration, drawn attention to throughout) was also based on a French prescription (or what was perceived to be one) – that the play occur on a special or long-awaited day. Neander describes the prescription thus in the *Essay of Dramatick Poesie*:

One of these advantages is that which *Corneille* has laid down as the greatest which can arrive to any Poem, and which he himself could never compass above thrice in all his Playes, *viz.* the making choice of some signal and long-expected day, wherepon the action of the Play is to depend.   (*Works*, XVII: 62)

In *An Evening's Love*, the "special day" is the last day of Carnival, the day before the advent of Lent, when all merriment and jollity will cease and a climate of mournful self-denial will commence.[14] Most importantly, at least as far as stage conventions are concerned, marriage is prohibited until Lent expires. Hence the lovers are under considerable pressure to marry and bed before Lent's arrival the next morning, after which time the marriage (and pendant consummation) must be postponed an unendurable forty days. Dryden's characters frequently express concern over the shortness of time; "this being the last Evening of the Carnival" (*Works*, X: 244), Wildblood reminds us as he serenades. "In one half-hour I have learnt to Cant with an indifferent good grace" says Bellamy, accounting for his sudden acquisition of the language of astrology. Maskall bounds the frame of the entire drama thus:

if the business had gone on till to morrow, when *Lent* begins, you would have grown so peevish (as all good Catholicks are with fasting) that the quarrel would never have been ended.   (*Works*, X: 288)

The extreme compression of events occurring all on a Cornelian "special day" yields a play of amazing bustle; the three Englishmen spot, woo, win, and marry their women – with all the attendant sub- and by-plots, including the astrologer and Jacinta-masquerades, swordfights, gaming, masques, songs, and dances – in the space of a single evening. No other drama of Dryden's moves with this rapidity.

By means of such ingenious improvements, Dryden demonstrates that French material prospers better under English than Gallic rule, for a French prescription is used to improve a French play beyond what the French themselves could manage – one more proof, if proof were needed, that this dramatic property is in better hands under the care of its new, though "unjust," ruler.

Marvelously crafted as a comparison with Corneille's *Feint Astrologue* shows *An Evening's Love* to be, many of Dryden's contemporaries were disturbed by what appeared to be, without more careful consideration, simple theft. In a reply to these critics, Dryden makes no bones about having taken the story, or his right to do so:

'Tis true, that where ever I have lik'd any story in a Romance, Novel, or forreign Play, I have made no difficulty, nor ever shall, to take the foundation of it, to build it up, and to make it proper for the *English* Stage.
(*Preface* to *An Evening's Love, Works*, X: 210)

Dryden mounts an elaborate defense against charges that his plays are stolen in the *Preface* to *An Evening's Love*; he proposes four related strands of argument to explain why taking the poetic work of others is laudable, customary, authorized by the great names of poetry, and to be considered "conquest" (as distinct from theft). The first thread of his argument is exactly similar to Corneille's final argument in his defense of the *Cid*: that his thefts have pleased "him" whom all drama must please.[15] Dryden does not identify the "him," but the reference to Caesar in the quotation from Juvenal might permit us to think it the king:

There is one answer [to my accusers] which I will not make; but it has been made for me by him to whose Grace and Patronage I owe all things,
    Et spes & ratio studiorum, in Caesare *tantum,*
and without whose command they shou'd no longer be troubl'd with any thing of mine; that he only desir'd that they who accus'd me of theft would always steal him Playes like mine.   (*Works*, X: 210)

In a monarchy – and in a theatrical climate – where the king's likes and dislikes constituted "a kind of law,"[16] to say that one's "incorrect" productions had pleased the king was to plead an overridingly higher standard of correctness against which there could be no serious argument.

Dryden's second line of defense is that the plot is the least part of a successful literary production; the author's wit and fancy are what set the work off, and these, Dryden untruthfully insists, he has never borrowed.[17] More accurately, he goes on to claim that the demands of English taste are such that any borrowed foundation of a play must be so reworked as to make it all but completely new:

... since no Story can afford Characters enough for the variety of the *English* Stage, it follows that it is to be alter'd, and enlarg'd, with new persons, accidents, and designes, which wil almost make it new.   (*Works*, X: 212)

Thus the "improving" of a seized-upon work is enough, in the language of Dryden's critical vocabulary, "almost" to "make it new." He shifts the argument here from the ethics of imperialism to the more radical notion (which we see embodied in the character of *An Evening's Love*'s Aurelia) that theft, *per se*, is artistically indefensible; only remaking appropriated material until it is "almost new" both satisfies the demands of England's particular taste in drama and removes the stigma of simple plagiarism.

Taking the preceding approach a step further, Dryden mounts a potentially radical defense of poetic appropriation. He reasons that, since the value of any poem lies in the "ornamentation," the story itself is, if not valueless, the least part of the poetic enterprise, a property as common to the nation of poets as language. Here, in the most far-reaching of the four arguments, Dryden attacks the entire notion of poetic property, arguing instead that the poet is a craftsman who fashions beautiful artifacts with materials that pass through his hands but do not belong to him, materials which, valuable or not as they may be, are the least valuable part of the finished artifact:

... the employment of a Poet, is like that of a curious Gunsmith, or Watchmaker: the Iron or Silver is not his own; but they are the least part of that which gives the value: The price lyes wholly in the workmanship.   (*Works*, X: 212)

And in the following lines, from the *Epilogue* to *An Evening's Love*, Dryden uses a similar metaphor of poetic currency passing altered through the hands of the artisan:

> He [the poet] still must write; and Banquier-like, each day
> Accept new Bills, and he must break, or pay.
> When through his hands such sums must yearly run,
> You cannot think the Stock is all his own.   (*Works*, X: 314)

Dryden vigorously attacks the concept of poetic property, holding that the finished work of one's predecessors becomes the essentially valueless raw material from which one fashions one's own work, which then, it is to be assumed, becomes near-valueless material in the hands of one's successor artisans; if pursued far enough, such an approach would have made unnecessary Dryden's reliance on a poetic lineage, with its attendant literary history.[18] Had he articulated some of the implications of this approach, he might have argued that we could think no poet's stock "all his own," that all poetry was the reworking of anterior poetry, that pure "ownership" of a poetic artifact, and hence, "pure" poetry, was an impossibility. But, like so much in Dryden's criticism, it is a tantalizing suggestion, seemingly thrown out upon the instant, mused upon an instant longer, and passed over in a rush upon the next point.

In his third line of defense, Dryden argues that he has done no more than what all great poets have done in translating the works of their own predecessors. To illustrate this he inventories a roll of ancients who borrowed from others yet more ancient: Virgil from Theocritus, Hesiod from Homer, Terence from Menander. Moving forward in time, Dryden cites Tasso's borrowings from Homer and Virgil, Shakespeare's from Cinthio's *Hecatommithi*,[19] Beaumont's and Fletcher's from the Spanish novelists, and Ben Jonson's from all the ancients.

The fourth and most briefly stated of Dryden's justifications is grounded in Ben Jonson's takings from the ancients. Reverting to a nationalistic mode in which the seizure of what enriches the *patria* is justified by the *patria*'s enrichment, Dryden writes of Jonson's borrowings (and by extension, of his own):

no man has borrow'd so much from the Ancients as he has done: And he did well in it, for he has thereby beautifi'd our language.   (*Works*, X: 212)

Pillage is justified, Dryden argues, because when it is successfully done the home state is enriched with the ornaments of others; "he has thereby beautifi'd our language."[20]

This, so briefly suggested, is the final argument of Drydenian imperialism, unnecessary for him to dwell upon since it underlies the other three arguments. Poetic imperialism, he claims, is justified by the mere fact of its increasing the overall poetic wealth of the native country. To justify poetic imperialism one need say no more than that a poet, by his takings, has "beautifi'd the language," as British privateers preying upon the Spanish plate fleet claimed only that they enriched the treasuries of the king, and as the Spaniards, in turn, claimed as they extracted the wealth of the native Americans.

In these four related arguments justifying the appropriation of poetic property from others (and especially others of other nationalities), Dryden shows himself keenly aware of the proprieties of poetic depredation. He demonstrates his awareness of the "correct" modes of poetic borrowing representationally (within the drama) as well as discursively (in prefatory material). One type of representation concerned with borrowing which recurs often in Dryden's work is the depiction of the failed or second-rate borrower, a character type with which Restoration audiences are greatly fascinated, and a type of which Dryden gives us some of the greatest examples.

An example of the "failed borrower" character in *An Evening's Love* is Aurelia, the object of Don Lopez's affections. Aurelia is modeled after Cathos and Magdelon, the affected ladies of Molière's *Précieuses Ridicules* (1659), and, like her models in the much-imitated Molière play, her humour is that she imports language verbatim from one sphere to another. Finding her native language inadequate to express her desired social status, she seeks to adopt a new language, composed of elisions (Ma'am for Madam, Parn for pardon), the too-frequent use of "furiously," elaborate circumlocutions for simple objects, and a number of importations from the French. Not only are many of her affectations of speech borrowed from the French language, but her very character, and whole speeches, are borrowed without acknowledgment from the Molière play.

In the following conversation between Aurelia and her maid, each of Aurelia's lines contains some affectation of speech; two (and possibly all) of the three are borrowed from the French either at the level of French vocabulary ("spiritual" for "clever"), or are borrowed closely from Molière's *Précieuses*:

Aurelia. How am I drest to night, *Camilla*? is nothing disorder'd in my head?
Camilla. Not the least hair, Madam.
Aurelia. No? let me see: give me the Counsellor of the Graces.
Camilla. The Counsellor of the Graces, Madam?
Aurelia. My Glass I mean: what, will you never be so spiritual as to understand refin'd language? (*Works*, X: 250–51)[21]

Here is Dryden's unacknowledged model in Molière:

Magdelon. Vite, venez nous tendre ici dedans le conseiller des grâces.
Marotte. Par ma fois, je ne sais point quelle bête c'est là: il faut parler chrétien, si vous voulez que je vous entende.
Cathos. Apportez-nous le miroir, ignorante que vous êtes, et gardez-vous bien d'en salir la glace par la communication de votre image.

(*Les Précieuses Ridicules*, vi)[22]

The passage shows two kinds of borrowings from the French; the first type, in Aurelia's language, is borrowed intact from the vocabulary of France, and is accordingly ridiculous as it is mal-absorbed. The larger borrowing of the entire speech from Molière – a secret, or at least an unannounced, borrowing – draws no attention to itself in the context of the play. It is reworked into English so that language which is foregrounded in the French remains foregrounded in the English, but with differences that suit the context both of the play and of English culture. It would not have done to have an English maid speak so to her mistress, nor would it have been in character for Aurelia to waste such a delicious insult ("gardez-vous bien d'en salir") on her maid, unobserved. The reader is ever aware of Aurelia's affectations of borrowed language, never Dryden's.

Aurelia, as an intermediary between the old "low" culture of her maid and the new "high" culture she wishes to assume by introducing more polite kinds of language into her circle, shares certain similarities with her raptor, Dryden, similarities of which Aurelia herself is a kind of inverted instance. Aurelia, though borrowed, is herself a borrower, and to that extent is an image in miniature of Dryden; what she does – badly – to language is what Dryden does – well – to Molière in the act of borrowing her. Aurelia is a kind of importer–exporter in language, introducing forms of speech, nominally French, intended by her to demonstrate her membership in an elect group presumed to exist outside the play's action (for we assume that she does not invent this affected speech, but exports it from a circle where it is currently in use).[23] By his borrowings (and in particular, in his borrowing of Aurelia), Dryden shows a similar determination to innovate, not by the fruits of his own endeavors, but by introducing what is taken from others. Through Aurelia a myth of imperialism is transmuted yet again, this time into another kind of parody of itself, the greedy barbarian taking what she does not understand (and what she has not made her own by understanding) and introducing this borrowed material in an undigested form.

In the undigestedness of Aurelia's innovations we see Dryden's principal differences from her: she imports uncritically and whole, thinking to present an elevated image of herself merely by importing what had value elsewhere; the language is borrowed but not conquered, quoted but not remade. Dryden, on the other hand, claims to have gone (and apparently has gone) to some trouble to make his poetic booty "his." He describes the inadequacy of simple conquest and the subsequent degree of reworking in the *Epilogue* to *An Evening's Love*, reporting his own speech in the third person:

> But should he all the pains and charges count
> Of taking 'em [French plays], the bill so high wou'd mount,
> That, like Prize goods, which through the Office come,
> He could have had 'em much more cheap at home.   (*Works*, X: 314)

Dryden again emphasizes that "pains and charges" are needed for successful "taking"; uncritical importation of language or dramatic forms will result in failure as pretentious and comic as Aurelia's.

Though the distance between Aurelia and Dryden is large, it is by no means infinite; with her he parodies himself and his process of "conquering" by showing us, not a conqueror, but an industrious importer whose principal characteristic is exactly what Dryden's enemies accused him of: plagiarism. He mocks her failure to assimilate what he has assimilated so well, and with such "pains and charges." The proud imperialist reminds us yet again: not till an importation is reworked, improved, made one's own, truly translated into one's own language, does it cease to be ridiculous.

Aurelia is a naive plagiarist; she takes a language not hers and offers it as her own, as if such unlicensed importation of language will elevate her social status. Dryden knows better, as do we; he knows that the only kind of appropriation that is artistically justifiable is what the character of Aurelia represents herself – a theft which is a victory, not surreptitiously offered as one's own, but a seizing, reworking, and improving upon the work of others. In the *Prologue* to *Albumazar* (1668), Dryden shows us a world in which authors, like Aurelias, take from others only to claim what they take, unaltered and untransformed, as their own:

> But this our age such Authors does afford,
> As make whole Playes, and yet scarce write one word:
> Who in this Anarchy of witt, rob all,
> And what's their Plunder, their Possession call;
> Who like bold Padders scorn by night to prey,
> But Rob by Sun-shine, in the face of day.
> Nay scarce the common Ceremony use,
> Of stand, Sir, and deliver up your Muse;
> But knock the Poet down; and, with a grace,
> Mount *Pegasus* before the owners Face.   (*Works*, I: 141)

In the "Anarchy of wit," which is Dryden's literary milieu, only "conquerors" such as Ben Jonson and Dryden, not mere petty thieves of verse, have the required poetic strength to refashion their appropriated poetic material. Dryden's quarrel with these "bold Padders" is not that they are bold (after all, "bold" is his favorite adjective to describe himself), or that they steal (for Dryden admits to taking plots from others), but that in stealing, they "scarce write one word"; they do not make what they have stolen their own by a secondary appropriation which is, in effect, a new act of creation. Language, like plots, must not simply be transported from one place, from one poet's work, from one country, to another; the raptor must make his prey his own. By the characterization of Aurelia, Dryden shows himself splendidly capable of just such a profound seizing of another's work.

As we exit the play through the back door of the *Epilogue*, Dryden introduces another Aurelia-figure whom we are to imagine as seated, not on-stage, but among ourselves:

> Up starts a *Monsieur* new come o're; and warm
> In the *French* stoop; and the pull-back o'th' arm;
> *Morbleu* dit il, *and cocks*, I am a rogue
> But he has quite spoil'd the *feint Astrologue*.   (*Works*, X: 313)

Dryden's miniature of the misborrowing English "Monsieur" is a little gem; we see the fop's attitude exactly staged, stooped over so, arm held back thus; his language is a marvelous blend of English and French (rhyme of "rogue" and "astrologue"); his accusation of spoiling-by-translation is false, but exactly the cultural crime of which he is himself guilty, for he has imported a set of forms (social and linguistic, instead of dramatic), and, in so doing, has parodied whatever value they might have had in France. Concluding the play with the English Monsieur completes the circle of representations of borrowing; the failed importer/audience member scorns the work of the behind-stage creator–borrower of the on-stage verbatim importer; fiction is heaped on fiction in a tableau of figures who seem almost frantic to import, to blazon forth their importations, figures who finally remain ridiculous by failing to make these importations their own. Standing back like a puppeteer behind a stage, the age's great English cultural imperialist can afford to let his parodies mock him.

Notes

1 *Works*, XVII: 57. Unless otherwise stated, all quotations from Dryden's works are from the California edition, *The Works of John Dryden*, ed. H. T. Swedenberg et al., 20 vols. (Berkeley and Los Angeles: University of California Press, 1955–) and follow the pattern just given.

2 I have found Edward Said's *Orientalism* (New York: Vintage Books, 1979) useful in identifying ways in which one culture (mis)represents what it finds of interest in another.

3 "The vices and virtues of Augustan poetry are the vices and virtues of buccaneering millionaires," writes Doody in *The Daring Muse* (Cambridge: Cambridge University Press, 1985), p. 18. She observes that the "Augustan Age" coincides with England's "first great age of imperialism," p. 15.

4 Earl Miner writes of Dryden's vision: "English imperialism of the next two centuries has been envisioned and its ideals provided." ("Forms and Motives of Narrative Poetry," *John Dryden*, ed. Earl Miner [Athens: Ohio University

Press, 1975]), p. 245. Steven Zwicker reads this vision much as he reads the rest of the poem: as a secularizing of biblical typology. See *Dryden's Political Poetry* (Providence: Brown University Press, 1972), pp. 78–83.

5 I include *Marriage A-la-Mode* in this list, since one of the several type of battles described therein is the battle between the English and French languages and dramatic forms, waged in the person of Melantha, who is accorded a comically rueful victory in "Sicilian" society.

6 Gerard Langbaine calls Dryden "this Poetick *Almanzor*." Langbaine, *An Account of the English Dramatick Poets* (1691), ed. John Loftis (Los Angeles: Clark Memorial Library, 1971), p. 133.

7 For an extended discussion of Dryden's manner of taking from Corneille, see chapter one of my forthcoming *The Imperial Dryden: The Poetics of Appropriation in Seventeenth-Century England* (Athens: University of Georgia Press, 1993).

8 See N. B. Allen's *The Sources of John Dryden's Comedies* (New York: Gordian Press, 1967), pp. 156–70; also his much more sympathetic treatment in "The Sources of Dryden's *Mock Astrologer*," *PQ*, 36 (1957): 453–64; and Dryden's *Works*, X: 434–43. Allen's earlier discussion of *An Evening's Love*, though competent, is marred by the belief that the play is not very good, a belief which further study seems to have altered.

9 Langbaine has this to say of *An Evening's Love*:

Evening's Love, or *The Mock Astrologer*, a Comedy acted at the Theatre-Royal by His Majesties Servants, printed in quarto *Lond.* 1671. and dedicated to his Grace *William* Duke of *Newcastle*. This play is in a manner wholly stollen from the *French*, being patcht up from *Corneille's Le Feint Astrologue*; *Mollière's Depit amoureux*, and his *Les Precieuses Ridicules*; and *Quinault's L'Amant Indiscreet*: not to mention little Hints borrow'd from *Shakespear*, *Petronius Arbiter* &c. The main plot of the play is built on *Corneille's*, or rather *Calderon's* Play call'd *El Astrologo fingido*. (*Account ...*, p. 163)

10 In the *Discours des Trois Unités*, Pierre Corneille writes:

... j'accorderais très volontiers que ce qu'on ferait passer en une seule ville aurait l'unité de lieu. Ce n'est pas que je voulusse que le théâtre représentât cette ville toute entière, cela serait en peu trop vaste, mais seulement deux ou trois lieux particuliers, enfermés dans l'enclos de ses murailles.
Pierre Corneille, *Oeuvres complètes*, ed. Georges Couton, 3 vols. (Tours: Gallimard, 1980–87), II: 188.

... I should be very willing to concede that a whole city has unity of place. Not that I should want the stage to represent the whole city, that would be somewhat too large, but only two or three particular places enclosed within its walls.
Pierre Corneille, *Of the Three Unities*, trans. Donald Schier, *The Continental Model*, ed. Scott Elledge and Donald Schier (Ithaca: Cornell University Press, 1970), p. 113.

11 Dryden also adapted *Sir Martin Mar-all* (1667) and *Amphitryon* (1690) from Molière's *l'Etourdi* (1655) and *Amphitryon* (1668), his *Oedipus* (1679) from Corneille's (1658–59), and the serious plot of *Marriage A-la-Mode* (1673) from George and Madeleine de Scudéry's *Le Grand Cyrus* (1649–53).

12 *Works*, X: 210–13.

13 See Allen, *Sources* (156–57), and Maximillian E. Novak's judicious Commentary in *Works*, X: 438–39.

14 A time used before in Thomas Porter's *The Carnival* (1664) and later in Behn's *Rover* (1677).

15 In the *Lettre Apologétique du Sieur Corneille* ..., Corneille writes:

> ... ne vous êtes-vous pas souvenu que *Le Cid* a été représenté trois fois au Louvre, et deux fois à l'Hôtel de Richelieu? Quand vous avez traité la pauvre Chimène d'impudique, de prostituée, de parricide, de monstre, ne vous êtes-vous pas souvenu que la Reine, les Princesses et les plus vertueuses Dames de la Cour et de Paris l'ont caressée en fille d'honneur?   (Corneille, *Oeuvres*, I: 847).

> (... didn't you remember that *Le Cid* was acted thrice at the Louvre, and twice at Richelieu's palace? When you treated poor Chimène as a shameless woman, a prostitute, a parricide, a monster, didn't you remember that the Queen, the Princesses, and the most virtuous Ladies of the court and of Paris had received and caressed her like a maid of honor? [My translation.])

16 In the *Defence of the Epilogue*, Dryden ascribes the refinement of the entire age "to the ... King; whose example gives a law to it" (*Works*, XI: 216).

17 Dryden lifts and translates whole speeches and scenes from Molière, Quinault, and Thomas Corneille, and inserts them verbatim and near-verbatim into *An Evening's Love*. See *Works* X: 437–39 for some parallel passages showing nearly verbatim translations from French to English. An article which, in my judgment, fails to demonstrate the assertion of its title, is Angel Capellan's "John Dryden's Indebtedness to Pedro Calderón de la Barca in 'An Evening's Love or The Mock Astrologer,'" *RLC*, 49 (1975), 572–87.

18 Ralph Cohen feels Dryden's modes of reception of anterior poets might form the basis for a more sophisticated view of poetic inheritance:

> Dryden's view of imitations of models implied a concept of intertextuality as more than a mere verbal enterprise, and it may prove more valuable to us than our own purely linguistic view of intertextuality.
> *New Homage to John Dryden*, Phillip Harth, Alan Fisher, and Ralph Cohen (Los Angeles: Clark Memorial Library, 1983), p. 85.

19 Dryden says he himself read *Romeo and Juliet* in Cinthio's Italian. As George Watson points out, the *Hecatommithi* was indeed a source for *Othello*, but not for *Romeo and Juliet*. See Dryden, *Of Dramatic Poesy and Other Critical Essays*, ed. George Watson, 2 vols. (London: Everyman, 1962), I: 154.

20 Dryden referred to himself as "a Man, who have done my best to improve the Language, & Especially the Poetry"; Samuel Johnson evidently concurred, concluding his appraisal of Dryden's accomplishment: "What was said of Rome adorned by Augustus, may be applied by an easy metaphor to English poetry embellished by Dryden – *lateritiam invenit, marmoream reliquit*, he found it brick, and he left it marble." John Dryden, "Dryden to Mrs. Steward," (1699), *The Letters of John Dryden*, ed. Charles E. Ward (Durham: Duke University Press, 1942), p. 123; Samuel Johnson "Life of Dryden," *Johnson's Lives of the Poets: A Selection*, ed. J. P. Hardy (Oxford: Clarendon Press, 1971), p. 200.

21 Although the *Oxford English Dictionary* credits Dryden with the first English use of "spirituel" in *Marriage A-la-Mode* (1673), the speech which follows in the text dates from three years earlier. The earliest use the *OED* gives of "spiritual" (spelled with an 'a') to mean "clever, smart, witty" occurs in 1791.

22 I would translate the French:

> *Magdelon.* Quick, come and set us up the counsellor of the graces.
> *Marotte.* By my faith, I don't know what stupidity that is; you have to speak
> christian if you want me to understand you.
> *Cathos.* Bring us the mirror, know-nothing that you are. And take care not to
> dirty it by the communication of your image.
>
> (Molière, *Oeuvres Complètes*, ed. Georges Couton, 2 vols. [Bruges: Gallimard,
> 1971], I: 271).

23 Perhaps it contains some points of contact with the kind of imported French
Dryden so often said he despised and so often used himself. See the *Defence of the
Epilogue, Works* XI: 211, for Dryden's assault upon a vocabulary he elsewhere
favors.

3

Ovid reformed: issues of Ovid, fables, morals, and the second epic in *Fables Ancient and Modern*

EARL MINER

As the preceding chapters have shown, a major feature of Dryden's career is his engagement with many authors, whether forerunners or contemporaries. Dryden's financial and other problems after the Revolution of 1688 led him first to the theater and then, on an increasing scale, to translation. Before his *Fables* (1700), he engaged in two major poetic translations, the *Satires* of Juvenal and Persius (1693) and the monumental *Virgil* (1697), which we have yet to understand. Looking back over his career, we see (on smaller scale) translations of Theocritus, Horace, and Lucretius. *Fables Ancient and Modern* is remarkable for its attention to two medieval–modern writers, Chaucer and Boccaccio, along with two ancients, Homer and Ovid. What follows here is an attempt to describe Dryden's reformation of the poet of changing forms, Publius Ovidius Naso.

His first published translations were of three poems from Ovid's *Heroides* included in the joint venture, *Ovid's Epistles* (1680). In the account he prefixed to *Annus Mirabilis* (1667), he had held that Ovid's Dido in the *Heroides* was a creation superior to Virgil's in the *Aeneid*. And in the *Essay of Dramatick Poesie* (1668), he praised Ovid's natural talents for drama. From these earlier writings to the end of his life, he keeps mentioning Ovid and, from time to time, translating him. If we can judge from frequency of publication in the seventeenth century, his taste was widely shared. Ovid is more frequently published than Homer, Virgil, or Horace, all of whom Dryden, as well as others, seems to have found greater or more respectable than the author of the *Amores*, from which, however, he also translated a couple of examples.[1] It should come as no surprise, therefore, that he should have turned to the *Metamorphoses* in selecting earlier stories for translation in *Fables*.

The preface to *Fables* is not most memorable for what it has to say of

Ovid, if only because Dryden so eloquently expresses his affection for Chaucer and seeks to arouse interest in a prospective translation of Homer. In fact, the Chaucerian poems bulk more largely, running to 4,556 lines to the 3,756 lines of the Ovidian poems, a comparison expressive of Dryden's patriotic esteem for Chaucer as the Homer of English verse.[2] But one of the five Chaucerian stories, *Palamon and Arcite* (The Knight's Tale) consists of 2,431 lines, making it nearly three times as long as the next lengthiest of the other fables, and it accounts for more than half the lines of the Chaucerian stories. (The lengthy pseudo-Chaucerian *Flower and the Leaf* goes yet farther to diminish the weight of Chaucer in *Fables*).

Apart from numbers of lines, Ovid is represented most numerously in *Fables* by the presence of eight selections, compared with the five from Chaucer, three from Boccaccio, one from Homer, and four from Dryden himself. Moreover, the most numerous selections from Ovid are the only ones that appear in the order of occurrence in their original.[3] The *Character of a Good Parson* (an "imitation" rather than a translation in the sense of the others) was taken, of course, from the General Prologue to *The Canterbury Tales* and yet appears as the last of the five Chaucerian fables included. The three stories from Boccaccio similarly occur out of their original sequence, and even the four poems originating with Dryden do not appear in order of composition, since "Alexander's Feast" (1697) and "The Monument of a Fair Maiden Lady" appear toward the end of the collection, whereas the more recent poems to the Duchess of Ormonde and John Driden of Chesterton are first and third. Because the *Metamorphoses* itself appears so episodic, it might seem that the ordering of *Fables* on the *Metamorphoses* matters little.

Current interpreters hold that Dryden's *Fables* is an integrated collection.[4] And, if Ovid matters to its practice and conception, we must seek to understand how Dryden conceived of the *Metamorphoses*. The thesis held here is that – by deliberate reformative practice – in his *Fables* Dryden renovated the *Metamorphoses* for his epic as, in writing *Paradise Lost*, Milton had renovated the *Aeneid* and therefore Homer, whose two poems Virgil had renovated. The implications of this are somewhat doubtful, but potentially very great.

Perhaps the first obstacle to understanding is the nature of Ovid's work itself, for, if it has no integrity, how can any work modelled on it be said to have the unity that recent criticism has argued or shown for *Fables*? And prior to the question of unity, for Dryden and Ovid alike, is the question of authority. In his preface to the *Fables*, Dryden remarks, "I can remember nothing of *Ovid* which was wholly his."[5] Classicists assume as much, even when exact sources cannot be shown. The point about Ovid emerges again in the comparison with Chaucer: "neither were great Inventors: for *Ovid* only copied the *Grecian* Fables, and most of *Chaucer*'s Stories were taken from his *Italian* Contemporaries, or their Predecessors" (IV: 1450). Given his admiration for these two poets, Dryden clearly did not think invention or originality a sole or necessary factor for poetic greatness (in this differing from Samuel Johnson). Similarly, he seems to imply that his own heavy indebtedness in *Fables* does not foreclose greatness or deprive his work of integrity (in this resembling Ben Jonson). Such being the case, our first order of business must be trying to describe the nature of Ovid's greatest work.

Ovid's perpetual poem

Ovid claimed that the *Metamorphoses* is a "perpetuum . . . carmen" (Book 1, line 4). The meaning of "perpetual" has enough ambiguity for Dryden to have rendered the Ovidian phrase (in *Examen Poeticum*, 1693), "And add perpetual Tenour to my Rhimes." The Loeb translator gives "my song in unbroken strains."[6] That is, Ovid ceaselessly moves forward, from the beginning (of the world) to the end (in his own times). We ought to bear in mind that "perpetual" also means general, universal, dealing with the world comprehensively, as is implied by Ovid's use of a similar word at the end of his poem – which Dryden had in mind in translating the opening.

parte tamen meliore mei super alta *perennis* astra ferar.

(Loeb: "Still in my better part I shall be borne immortal far beyond the lofty stars.")[7]

No more than Virgil before his death had Ovid tidied up his poem when he went to exile. In fact, he burnt his copy, later regretting the act and getting a copy, or copies, from friends. Dryden did finish his *Fables* and so might have claimed to have written a perpetual poem in all these senses.

The concept of the perpetual poem reconciles highly episodic writing with unity of total conception. The *Metamorphoses* is, in fact, more miscellaneous than the *Fables*. As one classicist has written of Ovid's masterpiece, "there are some fifty stories long enough to rank as epyllia and some two hundred others that are treated more cursorily or merely referred to."[8] Not only that. The longer stories incorporate other plot material, as was quite traditional: all extant epyllia dating from before Ovid except Theocritus' *Hylas* have an inset story or stories or narrative digression that may be unconnected with the main story; sometimes the main story was merely a device for introducing a far longer inset tale.[9] None of this falsifies Ovid's claim that he will write "ab origine mundi / ad mea ... tempora." In fact he does begin with creation and end with the reign of Augustus. Yet most of his stories are so divorced from the world as we know it that discernible chronology is basically infeasible. It is only with the Trojan war in Book 12 (included entire by Dryden) that Ovid enters human history from Troy, to the founding of Rome, and so "to my own times." Fully two-thirds of the *Metamorphoses* is unhistorical, even by the more relaxed standards of Dryden's time. In that sense, "perpetual" refers to what Ovid made by narration, rather than to any modern historiographical conception.

As we all know, where problems occur interpretation becomes an explicit, necessary act. Renaissance commentators on Ovid draw on earlier critics and add their own emphases. The most important English interpreter of Ovid before Dryden was George Sandys, whose second paragraph of address "to the Reader" explains his purposes in the commentary portions of *Ovid's Metamorphosis*:

> I have also endeavored to cleare the Historicall part, by tracing the almost worne-out steps of Antiquitie; wherein the sacred stories afford the clearest direction. For the first Period from the Creation to the Flood, which the Ethnickes called the Obscure, some the Emptie times; and the Ages next following which were stil'd the Heroycall, because the after deified Heroes then flourished; as also the Fabulous, in that those stories convayed by Tradition in loose and broken Fragments, were by the Poets interwoven with instructing Mythologies, are most obscurely and perplexedly delivered by all, but the supernaturally inspired Moses.[10]

Since, in his preface to *Fables*, Dryden referred his readers to the life of Ovid given by Sandys, and to his interpretations, he could only have been well familiar with *Ovid's Metamorphosis* and better able to make sense of such remarks than most of us today.

Making sense ourselves involves difficult problems of interpreting Ovid and Dryden. It seems prudent to deal first with the least complex, the historical pattern that Sandys discovers in Ovid's poem. His postulation has been confirmed by modern classicists. The order follows:

> Prologue, Book 1, lines 1–4
> Introduction: The Creation and Flood, Book 1, lines 5–451
> Part I. Gods, Book 1, line 452 to Book 6, line 420
> Part II. Heroes and Heroines, Book 6, line 421 to Book 11, line 193
> Part III. Historical Persons, Book 11, line 194 to Book 15, line 870
> Epilogue, Book 15, lines 871–79

To such an outline modern classicists add the caveat that Ovid enters numerous digressions and interpretations.

Such a pattern or "history" takes on special significance when we consider that all Dryden's Ovidian selections for the *Fables* come from the eighth and later (eleventh to fifteenth) books. One reason for the selection may have been that in 1697 there appeared a translation, by several hands, of the first five books; perhaps Dryden wished to take fresh ground for his work. But it is certain that he chose to reject the "Obscure"or "Emptie times" as his subject. Since he had translated the opening book of the *Meta-morphoses* seven years earlier for *Examen Poeticum*, he might have re-used that as readily as he did the previously published "Alexander's Feast" (1697). It seems clear that he had no wish to meddle with Ovid's creation, flood, and gods – in those "Emptie times." He was after a heroic, historical Ovid in order that his own perpetual poem might deal with humanity. And, if he included religious elements, those would involve either the Christian scheme or rejections of the pagan gods, unless those might be used to figure the Christian godhead. In this respect, Dryden took what we shall discover is a traditional means of Christianizing his pagan poet.

As Sandys' historical conceptions show, Dryden also considered the *Metamorphoses* to be a heroic poem. The characters of the second segment are "Heroycall" in the sense of being exalted individuals, usually demi-gods, and chiefly those celebrated by Homer or by Virgil and other Augustan poets. What did not fit by way of subject – most notably the long explication of Pythagorean philosophy in Book 15 – fitted historically by attribution to the early Roman king, Numa.[11] All too human love stories could be included as insets entered into epyllia, or as specimens of the "heroical" love Ovid celebrated in the *Heroides*.

Dryden's account of his composition of *Fables* implies an associative process of composition. He began, he said, with

the first book of *Homer's Iliads* ... [and then turned to] the Twelfth Book of *Ovid's Metamorphoses*, because it contains, among other Things, the Causes, the Begin-ning, and Ending of the *Trojan* War: Here I ought in reason to have stopp'd; but the Speeches of *Ajax* and *Ulysses* lying next in my way [at the beginning of Ovid, 13], I could not balk 'em.   (IV: 1444)

The context of these remarks suggests that the composition involved a chain of association that included the other authors. It seems significant that the process of composition was associational, but that the process of ordering the individual translations was more deliberate – and different. (Dryden does not begin *Fables* with Homer and Ovid.) Moreover, only to the selections from Ovid did Dryden prefix headnotes explaining connec-tions. His notes might characterize "inartificial Connexions" (*Meleager and Atalanta*) or "admirably well connected" episodes (*Pygmalion and the Statue*). Integration was clearly on his mind, and that included conception as well as execution. We may think many individual fables to be romances, but Dryden's emphasis is on the heroic. The Knight's Tale, which he most admired in Chaucer, "is of the *Epique* kind" (IV: 1460). Since he seems to have thought even *Cinyras and Myrrha* to be heroic (see the context, IV: 1444–45), that is obviously a way of declaring the perpetual poem an epic. If so, *Fables* is unmistakably a heroic collection of otherwise discrete poems or parts of poems.

Obvious as it may be, the fact that all is in verse is one of the little noted implications of his famous phrase on his easy choice of verse over "the other Harmony of Prose" (IV: 1446), since he conspicuously translates Boccaccio's prose novelle into the higher harmony of poetry in making his own heroic, perpetual poem.

Ovid and the fable

Dryden's word for his stories, "fables," is not innocent of meaning. For one thing, fables constituted, for Quintilian and others, one kind of *narratio*, along with *historia* and *argumentum*. Of the three kinds of narration, history concerned actual fact; argument presented something that resembled the actual (as also having its more familiar meaning); and fable dealt with the made up, the fictional, requiring no resemblance to fact.[12] In *Fables* we may find historical touches, especially in the poems to the Duchess of Ormond and to John Driden, and (by the standards of the time) in the Ovidian selections from Book 12 onward. Argument is found in many of the same poems. The fabulous must include *Pygmalion and the Statue* and those parts of the *Metamorphoses* before Book 12, and not a little taken from Chaucer. It does not seem likely that Dryden ever envisioned for his title *Narratives*, *Histories*, or *Arguments* (ancient and modern), but there were other real possibilities. As he was ending his work, he wrote Pepys about his having translated "as many fables from Ovid, and as many novels from Boccaccio, and tales from Chaucer, as will make an indifferent large volume in folio."[13] Of the three possible terms, Dryden takes the one he associates with Ovid.

In fact, his term is as exact for Ovid as are "novelle" and "tales" for the two other authors. A look at any Renaissance or seventeenth-century edition of Ovid will show the *Metamorphoses* divided into fables within the fifteen books. The episodes or fabulae are not always distinguished as the same numbers of lines, but the term is uniform in vernacular versions as well. A popular folio in French, which Dryden might have seen, and with which we shall be concerned, shows in its title approaches to Ovid in the latter half of the century:

Les Metamorphoses d'Ovide, en Latin et François, divisées en xv. livres. Avec des nouvelles Explications Historiques, Morales & Politiques sur toutes les Fables, chacune selon son sujet; de la traduction de Mr. Pierre Du-Ryer ... Edition nouvelle (Brussels, 1677).

We shall be seeing the importance of various phrases in this title, and it is worth recording that (according to The British Library Catalogue) this work appeared as late as 1728.

Dryden mentions having used the Dauphin (or Delphin) edition, a printing of which appeared from Oxford in 1696: *P. Ovidii Nasonis Metamorphoseon Libri XV ... Recensuit Joh. Freind Aedis Christi Alumn.*[14] After the dedication and the address to readers, there appear four pages of contents under the head "Index Eorum quae in unoque Libro et Fabula Metamorph. Ovid. continentur." Since both the Dauphin and *Les Metamorphoses* versions are of obvious French origin, they may be worth a small comparison. Both agree that the story of Meleager and Atalanta is the fourth fable of Book 8, that there are seven fables in Book 12, etc. But the vernacular version gives the story of Myrrha as fables 10 and 11 in Book 10, whereas the Dauphin accounts it the ninth. In short, the concept of fables was as importantly identified with Ovid as with Aesop, and it will be obvious that the *Metamorphoses* rather than the beast fable used (in part) for *The Hind and the Panther* provides the new model. And, since Ovid's work is so discontinuous in some ways, the episodes were honored (with differing judgments as to their length) by name as fables. Ovid's boast of writing a perpetual poem assumes at once a range of subject and a view of it, a larger continuity.

The approach to continuity and, within it, discontinuity determine the kind of narrative being created.[15] Before asking how like or unlike Dryden is to Ovid in this respect, we should concern ourselves with the nature of the integration of *Fables*, a subject that has been explored a number of times.[16] Dryden obviously drops Ovid's opening and closing passages, which deal with the poem Ovid was writing, as if Dryden had to claim his own English ground. Part of his integration involves a use of recurrent subjects that resembles Ovid's in their range, but differs from his in many constituents. There are: heroism; love in numerous versions; families; sage old people; rash young people; tyrants; government; history; philosophy; and the very Drydenian as well as Ovidian subject, art or the artist. By taking the second, rather than the first, half of the *Metamorphoses* as his model, he emphasizes human nature over the kind of myth found at the beginning of Ovid's poem. Dryden's characters struggle in various ways to achieve their desires for a good life, whether that be an exemplary *vita bona* or a more hedonistic, at times selfish, *vita beata*.[17]

Conceptions of the good life require some adjustment between the pagan character of many of the stories and Dryden's own Christianity. Pagan philosophy is allowed its fullest say near the beginning and end of *Fables*: the second of the twenty-one, *Palamon and Arcite*, and the eighteenth, "Of the Pythagorean Philosophy." The death of Arcite seems to require the consolation of philosophy. First Theseus is comforted by his father, Egeus (Part 3: lines 877 ff.), with Stoicism. Theseus later comforts his court with a Boethianism expanded by Dryden to include Lucretianism (Part 3: lines 1024 ff.). The addition involves expansion and also a de-Christianizing of Chaucer's Theseus. This change has a partly historical end Chaucer had no need of: staying within the pagan terms of ancient times. No such de-Christianizing was necessary for "Of the Pythagorean Philosophy." Dryden's correction is spiritual as well as historical in motive. It is striking that *Palamon and Arcite*, much the longest fable, is set between two Christian poems, "To the Dutchess of Ormond" and "To My Honour'd Kinsman."[18] Similarly, "Of the Pythagorean Philosophy" is immediately corrected by *The Character of a Good Parson*, which is much expanded over Chaucer's few lines, and by the penultimate fable, "The Monument of a Fair Maiden Lady."

Every reader who assumes the integration of *Fables* and follows Dryden's development of ideas and motifs finds a shock in the concluding poem, *Cymon and Iphigenia*, a splendid but bleak close. After two ideal figures – the Parson and Fair Maiden Lady – we have Cymon growing by love-as-education from being the brute that his name implies. So far, so good. Then he seizes Iphigenia (pron. i-ph-i-JEEN-ia) from the ship taking her to her betrothed in Rhodes. A storm ironically drives Cymon's ship to that very place, where he is imprisoned. Since a magistrate wants another woman, who is to be married alongside Iphigenia, he plots with Cymon. The two of them and their men wrench the women from their nuptial feast, leaving behind many people slain, fleeing to Candy (Crete) rather than stay in Rhodes or return to Cyprus. The fable, and therefore also the *Fables*, concludes:

> A War ensues . . .
> Both Parties lose by turns; and neither wins,
> 'Till Peace propounded by a Truce begins.
> The kindred of the Slain forgive the Deed,
> But a short Exile must for Show precede;
> The term expir'd, from *Candia* they remove;
> And happy each at Home, enjoys his Love.   (lines 633–40)

This is the bleakness of the human comedy Dryden displays. The virginal Fair Maiden Lady and Good Parson may be ideal, and they are certainly models for our lives under the Christian dispensation. But neither the unmarried clergy of England's past, nor an unmarried woman of England's present, can translate idealism into procreation. Their perfections judge Cymon and the ending of the work. How different would be a collection that ended instead with the poem to the Duchess of Ormond! Yet in his "Poeta Loquitur" at the beginning of *Cymon and Iphigenia*, Dryden returns in fact to the Duchess (and all "the fair") to say that his story shows how love will educate.[19] This return to the Duchess both shows Dryden's integrative purpose and poses problems of interpretation.

This stage of our inquiry may close with attention to Ovid and to the scale of various epics. Ovid, we are told,

> attempts no less a task than the linking together into one artistically harmonious whole all the stories of classical mythology ... The poet has seized upon every possible thread of connexion as he passes from cycle to cycle of story; and where this connexion is lacking, by various ingenious and artistic devices a connecting-link is found.[20]

Dryden shows unparalleled concern with Ovid's links, to the point of adding headnotes to his translations – but solely to those derived from Ovid, not from Chaucer or Boccaccio – additions that would certainly have been appropriate enough, given the nature of *The Canterbury Tales* or the *Decameron*. And they apply to connections in Ovid, not in Dryden (unless he takes over successive units). Thus the "Connexion to the Former Story" at the beginning of *Meleager and Atalanta* links it not to Dryden's preceding poem to John Driden but to events in *Metamorphoses*, 8. There is one non-Ovidian exception in the clear link at the beginning of *Fables*, with the title "To Her Grace the Dutchess of Ormond With the Following Poem of Palamon and Arcite, from Chaucer." This link is strengthened by an elaborate comparison of the Duchess to Chaucer's Emily, of her husband to Palamon, and of Theseus to William III. This last identification continues into the initial part (alone) of *Palamon and Arcite*, where Dryden adapts Chaucer to make Theseus (William) a warlike, bloody conqueror. Dryden often makes changes that help integrate his larger narrative, and in one respect his task is simpler than Ovid's. If only he could find some conception of continuity, it would be easier to connect his twenty-one fables than Ovid's far more numerous ones.[21]

We shall be considering further the kind of integration already suggested, but for the moment we may conclude that with his *Fables* Dryden made an epic that at last reconciled him to his age, his version of *Paradise Lost* written after his cause, like Milton's earlier one, had gone down in defeat. Both poets had had their triumphs, which involved politics as much as poetry. And doubly handicapped as they were (Milton blind and

Dryden crippled), both faced a new ruling order as something like exiles in their own country.[22] Whatever was the case with Milton, Dryden clearly had Ovid and the Roman poet's more literal exile on his mind.[23]

The evidence derives from writings from the outset of the reign of James II and thereafter. In the penultimate stanza (17) of *Threnodia Augustalis* (1685), Dryden recalls the last book of the *Metamorphoses* to draw a comparison between the recently dead Charles II and the now succeeded James II: "As after *Numa*'s peaceful Reign, / The Martial *Ancus* did the Scepter wield . . ." (lines 465–66). During the reign of William and Mary, he wrote "A Panegyrical Poem" on "the Late Countess of Abingdon." Dryden's beginning of *Eleonora* (1692) addresses the Earl of Abingdon and compares his personal situation as a poet to that of troubled Ovid:

MY LORD,

The Commands, with which You have honour'd me some Months ago, are now perform'd: They had been sooner; but betwixt ill health, some business, and many troubles, I was forc'd to deferr them till this time. *Ovid*, going to his Banishment, and Writing from on Shipbord to his Friends, excus'd the faults of his Poetry by his Misfortunes.   (II: 582)

Dryden was not aboard ship, at least literally, but shipwreck had long been a personal metaphor for the possible suddenness of human disaster.[24]

Of course he may have written such things and then have put Ovid from his mind. But both the *Metamorphoses* and the *Fables* are of the particularly mixed scale that may be called the epic as cento. The fable as unit may be brief, in both cases. But Dryden's perpetual poem constitutes what is perhaps the longest heroic poem of the classical line in European literature. Whatever else the numbers mean, they testify to the kind of scale Dryden employed.

Poem	Number of parts	Number of lines
Iliad	24	15,600
Odyssey	24	10,912
Argonautica	4	5,835
Aeneid	12	9,896
Metamorphoses	15	12,015
Paradise Lost	12 (10)	10,811
Fables	21	22,356

The ambition is obvious. Here, in a way not even translating all Virgil could represent, was Dryden's heroic coming to terms with his age.

Interpreting *Fables*

Such a claim presumes that Dryden was not interested merely in telling (retelling) interesting stories. Nor was he interested merely in formally integrating them, since a concern with features (possibilities, failures, renewals, further vicissitudes) of the good life goes beyond forging links. For this topic the conception of a fable enters again, Ovid matters again, and larger issues are involved again, even if full certainty is infeasible. In a word, we shall have to face in the end what Dryden meant, or came to mean, by the *morals* of his works.

Precisely because narrative in fabulae was thought remote from truth or fact, some other truth was sought. When there is a problem, real or seeming, it becomes the business of the reader to interpret. The Ovidian fable was assumed to share with the Aesopian a meaning beyond its plot. Having read George Sandys' *Ovid's Metamorphosis*, Dryden was aware that the "mythologizing" of his predecessor comes in commentary (on fables in numbered books) gathered together at the end of each of the fifteen books. If he read *Les Metamorphoses* or other similar French versions, he would have found the Latin with a French prose translation and, at the end of a fable or group of fables, those "Explications Historiques, Morales et Politiques" spoken of in the title. It seems certain that Dryden had also read the most popular of English mythographers, Alexander Ross, whose *Mystagogus Poeticus* became complete in its second edition (1648) and thereafter was republished several times.[25] Ross proceeds by alphabetizing individuals who appear in various classical stories, notably Ovid's *Meta-morphoses*. In any event, with a French and two English interpreters, we should be able to judge in what ways fables could be interpreted by Dryden and his contemporaries.

There is no need to deal exhaustively with Dryden's Ovidian selections, since the method becomes clear from a few representatives. Dryden's first selection is his fourth fable, *Meleager and Atalanta* (*Metamorphoses*, 8). Sandys has the following gloss on the Caledonian Boar of that story: it was

sent by *Diana* as a punishment for her neglected sacrifice. For there is no evil befalls unto man, but either proceeds from his omission of divine duties, or actual impietie. And although they often seeme to proceede from naturall causes, in that concealed from our understandings; yet are they ever inflicted by the Supreme appointment.[26]

As a kind, swine offer an emblem (*in malo*) of people "who delight in un-cleannesse, and detest the contrary" (p. 387). The boar is a "salvage and inhumane theife," an enemy of Greece, as "Sparticus" was of Rome (*ibid.*). The story reaches its bloody climax as Meleager's mother decides against her son and for her brothers, causing his death. "So *Meleager* dyes by the impietie of his mother; by her desperate hands on her selfe revenged" (p. 390).

Ross discusses only Atalanta, having in mind her subsequent life as well. But he also treats her part in the chase of the boar and her being loved by Meleager. In *Mystagogus Poeticus*, he comments that

whilest *Atalanta* was employed with *Diana* in hunting, she kept her virginitie, and did help, yea, was the first that wounded the Chaledonian Boar; but when she gave her self to idlenesse, shee fell into lust and profaneness.   (p. 33)

A draft of this had appeared in the predecessor volume, *Mel Heliconium* (London, 1646), whose comment begins with a sentence now inserted into *Mystagogus Poeticus*:

Here we have the picture of a whore, who runnes swiftly in the broad way that leadeth to destruction; if any thing stay her course, it is wise counsell and admonition; for wisdom is presented by gold.   (p. 33)

This interpretation bears on her race and her defeat in it when Hippomanes (or Meilanion) distracts her with the golden apples furnished by Venus. Far from being a delusory temptation, gold represents wisdom, according to Ross, who adds (*in bono*), "Let us with *Atalanta* run the race that is set before us, and wound the boare of our wanton lusts" (p. 42). In short, Ross follows the long tradition of allegorizers or interpreters by explication both *in bono* and *in malo*. The French version by Du Ryer compares the Caledonian Boar and its ravages with the punishment on Pharaoh for his impiety and with the plague sent because of David's sin. (The Christianizing here as well needs no underscoring.)

Such a range of interpretation seems inconsistent, even crazy. Let us continue. Of *Baucis and Philemon* (Book 8), Sandys tells us that the pious couple offers "the patterns of chast and constant conjugall affections; as of content in povertie; who make it easy by bearing it cheerfully" (p. 391). He adds that "this our fable was devized to deterre from inhumanity, and perswade to hospitality" (p. 393). He comments on their desire to have their poor house made a temple and to serve in it together as long as they live, as also on Jupiter's divine vengeance upon the impious people of the area. He explains: "their poor cottage [alone] was preserved; and chaunged by the remunerating Gods into a glorious Temple. As the body is the Temple to a virtuous soule [1 Corinthians 6: 19]; so is that house to the body where religion and piety is [*sic*] exercised" (pp. 393–94). Ross has nothing to say on this couple. *Les Metamorphoses* resembles Sandys in holding that

La maison de ces bonnes gens est metamorphosée en Temple, pour apprendre à tout le monde, que la maison d'un homme de bien est veritablement un Temple, où Dieu est tousiours present.   (p. 268)

The French commentator does not speculate, as Sandys does, that Ovid's story probably came from Holy Writ, where Lot is said to entertain two angels, who conduct him and his wife out of Sodom (p. 393; the Christianizing may be noted one last time).

Pygmalion and the Statue (Book 10) leads Sandys to speculate on the animation of the statue by Venus: "perhaps the life which was given it by the Goddesse, was no other then the grace and beauty of the figure; which *Apelles*, in his pictures, called the *Venus*" (p. 484). When the statue comes to life and blushes over Pygmalion's caresses, her change in color is "The ensigne of native Modesty, & the colour of vertue" (p. 485). Allegorical reading is the only consistency in this. Ross passes by this story as well as the former. *Les Metamorphoses* again resembles Sandys' gloss. It stresses that it is God who sanctions marriage (Venus becoming, *in bono*, a pagan type of the Christian deity, a method Ross often uses), and the whiteness of the ivory "est une marque de la chasteté" (p. 324). Venus somehow serves as helpmate to chastity in this seemingly incoherent gloss.

For various reasons, extraordinary attention is shown the story of *Cinyras and Myrrha* (Book 10). It seems odd, given that the unsavory fable tells of Myrrha's incestuous enjoyment of her father, his anger on discovery, her flight, her metamorphosis into the myrrh tree, and her giving birth to Adonis. Sandys comments that her desires should be "imputed to infernall *Alecto*, or the Divell, who begets in the impious soule, deserted by Vertue, such hellish affections" (p. 485). On Cinyras' drinking wine before enjoying his daughter, Sandys finds a comparison with Lot, "who then lay with his two daughters (wherewith this fable agrees in sundry particulars)" (p. 487). On the tree's giving birth, Sandys has what seem some highly ingenious things to say:

The tree, according to the time of women, is delivered of *Adonis*; which signifies sweetnesse, and may be taken for that fragrant gumme; as the story of *Myrrha*'s affecting her father, for the sun, the father of all vegitables; this plant delighting, and fructifying onely with immoderate fervor, which chaps the rine, and opens a passage for that delicate liquor [the myrrh].   (p. 364)

Ross says much the same: "*Myrrha* begot *Adonis* of her own father, because the Myrrhe by the heat of the Sun, which is the common father of all trees, chapps and cleaves in the rine, and sends that liquor which we call Myrrhe" (p. 300). *Les Metamorphoses* differs only in adding a Catholic touch. The weeping tree signifies repentance, and Myrrha resembles "la

Magdelaine ... diffamée par ses vices, & rendu glorieux par son repentir"
(p. 333).

Such patterns of interpretation run throughout the commentaries on
the other fables taken from Ovid.[27] But enough examples have been given
to show that from Sandys, who wrote before our poet was born, to the
popular and egregious Ross who wrote during his lifetime, and to the
commentary of *Les Metamorphoses* (which continued to be reprinted well
after Dryden's death), there was a continuous tradition that mytholo-
gized, told the mysteries, or offered explications. By their nature, "fables"
required interpretive glosses, and those did not always deal with matters
that come first to our minds.

The question for us is, of course, what kinds of meaning Dryden
expected *his* fables would be construed to bear. Those who think them
simple stories do so in the face of abundant historical evidence to the
contrary, indeed in the face of Dryden's own statement in the preface to
Fables:

I have endeavour'd to chuse such Fables, both Ancient and Modern, as contain in
each of them some instructive Moral: which I could prove by Induction, but the
Way is tedious: and they leap foremost into sight without the Reader's Trouble of
looking after them.   (IV: 1447)

We must take Dryden seriously: a choice *not* to read fables for morals
would have required justification in his time. If this be questioned, the
doubters should consider his slightly younger contemporary, one of the
bright (or glaring) lights of the Royal Society, Robert Hooke (1635–
1703). In *The Posthumous Works of Robert Hooke*, edited by Richard Waller
(London, 1705), there is a now forgotten lengthy composite essay, *A
Discourse of Earthquakes* (pp. 279–450). Waller's notes explain that the
Discourse began as a treatise written about 1668, which was followed by
lectures on the same subject some twenty years later. In editing them
Waller preserved a remarkable section (pp. 377–403) that glosses the early
parts of the *Metamorphoses*: creation, flood, restitution, and the like. There
is no proof that Dryden heard the lectures or saw the manuscript. My point
is rather that the irascible originator of "Hooke's Law" on stress was
thinking in terms very like those of Sandys and others.

In fact, Hooke begins just like Sandys, with discussion of the periods,
and in fact the same periods, of human history.

Varro has distributed the ages of the world into three, *viz.*, the *adēlon, mythikon,* and
historikon [the dark, the mythic, and historical]; of the *adēlon*, we know nothing
from Heathen Writers; of the *mythikon* we must look for an account from the Fables
of the Poets, *Homer, Hesiod, Ovid,* &c. *Ovid*, to pass by *Hesiod* and *Homer*, is said to

have imitated the Greek Poet *Parthenius*, and has left us a very large History of the changes that had anciently happened in the World.

(p. 377: repunctuated and the Greek corrected)

Hooke maintains that "the Metamorphosis of *Ovid* was a continued account of the Ages and Times of the duration of the Earth" (p. 379). The ages are in part traditional. Hence, up to *Metamorphoses*, 1: 312 Ovid shows the golden age, next the silver, and so on. But with the gigantomachy, Hooke becomes more and more interested in supplying "Explications," in "mythologizing," or being an "Interpreter" of "Mysteries" – to use a few of the terms employed by the French and English sources we have followed. It will be apparent that there was full agreement on the need for allegoresis (allegorical interpretation) of fables, a common range of method, and to a large degree a common fund of lore used, even if the method has latitude for differences from "Interpreter" to "Interpreter."

Hooke's own interest often shifts between what seems modern and what seems bizarre, because in our view both extremes characterize his thought.[28] For example, the story of Lycaon catches his attention (*Metamorphoses*, 1, 163–243). Ovid associates Lycaon with the last age before the flood. This Arcadian king behaved so impiously to Jupiter that he was changed into a wolf, even as Jupiter then destroyed all but a single pair of humanity. Hooke recounts this in a section, "The Fable of the *Lycaon* explain'd" (pp. 382–84), from which we also learn, "Lukaōn, as the word signifies, is Dissolution." That is, the fable means the earth is then in a state of fiery eruptions that require putting out. Hence the reason why Ovid follows that fable with his flood. "I would observe to you," Hooke remarks, "the Cohaerance and Connexion of the Mythologies, as they are ranged in this first book" (p. 385). With a skillful interpreter, we find sense in anything.

Our interpreter subsequently relates that Flood (p. 386), and then proceeds to the Python (p. 387). It will not be as self-evident to readers now as it was to the scientist Hooke then that in these passages Ovid is telling how the wet places corrupted and turned pestilential; or that next there was a drying-period, followed by the emergence of trees and woods (the Daphne story) and grass in the fields (the attributed point of the Io story). Juno, we hear, finds vapors drawn up and sets Argus to watch the stars by night. But Mercury, "or the light of the Morning," cuts off Argus' head, "that is, makes the Stars disappear and the Sun return." So the scientist's mythologizing goes on, hardly foretelling the interpretations advanced by classicists today.

To a skeptical mind, the obvious question is why Ovid did not say such things if that is what he meant. Far from trying to break *his* hermeneutic circle, Hooke offers two of them. His first:

> I have, in some of my former Discourses, indeavoured to shew some Probabilities, that the Mythologick Stories of the Poets did couch under those monstrous and seemingly impossible representations of Actions performed by humane Powers, some real and actual Catastrophies that had been caused by [on?] the Body or Face of the Earth by other Natural Powers, of which the *Aegyptians, Chaldeans, Greeks,* or some other learned Nations had preserved some Histories or Traditions among the more learned part of them; which, that they might the better conceale their Knowledge, and keep it to themselves, and abscond it from the Vulgar, and such as were not initiated and admitted into their Fraternities, they had contrived and digested into fabulous Stories, which, as they might serve to amuse and awe the Vulgar by the Daemonology they had thereupon superstructed, so they might serve to instruct and inform the Adepti.   (p. 394)

On the rhapsody goes, using arguments long since familiar. The one element of special interest here is the relation Hooke assumes between the fable and *history*. Little else is consistent. Yet within two pages he turns from saying that the adepts use fables to *conceal* their meaning from the vulgar, to maintaining instead that the Greeks turned "all their Histories into Mythologick Poetry" (his example is Plato's *Timaeus*, not the first history to come to mind), in order that the young could remember them the better by reason of "extravagant Marks" and "Pleasure" (p. 396). Concealment in obscurity yields to open or obvious pedagogy.

Like many a mythographer before him (Bacon's *Wisdom of the Ancients* offers a close precedent), Hooke takes pains to insist that history (truth?) will not be found in every fable. Because some

> are repeated and believed Fables which are true Histories, others are believed true but are really Fables: Some are believed Fables and are really so, and others are believed true and really are so. But of this fourth Head I fear is the smallest number.   (pp. 396–97)

Quite apart from his distinction between fable and history undoing all his previous interpretations, Hooke can be caught up in his scientific glossing of the wisdom of the ancients, now on Perseus (according to Lemprière's *Classical Dictionary*, 1788 ff., "*Met.* 4, *fab.* 16. 1[ib]. 5, *fab.* 1, &c."). He glosses "*Perseus* from *perizeo, circumferveo,* I take to signifie hot inflamed Air or Lightning," and so on and so forth (p. 297).

Since we do not read Ovid by those canons today, there had to have been a period when belief in such interpretation waned and then disappeared. As far as my study reveals, that shift occurred in the next century. In 1720, Samuel Garth brought out *Ovid's Metamorphoses,* a composite translation by himself, Dryden, Addison, and others. His preface shows an attitude with which Dryden would have been sympathetic.

The characters of the Gods of the old Heroick Age represented them unjust in their Actions; mutable in their Designs; partial in their Favours; ignorant of Events; scurrilous in their Language. Some of the superior Hierarchy treating one another with injurious Brutalities, and are often guilty of such Indecencies and Misbehaviour as the lowest of Mortals would blush to own.   (pp. xv–xvi)

Garth differs, however, from seventeenth-century interpreters in holding that "The Commentators may endeavour to hide those Absurdities under the Veil of Allegories" (p. xvi). For "Allegories should be obvious, and not like Meteors in the Air [so much for Hooke], which represent a different Figure to every different Eye" (*ibid.*). Garth *is* willing to comment on Ovid's fables, as in this comment on Baucis and Philemon: the tale is "most inimitably told" by Ovid, who "represents a good old Couple; happy, and satisfy'd in a cleanly Poverty; hospitable, and free [generous] of the few things, that Fortune had given them; moderate in Desires, affectionate in their conjugal Relation; so religious in life" (p. xvii). This may not differ entirely from commentaries in the preceding century. But it is more literal, more modern, in taking the story to mean what it seems to us to mean. We hear nothing from him about the body as the temple of the Holy Ghost. Ovid is Roman Ovid, not a writer needing to be allegorized to fit *a priori* Christian assumptions.

Our overwhelming question is: where does Dryden stand in all this? There is no doubt that he knew and used the lore beloved by Ross and others but dismissed by Garth. In *Threnodia Augustalis*, for example, there appears the following fable:

> But, like an Hurricane on *Indian* Seas,
>   The Tempest rose;
>   An unexpected Burst of Woes:
> With scarce a breathing space betwixt,
> This *Now* becalm'd, and perishing the next.
> As if great *Atlas* from his Height
> Shou'd sink beneath his heavenly Weight,
> And, with a mighty Flaw, the flaming Wall
>   (As once it shall)
> Shou'd gape immense and rushing down, o'erwhelm this neather
>   Ball;
> So swift and so surprizing was our Fear:
> Our *Atlas* fell indeed; But *Hercules* was near.   (lines 24–35)

We can gloss crucial references by attention to Ross, *Mystagogus Poeticus* (first edn., London, 1647; 6th, 1675). Under "Atlas" we find: "A King is the Atlas of his Common-wealth ... by the means of his knowledge the Kingdome is supported"; and under "Hercules": "Hee helped Atlas to support the heaven" (cf. Dryden, line 30) and is "the type of a good King ... who should support the heaven of the Church." In other words, when Charles II died, James succeeded him as "the type of a good King" – with the pagan fable of Hercules taking on Atlas' burden of the world (interpreted *in bono*) to prove it. Then there is the beast lore of *The Hind and the Panther*. (On these two poems, see the commentary in the California *Dryden*, III).

Dryden shows that he knew Sandys' Ovid, and that in his *Fables* he required morals. What should we conclude? If we take him at his word, as I feel we must in the absence of contrary evidence, we must place him somewhere in his century's lines of moralizers of fables.

As it happens, we are not without auxiliary evidence. In 1697, the year of his *Virgil*, Dryden was one of a group of people involved in a three-volume translation published in London:

The Annals and History of Cornelius Tacitus ... Made English by several Hands. With the Political Reflections and Historical Notes of Monsieur Amelot De La Houssay, and the Learned Sir Henry Savile.[29]

The substantial first volume of the *Annals* (1, 1–159) was translated by Dryden, so that its copious "reflections" and "notes" may be suggestive of his sense of possible historical signification in 1697, even in this group enterprise. The very first sentence in the translation begins: "ROME was govern'd at the first by Kings. Liberty and the Consulship were introduc'd by *Lucius Brutus* ..." At the foot of the page are, first, the numbered notes labelled "Politick Reflections," and below those, the lettered notes, designated "Historical Notes." Thus, the word "Kings" is glossed with the following "Politick Reflections":

When once the Regal Power begins to degenerate into Tyranny, the people aspire to Liberty; and when once a *Brutus* appears, that is, a Head who is capable to give it, they seldom fail to shake off the yoke, not only of the King, who Tyrannizes, but also of the Regal Power, for fear there come another King, who might tyrannize also. *Occultior non melior* [more concealed, not better].   (Tacitus, p. 1)

This differs from Dryden's familiar earlier support of kingship (and notably from his extreme "Postscript" to *The History of the League*). But after the revolution of 1688, Dryden and others had to think again about the terms of royal rule. Our poet's change of mind can be readily judged by comparison of what is usually termed "the passage on government" in *Absalom and Achitophel* with the passage on the true member of parliament in "To My Honour'd Kinsman" (lines 171–94).[30] So it is not surprising that he would associate himself with something less than total support of kings in political reflections on Tacitus.[31] What is of greater import for this chapter, however, is Dryden's evident consent that history as well as fables benefitted from moral interpretation. Take, for example, the first note, glossing "Kings":

viz. *Romulus* its founder, who, according to *Tacitus*, rul'd with absolute Power; *Romulus ut libitum imperitaverat. Ann. 3.* Numa, who Establish'd a Form of Divine Worship, with High-Priests, South-Sayers, and Priests.   (Tacitus, p. 1)

Numa is dealt with at length in Dryden's selection from *Metamorphoses*, 15.

Near the end of Dryden's portion of the *Annals*, we come to a particularly arresting example, one in which the "history" itself contains a moral.

For it was a Maxim of *Tiberius*, To let the Governours grow old in the Provinces which they commanded, and many of them died in Possession of these Places they held, whether Military or Civil.   (pp. 154–55)

It is worth speculating in advance what gloss, what reflection Dryden's contemporaries would include on this sentence. What we discover is at once more historical and fabulous than the text glossed.

In *France*, where the Offices are for Life, the Maxim of *Tiberius* hath the Approbation of all the great Men, inasmuch as it favours their Interests; but it is against that of the Prince, who, in some sort, ties up his own Hands, in giving what he cannot take away; and likewise against that of the Publick, where more Persons would be gratified and requited, if Places were triennial, as in *Spain*. The Fable of the Fox, which being fallen into a Pit, where the Flies sorely stung and tormented him, refus'd the assistance of the Hedgehog, who profferred to drive them away; Because (saith he), if you drive away these, others will come half starv'd, and exhaust all the Blood I have left. This Fable, I say; which Tiberius alledg'd as a Reason on which his *Maxim* was founded, concludes nothing in favour of Governments for Life; because the Fear of being no more employ'd, and the hope of rising from one Post to another more considerable will serve as a Curb and Restraint to Triennial Officers.   (p. 154)

The historical note has a brevity more like the style of Tacitus:

Cato the Censor's saying was, That to continue the same Persons long in Offices, did demonstrate, either that the Commonwealth afforded few that were fit, or that they made small account of Magistrates.   (p. 155)

The conclusion seems to be disarmingly simple. As he accommodated himself to glosses of histories, Dryden must surely have assumed that fables more urgently required allegorical – that is, moral – interpretation. At least, he says explicitly that that is how he designed his *Fables*. Moreover, if history as well as fables requires "Explications Historiques, Morales et Politiques," then all kinds of narrative (*historia, argumentum, fabula*) were alike in requiring – or perhaps it would be better to say that they were alike in benefitting from – explication and moral interpretation. The principle seems straightforward in its distinctly odd fashion. In practice, however, Dryden rarely supplies "morals" or allegoretic interpretations of his works. *Cymon and Iphigenia* is an instance in *Fables* when he does, and we shall shortly see another.

Granted that later in life he presumed that allegorical glosses were either necessary or helpful for all kinds of narrative, and for fables in particular, there is a further complexity. It may be phrased as a principle for interpreting fables: allegoresis is not equally necessary for all kinds of readers. *Cymon and Iphigenia* appears to be given a moral that is contrary to the implications of that fable itself. From the possible alternative explanations, we may consider three that are not necessarily conflicting: Dryden was inconsistent, disingenuous, or cognizant of the diverse needs of differing readers.

The "Morals" of Dryden's *Fables*

There may be muddle in the hermeneutic tradition within which the ageing Dryden worked as a translator and writer of narrative. It seems to me, however, that the tradition is more easily commanded than is responsible application of it. I find it difficult to be sure that my sense of the poet's methods is accurate, and yet more difficult to prove its accuracy. That is, for a Dryden to work within a tradition is not precisely the same as his accepting it entire. Nor is his revision of a tradition the same as his rejecting it.[32]

To assess the morals of *Fables*, we shall have to return to that perpetual poem. In Dryden's translation of Chaucer's Nun's Priest's Tale (*The Cock and the Fox*), he introduces numerous alterations, of which the most important for our purposes is his separating at the end Chaucer's own application of his story into a section labelled "The MORAL." The separation is not unlike the "Poeta Loquitur" prefixed to *Cymon and Iphigenia*, and the moral is as follows:

> In this plain Fable you th' Effect may see
> Of Negligence, and fond Credulity:
> And learn besides of Flatt'rers to beware,
> Then most pernicious when they speak too fair.

> The Cock and Fox, the Fool and Knave imply; }
> The Truth is moral, though the Tale a Lie.
> Who spake in Parables, I dare not say;
> But sure, he knew it was a pleasing way, }
> Sound sense, by plain Example, to convey.
> And in a Heathen Author we may find,
> That Pleasure with Instruction should be join'd:
> So take the Corn, and leave the Chaff behind.   (lines 810–21)

The "plain Fable" requires a gloss, partly from Horatian affectivism ("a Heathen Author"), partly from the parables used by Jesus, partly from Chaucer's corn–chaff distinction, which was itself based on a model of biblical exegesis adapted to secular works. In the common four-part division of the senses of scripture, the literal dealt with what happens, the moral with what we ought to *do* (my stress), the typological with what we ought to *believe* (again my stress), and the anagogical with the heavenly realm to which things tend.

Our understanding of these matters for the seventeenth century is still inadequate. But it appears that most earlier English writers of the century shared the Reformation emphasis on faith (belief) over acts (works), so that the typological significance then held greater importance (to Protestants) than the moral. Dryden's earlier works use typology, especially of the king and covenanted nation, with retrospective and correlative types by which a king might be a type of David, who was a type of Christ, so making the king Christotypical, as in the instance of Charles I for *Eikon Basilike* or of the king in *Absalom and Achitophel*. Dryden's later uses of types commonly tend more to involve individuals participating in the offices and imitation of Christ, as for example Anne Killigrew, Eleonora, and the Duchess of Ormond.[33] This brings Dryden's practice in the use of typology closer to pre-Reformation usage, which is to say that it involves his greater use of the moral sense of scripture (good works) and secular writing. Two major events appear to account for such change: his conversion to Roman Catholicism and the Revolution of 1688.

With his conversion, Dryden entered into a new relation with most of his readers. He was cut off from his former role of speaking for them, and from his former hope that by such speaking he might instill in his audience a faith that would lead the nation to new and great achievements. After his conversion, such poems as the Anne Killigrew Ode (if it is after) and the "Song for St. Cecilia's Day" exhibit the faith he retained in his art. But *The Hind and the Panther* was, he acknowledged, a "mysterious writ" (Part 3, line 2). It had been long since an English poet had used a figurative procedure with such strange features, such recondite lore. In spite of its title, *Britannia Rediviva* marks the end of Dryden's practice of putting politics at

the center, since the Revolution followed hard after. This important
change over these few years can be represented by lines from his two religious poems. *Religio Laici* bespeaks a Protestant emphasis on faith, belief:

> For *MY* Salvation must its Doom receive
> Not from what *OTHERS*, but what *I* believe.   (lines 302–03)

The comparable lines from *The Hind and the Panther* have a different
emphasis:

> Good life be now my task: my doubts are done,
> (What more could fright my faith, then Three in One?)(lines 78–79)

Faith has grown more passive in affirmation; good works have become the
active "task."

   The Catholic poem was written before the Revolution of 1688, and it is
almost solely thereafter that, in non-religious writing, we discover a
recurrent explicit concern with morals. In the preface to *Don Sebastian*
(1689) he says something of his tragedy that puts the interpretive issue
starkly to us:

This is not a Play that was huddled up in hast; and to shew it was not, I will
own, that beside the general Moral of it, which is given in the four last lines,
there is another Moral, couch'd under every one of the principal Parts and
Characters, which a judicious Critick will observe, though I point not to it in
this Preface.[34]

This statement more closely resembles Dryden's remark in the preface to
Fables – that "each of them" holds "some instructive moral" – than
anything else he wrote. And it is therefore appropriate that "The MORAL"
affixed to *The Cock and the Fox* is most closely approximated *in kind* (i.e.,
being emphatically moral rather than dominantly political, being open
rather than implicit) by "the general Moral" expressed in the concluding
lines of *Don Sebastian*:

> And let *Sebastian* and *Almeyda*'s Fate,
> This dreadfull Sentence to the World relate,
> That unrepented Crimes of Parents dead,
> Are justly punish'd on their Childrens head.

   This moral as to "Fate" and justice obviously deals with providential
causation, which is to say with problems of justice in a world divinely
ordained. The assumptions include both human freedom and the suffering
of the good. It is of no small significance that Dryden amplifies the
discussion of such issues beyond Chaucer's extent in his *Cock and the Fox*,
although he, no more than Chaucer, Milton, or Belial's seminar, can be

said to have settled those issues "Of Providence, Foreknowledge, Will and Fate, / Fixt Fate, free will, foreknowledg absolute" (*Paradise Lost* II: 559–60).

I am well aware that the morals Dryden wrote of as being "couch'd under every one of the principal Parts and Characters" of *Don Sebastian* have recently been conceived of in almost exclusively political terms. Such applications are certainly possible. The opening scene of that tragedy may be a recollection of the "king's disguise" poems of the interregnum or may be a prompt to English memory of an earlier king outside his own kingdom. These likenesses would mean more if Dryden's plays early and late did not actually feature the figure of a king or other royal figure in a vulnerable situation.[35] Yet that which seems to me to require most stress in our attempt to interpret *Fables* is that the moral provided by Dryden from the last lines of *Don Sebastian* is not political. More evidence than the fact of authorship by the poet of *Absalom and Achitophel* is required to establish political reflections, and particularly to argue for them alone. The examples require attention to an issue of principle: what, at heart, was meant by the "moral" of a literary work?

A quarter of a century before *Fables*, René Le Bossu had dealt with the centrality, indeed the priority, of the moral of a work in his highly influential work, *Traité du poème épique* (1675).[36] As Dryden paraphrases Le Bossu, "The first Rule" of an epic or tragedy "is to make the moral of the work"; only thereafter is the "whole action of the Play" devised, or the fable "designed" (XIII: 234). Le Bossu's general model has been taken as "an account of the literary work as a hierarchy of probable signs" and set forth in a figure:

Le Bossu and Dryden knew that Aristotle's "parts" of a tragedy (*Poetics*, ch. 6) began with action, or rather *mythos*, the "fable" in the diagram above. Dryden follows Le Bossu, who adds to Aristole's "hierarchy the prior requirement of a moral, which the fable 'allegorizes.'"[38] As we have been seeing, the moral might be political, but more often is not. In any event, *the moral is not a species of political allusion or parallel.*[39] The moral is taken to exist before the fable, which is why in interpreting Ovid the *Metamorphoses* was divided into fables whose morals were sought. That seems the main sense Dryden had in mind for his *Fables*, judging from his explanation, in his Preface, of his choices:

I have endeavour'd to chuse such Fables, both Ancient and Modern, as contain in them [sic] some instructive moral, which I could prove by Induction, but the Way is tedious; and they leap foremost into sight, without the Reader's Trouble of looking after them.   (IV: 1447)

That is, on the model given by Le Bossu, Dryden and his readers could easily interpret a given work in *Fables* by going back to its obvious, informing moral. Would that matters were so easy.

It does appear that we must allow for the importance of morals, allegory, and applications far more than criticism of late seventeenth-century literature has done, and that we must do so by attending to a wider range of possibilities. Not only that. We are faced with the need to account for a shift between *Don Sebastian* and *Fables*: Dryden moves from what (only?) "a judicious Critick will observe" to what is so obvious as not to require specification. Surely such a shift was first realized in great literature by Bunyan's *Pilgrim's Progress*, a moral allegory whose most famous question is, "What shall I *do* to be saved?" (Stress added.) This is not to suggest for a moment that issues of faith ceased to be important for Protestants like Bunyan, but that a new concern has also become central. Only later did socially more prominent, more "serious" writers like Dryden find themselves, as it were, Dissenters after the Revolution. In some ways, Sir Roger L'Estrange illustrates the shift best of all. Like Dryden, he turned to translation for financial support. And in 1692 he published his *Fables of Aesop and Other Eminent Mythologists; with Morals and Reflections*, adding *Fables and Storeys Moralized* in 1699, even as Dryden was completing *Fables*. We can gain a sense of the range of L'Estrange's second collection from two "Storeys" indexed under "A." Besides "Augustus Caesar and Virgil" there is "The Asses made Justice." L'Estrange obviously mines sources as much like Dryden's Ovid as Aesop, as much like Dryden's *Fables* as *The Hind and the Panther*. Not long thereafter some of the most conspicuous of later English allegory appears. By 1704 Swift had brought out his *Tale of a Tub*, and in 1726 *Gulliver's Travels*. In 1709 there appeared, with authorship attributed to Bernard Mandeville, *Bickerstaff's Aesop: or, the Humours of the Times, Digested into Fables*; in 1714 appeared what all allow to be his masterpiece, *The Fable of the Bees*.[40]

There are some real problems here. Nobody needs reminding that allegory is important to *The Pilgrim's Progress*, *The Fable of the Bees*, and *Gulliver's Travels*. But let us take examples from *Fables*, especially where "political meaning" may be discovered. In *The Cock and the Fox*, we read this concerning the sexual "Play" of Chanticleer and Dame Partlet:

> Ardent in Love, outragious in his Play,
> He feather'd her a hundred times a Day:
> And she that was not only passing fair,
> But was withal discreet, and debonair,
> Resolv'd the passive Doctrin to fulfill
> Tho' loath: And let him work his wicked Will.

It is reasonable to see in Partlet's "passive Doctrin" a reflection on those Anglican divines who professed a passive or neutral stance during the reign of James II. One need only compare the passage just given with others in *The Hind and the Panther*, Part Three (lines 665–66, 1061, 1261, but in particular line 134, with its sexual context). Yet such *allusion* does not require the claim of a political *moral* for the poem, as can be seen by reference to the moral Dryden separates for the conclusion of *The Cock and the Fox*.[41]

Let us consider another, more complex, example, the first poem in *Fables*, "To Her Grace the Dutchess of Ormond, with the Following Poem of Palamon and Arcite, from Chaucer." By his conflation of the Duchess with Chaucer's heroine and of her husband with Palamon, Dryden is able to offer the equivalence of "Conqu'ring *Theseus*" to William III. It has long seemed clear (to me, at least) that portions of the opening of *Palamon and Arcite* continue the Theseus–William identification, to the extent of criticizing King William and his unpopular, massive land wars.[42] But this is also only allusion, for, although it serves as a device to link the first two poems in *Fables*, the Theseus–William possibility soon fades from the "fable" of *Palamon and Arcite*; in short, it never was the *moral*.

As with personal "applications," larger matters encourage both connections and hesitations. For example, Dryden included "Alexander's Feast" in *Fables* between *The Flower and the Leaf* and Ovid, *Metamorphoses*, 12, on the Trojan war. The connection of the ode with its predecessor suggests a more amatory concern, as the connection with the latter suggests a more martial (although both are mixed). What then is the moral of the ode? Is it a political one, Alexandering William III down in a truthful ode? Or is it that: "None but the Brave deserves the Fair"? (line 15)? "Sweet is Pleasure after Pain" (line 60)? "War ... is Toil and Trouble; / Honour but an empty Bubble" (lines 99–100)? Or is it the same as that of "A Song for St. Cecilia's Day," "What Passion cannot MUSICK raise and quell" (presuming that *is* the moral of the "Song" – line 16)?

Before attempting to adjudicate among these possibilities, we ought to consider the highly varied nature of Dryden's larger figurative procedures. Who does not see the difference between the species of allegory, analogy, or metaphor – of sustained "parallel" – in *Absalom and Achitophel*, a figurative procedure that is all but "closed," and the very discontinuous allegory, or fable, or whatever one wishes to term the story of those beasts representing churches in *The Hind and the Panther*? But it has not been at all common to consider Dryden's plays or his verse narratives (apart from *Absalom and Achitophel* and *The Hind and the Panther*) as allegorical, or as fables, or as even works requiring "morals." Perhaps the reason is that Dryden just does not seem that simple, that much given to the a = b mentality that we tend to associate, in the abstract, with allegory and morals. In fact, Dryden suggests here and there that we must read figuratively in the senses we have been considering. The first line of the prologue to *The Duke of Guise* begins "Our Play's a parallel" (i.e., Guisards paralleling English Whigs). As we have seen, Dryden's prefaces to *All for Love* and *Don Sebastian* include talk of morals. The epilogue to *Albion and Albanius* (1685) is yet more specific and employs terms that have been recurring in this discussion:

> After our Aesop's Fable shown to day,
> I come to give the Moral of the play.   (lines 1–2)

"Fable" and "Moral." The problem comes down to this: what seems easy to conceive for Aesop or *Albion and Albanius* seems inadequate to *Fables* or any other complex work. Because students of Dryden and other late seventeenth-century English writers have simply not addressed the issues, it is necessary to provide at length the passage earlier excerpted from "The Grounds of Criticism in Tragedy," prefixed to Dryden's version of *Troilus and Cressida*:

The first Rule which *Bossu* prescribes to the Writer of an Heroic Poem, and which holds too by the same reason in all Dramatic Poetry, is to make the moral [sic] of the work; that is, to lay down to your self what that precept of morality shall be, which you would insinuate into the people; as namely, *Homer*'s (which I have Copy'd in my *Conquest of Granada*) was, that Union preserves a Commonwealth, and discord destroys it; Sophocles, in his *Oedipus*, that no man is to be accounted happy before his death. 'Tis the moral that directs the whole action of the Play to one center; and that action or Fable [sic], is the example [sic] built upon the moral, which confirms the truth of it to our experience: when the Fable is design'd, then and not before, the Persons are to be introduced with their manners [habitual moral conduct], characters [personalities] and passions.[43]

These remarks clarify some issues but not others. It is quite clear that Dryden conceives of the "moral" as the intentional foundation, or more simply the purpose, in writing a serious work. (It is less clear how widely the principles are to be construed. To comedies? To songs for plays?) The moral is, moreover, a species of affectivism, something the author desires, in Dryden's curious phrase, to "insinuate into the people." To call forth the authority of the *Iliad* and *Oedipus the King* can have been no idle gesture, but how adequate to those works do the stated morals strike us? We require knowing what Dryden means before we can decide whether to agree, and we have not asked even what it is we must know.

Is Dryden being somehow old-fashioned, moralistic? Are we missing something basic from his writing? Does Dryden shift what he means by "fable" and "moral"?[44] Or, do we have to make discriminations that his works, rather than his criticism, imply? In my view, we are not yet in a position to explain all these recurrences of "fable" and "moral," or to use these terms to explain Dryden's whole poetic and dramatic canon.[45] It does seem the case that we must face head on some features of these issues for a work whose title is *Fables Ancient and Modern*.

The "Poeta Loquitur" opening *Cymon and Iphigenia* constitutes one crucial passage. In its second half Dryden justifies, in his fashion, the treatment of love in *Fables*:

> But Love's the Subject of the Comick Muse:
> Nor can we write without it, nor would you
> A tale of only dry Instruction view.   (lines 24–26)

If the collection aims at something more attractive than "dry Instruction," it must yet be taken to use fables to some end of morals, significance, or import. There is nothing here inconsistent with Crites' definition of a play (really of literature) as the "just and lively Image of Humane Nature ... for the Delight and Instruction of Mankind."[46] That is, both passages presume that instruction must accommodate "delight" and be "lively" as well as "just." But context is the determining factor, and we must consider the lines that follow those just quoted (and then *their* context as well):

> Nor Love is always of a vicious Kind,
> But oft to virtuous Acts inflames the Mind.
> Awakes the sleepy Vigour of the Soul,
> And, brushing o'er, adds Motion to the Pool.
> Love, studious how to please, improves our Parts,
> With polish'd Manners, and adorns with Arts.
> Love first invented Verse, and form'd the Rhime,
> The Motion measur'd, harmoniz'd the Chime;
> To lib'ral Acts inlarg'd the narrow-Soul'd:
> Soften'd the Fierce, and made the Coward Bold:
> The World when wast, he Peopled with increase,
> And warring Nations reconcil'd in Peace.
> *Ormond*, the first, and all the Fair may find
> In this one Legend to their Fame design'd,
> When Beauty fires the Blood, how Love exalts the Mind.

Using the old trope of love as education, the passage provides a moral for the last poem in *Fables*. Yet, as has already been said of *Cymon and Iphigenia*, its action fails to sustain this equable moral. In short, neither this moral nor that for *The Cock and the Fox* can be regarded as anything other than reductive of fables very complex (*The Cock and the Fox*) or dissident (*Cymon and Iphigenia*). Of course we might infer additional morals: that concupiscence shortly yields to wrath (cf. *Palamon and Arcite* and other stories in *Fables*), wrath to sorrow, and sorrow to unjust rewards to victors in a world for which a Christian afterlife is the sole assurance of divine providence and of a human sense of justice. If Dryden meant those further morals, he does not explicitly supply them. That is one problem. Another is that the explicit morals he does offer seem bewilderingly simplistic.

The immediate issues are: why he offers a likewise simple moral to "*Ormond*, the first, and all the Fair"; and why that moral does not seem adequate, on its own terms, to *Cymon and Iphigenia*. What is immediate is also ultimate in implications for how we read Dryden and other earlier writers. There is a genuine possibility that he meant those simple morals seriously, and that we misread him and earlier Renaissance writers if we interpret them otherwise. If so, the moral of *King Lear* is that of *Gorbuduc*: kings should not bequeath divided realms. And the moral of *Paradise Lost* is precisely a justification of "the wayes of God to men."[47]

To state matters so starkly is also to expose their insufficiency to our modern view of literary interpretation and of the nature of literature. Of course, views are not proved simply by our holding them, and it seems intellectually responsible only to present evidence for an interpretation of Dryden's "morals" different from that which will be espoused here.

That is, we must take seriously the possibility that the morals of Dryden's *Fables* are in fact simple, embarrassingly so to modern taste. There seem to me three kinds of evidence. One is the lore of commonplaces ("Festina lente," "Sibi imperare imperium maximum" – Happy in slowness, To rule oneself is the greatest dominion), emblems, and tag lines. These are characteristic features of thought at the time and earlier. Second, none of Dryden's examples of morals requires extended, discriminating judgment. It is the works that are extended and that seem complex rather than the specific, explicit morals drawn about them.

The third kind of evidence is that provided by Boswell from Johnson's conversation. Boswell begins with his own observation.

I observed, the great defect of the tragedy of *Othello* was, that it had not a moral; for that no man could resist the circumstances of suspicion which were artfully suggested to Othello's mind. JOHNSON. 'In the first place, Sir, we learn from *Othello* this useful moral, not to make an unequal match; in the second place, we learn not to yield too readily to suspicion. The handkerchief is merely a trick, though a very pretty trick; but there are no other circumstances of reasonable suspicion, except what is related by Iago of Cassio's warm expressions concerning Desdemona in his sleep; and that depended entirely upon the assertion of one man. No, Sir, I think *Othello* has more moral than almost any play.[48]

Let us set aside what Boswell and Johnson seem to agree upon as a condition of a moral, that it could not gloss what carried full conviction. We are left with morals of such a surprising degree of simplicity that we are almost disgusted by their crudity in interpreting *Fables* or *Othello*. Perhaps Johnson – and Dryden – were satisfied with much less than we in discussing the significance of literary works. The possibility is a genuine one.

Yet it seems to me unacceptable, both for reasons that will follow and for one that may be given here. A critic contemporary with Dryden also concerned himself with the morals of *Othello*. It is the turn of Thomas Rymer:

> What ever rubs or difficulty may stick on the Bark, the Moral, sure, of this Fable is very instructive.
>
> 1, First, This may be a caution to all Maidens of Quality how, without their Parents consent, they run away with Blackamoors ...
>
> Secondly, This may be a warning to all good Wives, that they look well to their Linen.
>
> Thirdly, This may be a lesson to Husbands, that before their Jealousie be Tragical, the proofs may be Mathematical ...
>
> Nothing is more odious in Nature than an improbable lye; And, certainly, never was any Play fraught, like this of *Othello*, with improbabilities.[49]

Rymer's last sentence appears to deny the basis upon which Boswell and Johnson agree a moral is possible: not of that which is perfected but of interpretable imperfection.

Two other matters are more important for our immediate concerns. One is that Johnson deduces the very morals, and in the same order, that Rymer sarcastically, caustically raises only that they may be rejected as ridiculous. It would seem that either there is some major shift in outlook between Rymer and Johnson or that, in "talking for victory" on this occasion, Johnson deliberately made a positive use of Rymer's fault-finding. None of these considerations wholly disposes of the possibility that Dryden's morals were simple things to our view. Which is why, in conscience, I have raised the issue. But (to adapt an old saying), one would rather go wrong with Dryden than err with Rymer.

Fortunately, there is an alternative that allows us at once to accept the

simplistic morals and to transcend them. That possibility seems to me to be
hinted at as early as "The Grounds of Criticism in Tragedy" quoted
above, when Dryden speaks of "that precept of morality ... which you
would insinuate into *the people*" (stress added). It does seem that Dryden,
like Ben Jonson, distinguished among different audiences, between what
Jonson called "mere readers" (Dryden's "the people," as also "*Ormond,
the first, and all the Fair*"). I believe that Dryden felt that he had a more
various audience than he had presumed earlier in his career, and necessarily had to assume (as the very complexity of *Fables* implies) a second (or
third) more erudite, experienced, knowing audience.

It seems impossible to determine exactly when Dryden first assumed
that he was addressing radically varied groups of readers. In a sense that is
always the case. Moreover, it constituted a general problem for him,
Marvell, Butler, and Milton when writing in a public mode. There were
always others who would disagree, even over panegyric. Our immediate
issue differs, however, in its involving readers distinguished, not by
partisanship, but by ability and insight. Jonson's distinction between
understanders and mere readers, like Milton's hope for a fit audience,
however few, show that the concern persists throughout the century. We
may recall that Hooke thought (in one humor) that morals were a means
by which the adept "absconded" knowledge from the vulgar. Dryden's
own concern emerges forcibly as early as the "Epilogue" to *Aureng-Zebe*
(first performed November, 1675):

> Yet scatter'd here and there I some behold,
> Who can discern the Tinsel from the Gold:
> To these he writes; and, if by them allow'd,
> 'Tis their Prerogative to rule the Crowd.
> For he more fears (like a presuming Man)
> Their Votes who cannot judge, than theirs who can.   (38–43)

In a more general sense, his many prefaces and epistles dedicatory show
him in the act of seeking to reach out to true discerners and to educate
those amenable to literary tutelage.

With other writers, he shared the dangers of ignorance and prejudice,
which are at once distinct and related. In his political poetry, he also had
to risk disagreement with discerning readers who were readers of genuine
principle, albeit principles different from his. And yet none of these
hazards approached the problem represented by his conversion. Readers
of *Areopagitica* often fail to recognize Milton's typical English anti-Catholi-
cism, his exclusion of Catholic writings from that very freedom of the press
he advocates. The third part of *The Hind and the Panther* begins: "Much

malice mingl'd with a little wit / Perhaps may censure this mysterious writ." But Dryden describes the more varied audience that I have presumed with far greater detail in his dedication of his *Aeneis*.

Following Segraius (J. R. de Segrais), Dryden presumes that there exist "three Classes of writers." Each is described in detail. The "lowest Form" are "Mobb-Readers." The "middle sort of Readers" are those with "a farther insight" but yet without "the capacity for judging right," including those "young Gentlemen" who have been educated at a principal school and perhaps a university. Finally, there are "the most Judicious: Souls of the highest Rank, and truest Understanding. These are few in number …"[50]

Studies of readership in the late seventeenth century seem to agree that there was a growing number of women who read literature, people who, of course, had little formal education and who were barred from Dryden's Westminster and Cambridge. But Dryden seems to assume a somewhat differently varied audience, including what he might have conceived of to include women and half-educated men, along with the basically unlettered nobility. This middle group seems in fact to have constituted the majority of his readers. If so, there was some such range in his mind as that from "Mobb-Readers," a "middle sort of Readers" and judicious souls "of the highest Rank, and truest Understanding." It seems likely that in the last group, however sparse, he could envision an audience cognizant of far more complex issues that might be no less involved with "morals," but readers who would see beyond the trope of love as education.

I am suggesting that in "Dryden's final poetic mode" one finds a range of usually nonconflicting morals for various kinds of readers. At one end of this continuum he follows the mythographers of Ovid that I have exemplified by Sandys and others as offering certain simple, neat morals; at the other he posits morals that are far more complex. By his simpler or "Mobb-Readers," the sweet story of *Baucis and Philemon* might be taken to concern the rewards of pious hospitality. For his more subtle readers, the fable would also concern a stronger, higher providence that brings justice of a kind comparable to the Christian, but still a justice limited by its paganness to a final metamorphosis into trees rather than of bodies and souls for eternity. Similarly, *Fables Ancient and Modern* would show at large a series of disjunct, easier morals, even while to more capable readers its bleak ending in *Cymon and Iphigenia* shows that the human comedy is far more complex, much sadder than morals provided for "Mobb-Readers" could possibly show.

Above all, I believe we must presume that there is no total contradiction between simple morals and the complex implications of *Fables*. What is

easy and what is subtle are both present, if on a scale of importance to
Dryden and, he hoped, to judicious readers. It is true that Cymon benefits
by education through love, but it is also true that that old trope insuffi-
ciently accounts for the darkened world at the end of *Fables*. In this last,
and to some of us the greatest, work of his career, Dryden offers what is in
many ways his freest, simplest version of narrative, and yet a narrative
whose very clarities issue in complexities. In a sense it is an old and dying
man's most youthful, healthiest work, and one worthy of being set beside
even *Paradise Lost*.

Perpetual poem and second epic

We have been seeing (with whatever deductions for our poor sight) that
Fables Ancient and Modern owes a debt to the *Metamorphoses* in the stories
chosen, in being another perpetual poem, in the implications of what a
fable meant to seventeenth-century poets, and in terms of enduring ways of
interpreting fables. Among the other connections that might be drawn, this
chapter will conclude with one lacking in full proof, although to one reader
at least it seems sufficiently probable to warrant declarative syntax. As has
long been recognized, many a poet has found that epic ambitions have been
achieved by a poet of the same generation or just earlier, so leaving the
finder with the need to write the second epic of the age. Chaucer dealt with
the matter in his two principal poems, confessing his secondariness to the
Italians (and to Lollius!). Boccaccio was a second to Dante. And Ovid was a
second to Virgil. Boccaccio and Ovid faced the problem of writing the
second epic after highly unified first epics. Unless they turned to downright
parody, the only likely alternative was that of a more episodic kind. It seems
clear that Dryden found himself in the same position *vis-à-vis* Milton:

Spencer and *Fairfax* both flourish'd in the Reign of Queen *Elizabeth*: Great Masters
in our Language; and who saw much farther into the Beauties of our Numbers
than those who immediately followed them. *Milton* was the Poetical Son of *Spencer*,
and Mr. *Waller* of *Fairfax*; for we [the pronoun is not "they"] have our Lineal
Descents and Clans, as well as other Families: *Spencer* more than once insinuates
that the Soul of *Chaucer* was transfus'd into his Body; and that he was begotten by
him Two hundred years after his Decease. *Milton* has acknowledg'd to me that
Spencer was his Original; and many besides my self have heard our famous *Waller*
own, that he deriv'd the Harmony of his Numbers from *Godfrey of Bulloign* [Tasso's
Gerusalemme Liberata], which was turn'd into *English* by Mr. *Fairfax*.

(Kinsley, IV: 1445)

Who can doubt that Dryden adds himself to a clan of poets or that, in
presenting a narrative work of this kind, he places himself in lineal descent

from Chaucer, Spenser, and Milton?[51] The company kept posed problems, however. Milton was Dryden's contemporary, and any serious attempt at heroic narrative needed a model other than Milton or his model (Virgil, who incorporated the two Homeric poems).

Milton in 1660 and Dryden in 1688 were in remarkably similar plights. Both might have lost their lives, Dryden – were it not for highly placed Anglican friends – for being guilty of high treason in being "reconciled" to Rome. (After all, Pepys was sent to the Tower merely on false suspicion of being a papist.) Like Milton, Dryden had to reconstruct his literary world, which is to say renovate his personal, religious, political, and artistic life. Given his problems, and given the importance throughout his career of the heroic, it is not surprising that he should have turned to one of Milton's chief models, Virgil, to find some compensation in translation. The effort brought a degree of financial success, but, for all his changes, Dryden could not make Virgil's three works his own. For what was to be his last great effort, he could only turn to Virgil's successor, the second Augustan epic poet, Ovid, to be the second epic poet of his age after Milton. It is true that he offers the first book of the *Iliad* as a proposal for the public to pick up, as it is also true that he died before he could complete his *Ilias*. But we observe that the other writers he chooses – Chaucer and Boccaccio – are also poets of the second epic. All face a problem different from Virgil's, which was to create an equivalent of the two Homeric poems in the Latin tongue, and to renovate them with a Roman meaning. Virgil's was the problem of writing the first epic of the age, for all useful purposes the first in his nation and tongue. Spenser had enough temporal, personal, and literary distance from Chaucer – as did Milton from Spenser – not to have to write second epics. It was enough for them to engage in the task of another "first."[52]

After his conversion and the revolution of 1688, Dryden's position resembled Milton's in some other respects. Milton famously did not expect many readers, as he says of himself in addressing his Muse:

> though fall'n on evil dayes,
> On evil dayes though fall'n, and evil tongues;
> In darkness, and with dangers compast round,
> And solitude; yet not alone, while thou
> Visit'st my slumbers Nightly, or when Morn
> Purples the East: still govern thou my Song,
> *Urania*, and fit audience find, though few.
>
> (*Paradise Lost*, VII: lines 25–31)

Dryden expects more readers. But like Milton, and like Ben Jonson yet earlier, he distinguishes in effect between "mere readers" and the few fit understanders.

Milton's problem was passionate, religious, and ideological: explaining what had gone wrong with the Good Old Cause. He found that he could "justifie the wayes of God to men" only by giving up the solely English story (or his proposed Arthuriad) and by finding beneficent divine purpose in the totality of providential history. In writing the second epic, Dryden emphasized the human rather than the divine. We recall Dryden commenting that Milton's "Design is the Losing of our Happiness; his Event [outcome] is not prosperous, like that of all other Epique Works: His Heavenly Machines [God, the Son, angels] are many, and his Humane Persons but two" (*Works*, IV: 15). Dryden's "human persons" are many, and his "machines" few, although present in Christian as well as pagan versions. His outcome (defined in *Cymon and Iphigenia*) is prosperous, at least as far as all but fit readers are concerned. For them, human limitations are stressed. Yet the ideological energy of *Fables* is not negative – or easy to describe in simple political, religious, or even literary terms. Here is Chanticleer to Partlet on the nature of "Man":

> See, my Dear,
> How lavish Nature has adorn'd the Year;
> How the pale Primrose, and blue Violet spring,
> And Birds essay their Throats disus'd to sing:
> All these are ours; and I with pleasure see
> Man strutting on two Legs, and aping me!
> An unfledg'd Creature, of a lumpish frame,
> Indew'd with fewer Particles of Flame:
> Our Dame sits couring o'er a Kitchin-fire,
> I draw fresh Air, and Nature's Works admire:
> And ev'n this Day, in more delight abound,
> Than since I was an Egg, I ever found.
>
> (*The Cock and the Fox*, lines 455–66)[53]

Human solipsism is laughed at here, but Chanticleer's highly amusing matutinal satisfactions as a mere cock to a mere hen shed an ironic but finally and decisively affirmative glow on the human world and the human creatures in it. That affirmation is hard earned, but the aged poet's disappointments in his world and his belief that things would come right only in the afterlife did not prevent him from affirming the imperfect, from observing tracks of the eternal in the present.

That said, as I think it must be – emphatically – both Dryden's preface and the composite heroic poem that followed it suggest that he felt regret at having to write the second epic of his age, and regret also perhaps in having to compose a version of the Ovidian perpetual poem of changes. We have already seen how the most philosophical part of the *Meta-*

morphoses is corrected by two Christian poems. And, what is equally to the point, we have also seen how Dryden chooses to end with *Cymon and Iphigenia*, for which only the simple moral is cheerful in this poem by itself and as a conclusion to *Fables*. With such undoubted sadness for the human comedy goes a dry-eyed acceptance of the way that comedy must be, a sense that full hope is deferred: "For here we have no continuing city, but we seek one to come" (Hebrews 13:14). With that hope, it was possible for Dryden to find consolation for the human in the divine comedy, and to express warmth such as we readers feel even for much of what must be found wanting. With that hope, he perhaps found some consolation in a perpetual poem founded on immediate problems, animated by deferred hopes. Given Ovid's claim to immortality, and to episodic if unbroken song, we may select four words from the beginning along with the last word of his perpetual poem; for if he were a seer, Ovid might well have looked ahead to Dryden to say, "I shall live altered in new forms" (In nova ... mutatas ... formas ... vivam).[54] This pastiche seems particularly appropriate to Dryden's epic as cento. It recognizes the plurality of forms he draws upon. It signals his debt to Ovid and to traditions of interpreting Ovid. To be sure, Ovid's forms required reforming aesthetically into a new whole, and religiously into a Christian epic that ignored Ovid's first "dark" age in favor of fables credibly treating the human comedy.

These remarks have centered on *Fables Ancient and Modern*, a work I deem the greatest of the century after *Paradise Lost*, which it excels in major features of interest, of readability.[55] Aware as I am that some of the questions raised may be faulty, there is no hope for uniformly correct answers here. And the choice of subject produces a necessarily different Dryden from that revealed by his engagement with Ben Jonson or with French dramatists. The same principle that selection determines results applies to others besides myself. And those others include interpreters of Dryden before (and after) me. It applies indeed to Dryden's important successors as poets and critics. Few great poets can have been as generous to a strong immediate predecessor as Pope was to Dryden. In that fact we understand something winning about Pope and a dimension of Dryden otherwise unavailable.[56] But our last sighting of Dryden in this study is given us through the powerful mind of Samuel Johnson.

For Johnson, the fevers of the seventeenth century were something to be read about rather than recalled. For Dryden they were all too fresh in his mind as he contemplated the beginning of a century he only glimpsed. It was "time to begin a New," as he would write in *The Secular Masque*. Ovid served him well in his last great effort. With Ovid's *Metamorphoses* as a model to be reformed, Dryden answered his needs in writing the age's second epic. The Ovidian claim to a perpetual poem and to poetic immortality in changed forms could itself be altered. By a benign fate, reforming Ovid's own altered forms enabled Dryden to live on in *Fables Ancient and Modern*, another perpetual poem, one that has delighted additional centuries of readers far more various than the poet had dared hope. The miracle is that, in reforming Ovid, Dryden's own dark meditations were transformed into the bright sunshine of that summer holiday in which Cymon whistles for want of thought.

Notes

1 According to my count, in the two short-title catalogues of Pollard and Redgrave and Wing, the frequency of publication in the seventeenth century runs: Ovid 93 times, Virgil 54 times, and Horace 46 times. Although Ovid was most *popular*, Homer, Virgil and Horace must surely have been more highly esteemed. On the general subject, see Lee T. Pearcey, *The Mediated Muse: English Translations of Ovid 1580–1700* (Hamden, CT: Archon Books 1984); Dryden's renderings are somewhat palely treated as matters of style.
2 Virgil poses an interesting problem. He is not the father of Roman poetry. That was probably Ennius. But in terms of "the first" and "second epic," which will concern us later, he is second to Homer, but primary to Ovid, Dante, and others. Dryden does speak of the "same Degree of Veneration" due Homer, Virgil, and Chaucer in their national traditions: Preface to *Fables*, James Kinsley, ed., *The Poems of John Dryden*, 4 vols. (Oxford: Clarendon Press, 1958), IV: 1452–53; hereafter this edition, cited as Kinsley, is used unless otherwise noted.
3 In *Sylvae* (1685), the four passages from the *Aeneid* are out of their original order in the poem; the five from Lucretius are in their order, as are the three idylls of Theocritus. On features of the integration of these, see my commentary in H. T. Swedenberg, et al., eds., *The Works of John Dryden*, III (Berkeley and Los Angeles: University of California Press, 1969), 267 and 276–81 (Lucretius); this edition is cited hereafter as *Works*.
4 The first published interpretation of *Fables* as an integrated collection was mine in *Dryden's Poetry* (Bloomington: Indiana University Press, 1967), ch. 8. But at that very time, the late Judith Sloman was writing her excellent University of Minnesota dissertation and later printed or delivered at conferences a number of papers, including one, "Interpretation of Dryden's *Fables*," *Eighteenth Century Studies*, 4, (1971), 199–211, emphasizing epic and historical elements in the work. See also her posthumous *Dryden: The Poetics of Translation* (Toronto: University of Toronto Press, 1985), ch. 7. For details concerning her thesis and other relevant studies, see part 6 of David J. Latt and Samuel Holt Monk, *John Dryden: A Survey and Bibliography of Critical Studies* (Minneapolis: University of Minnesota Press, 1976). In his excellent discussion of individual poems and recurrent issues, *Dryden's Final Poetic Mode: The Fables* (Philadelphia: Pennsylvania University Press, 1988), Cedric D. Reverand II does not discuss the

morals of poems in *Fables* or issues of the second poet dealt with here. He takes issue with Sloman's thesis, and therefore implicitly with mine, that *Fables* should be read sequentially, and yet in his wish to show that one poem or issue qualifies or undermines another, he necessarily holds for a holistic conception. Relative to my concerns, he holds that Christian ideals have no special role in *Fables*.

5 IV: 1450. The burden of originality is beginning to be felt – more in the abstract than in practice.

6 The suggestion has been made to me that the primary meaning of "carmen perpetuum" is musical (see "song" here). But I see no warrant for that interpretation in classical or middle Latin. Moreover, in the Preface to *Fables* Dryden twice uses English equivalents in speaking of Chaucer: "He is a *perpetual* Fountain of good Sense," and he translated Chaucer "only that I might *perpetuate* his Memory" (Kinsley, IV: 1452, 1459; stress added). To be or to render "unbroken," "ceaseless" are the meanings Dryden clearly assigns, as had Ovid, to "perpetuum."

7 Loeb edition: Ovid, *Metamorphoses*, ed. Frank Justus Miller, 2 vols., 3rd edn. (London, 1977), II, 426 (15, 875–76; Loeb Classics).

8 L. P. Wilkinson, *Ovid Recalled* (Cambridge: Cambridge University Press, 1955), p. 145. This book was later shortened and published as *Ovid Surveyed*. In a tribute to Wilkinson, Charles Martindale has edited *Ovid Renewed*, fifteen chapters on Ovid himself or his reception by later authors. (See notes 19 and 24, below.) My title is indebted to this line of study.

9 *Ibid.*, p. 147.

10 Sandys' *Ovid's Metamorphosis. English'd, Mythologiz'd And Represented in Pictures* (Oxford, 1632). The first edition translating the complete poem appeared in 1626 and a pirated edition the next year. The 1632 edition is more valuable, since it includes the translation, mythologies, and figures. For reviewing quotations and citations, I have used the modern reprint (here pp. 8–9) edited by Karl K. Hulley and Stanley Vandersall (Lincoln: University of Nebraska Press, 1970).

11 With certain reservations, Numa Pompilius is taken by Sandys and Dryden to be a historical figure, the successor to Romulus (with whom Book 14 ends). After an account of Numa's teaching, Ovid considers principal Roman leaders down to the empire in his own times, as the opening of the poem promises. Dryden is at pains to stress "the Moral and Natural Philosophy of *Pythagoras*," taught by Numa, "which are, the most learned and beautiful Parts of the whole Metamorphoses" (headnote to "Of the Pythagorean Philosophy"). Subsequent reversals, as here, of italic and roman usage will not be mentioned. Similarly, henceforth citations are of Kinsley, IV, unless otherwise specified.

12 For a more detailed discussion of this, see *Dryden's Poetry*, p. 290.

13 Pepys' letter is quoted here from *Of Dramatic Poesy and Other Critical Essays*, ed. George Watson, 2 vols. (London: Everyman, 1962), II: 263; hereafter cited as Watson.

14 This is not the place to enter into the complex matter of the editions of his

authors Dryden used in *Fables*, a topic we may fairly expect the California *Works of John Dryden* to set forth.

15 For the role of such junctures and disjunctures in providing the force of narrative continuum, see my *Comparative Poetics: An Intercultural Essay on Theories of Literature* (Princeton: Princeton University Press, 1990), p. 210.

16 See n. 4.

17 Reverand (see n. 4) well discusses a number of these issues.

18 Recently the tendency among critics of Dryden has been, as it were, to use *Absalom and Achitophel* as the model of interpretation, and to search for political meanings. Those will indeed be found in "To My Honour'd Kinsman." But the right balance is struck by Alan Roper, who regards the ultimate allusive fields of both that poem and "To Her Grace the Dutchess of Ormond" as Christian: "The Kingdom of Adam": *Dryden's Poetic Kingdoms* (London: Routledge and Kegan Paul, 1965), pp. 104–35. And in developing his argument he acknowledges the similar one by Jay Arnold Levine, "John Dryden's Epistle to John Driden," *JEGP*, 3 (1964), 450–74.

19 In the *Poeta Loquitur* that leads off his last fable, Dryden declares he writes for "*Ormond*, the first, and all the Fair" to discover "how Love exalts the Mind" (lines 39, 41). I interpret the first phrase to mean (the Duchess of) Ormond (in) the first (instance and rank) and (all the rest of) the Fair (with her). It is also possible to interpret the phrase to mean (the Duke of) Ormond (in) the first (instance or rank) and (with him) all the Fair (including the Duchess). If so, Dryden would be returning to his dedication of *Fables* rather than to its first poem and the Duchess. But the easier, more natural interpretation of the succession, "Ormond, *the first, and all the Fair*" (reversing italics) seems to me to bear on the Duchess. The issue of one interpretation or moral for one audience and another meaning for another will be taken up later.

20 Ovid, *Metamorphoses*, ed. Frank Justus Miller, 2 vols. (Cambridge, MA: Harvard University Press, 1960), I: xi–xii (Loeb Classics).

21 Dryden would surely have agreed with the basic assumption of Brooks Otis, *Ovid as Epic Poet* (Cambridge: Cambridge University Press, 1966). Reviewing a recent study of the *Metamorphoses*, Charles Martindale comments on "the difficulty in talking about the poem except in terms either of generalization, or general topics, or of Ovid's modifications of the mythological tradition. A critical language for detailed discussion of local particulars throughout individual episodes remains a key desideratum," *Comparative Literature*, 42 (1990), 260. As we shall be seeing, Dryden inherited such a "critical language." But his use of it is not easily characterized.

22 In *Milton, Poet of Exile* (New Haven: Yale University Press, 1986), Louis L. Martz treats Milton's poetic versions of exile in a yet broader or freer sense than that used here.

23 On Ovid's still unexplained banishment and the poems on which information about his exile is based, see Hermann Fränkel, *Ovid: A Poet Between Two Worlds* (Berkeley and Los Angeles: University of California Press, 1969), chs. 12–18; and Harry B. Evans, *Publica Carmina: Ovid's Books from Exile* (Lincoln: University of Nebraska Press, 1983) on *Tristia* and *Epistulae Ex Ponto*.

24 See *Annus Mirabilis*, lines 137–40, for an earlier, and *Threnodia Augustalis*, lines 24–26, for a later, example of the metaphor.

25 In addition to Dryden's Ross-like application of pagan examples *in bono* and *in malo*, he would have known Butler's characteristic elevation of Ross to bad eminence at the beginning of *Hudibras*, 1, 2: "There was an ancient sage *Philosopher*, / That had read *Alexander Ross* over ... "

26 1970 edition (here and hereafter), p. 386. Note in particular the Christianizing.

27 The amplitude does vary, as in study today. For example, David Hopkins shows convincingly that Dryden's treatment of Ovid was more sympathetic in his translations than in some of his pronouncements. See "Dryden and Ovid's 'Wit out of season'" in Charles Martindale, ed., *Ovid Renewed* (Cambridge: Cambridge University Press, 1988), pp. 167–90. Hopkins does not dwell on Dryden's praise of Ovid, and he chooses to focus on the translation of *Metamorphoses*, 12, particularly on the battle of the Centaurs with the Lapiths. This is fresh territory. The curious thing is that he chooses an episode that Ross' method leads him to ignore, that Du Ryer says almost nothing about, and that Sandys treats in terms of the Centaurs' bestiality, using the Centaurs' names to make his point. Yet more oddly, although Hopkins is quite aware of the commentaries by Sandys and Du Ryer, he does not use them or, for that matter, American scholarship on Ovid in *Fables*.

28 In fairness to Hooke, it should be recalled that (like Dryden) Newton practiced judicial astrology; he labored over the chronology since the Creation; and he practiced alchemical experiments (while conveniently master of the royal mint). The successive publications of another Royal Society virtuoso, the Hon. Robert Boyle, would show at a glance the combination of what may seem to us credulity and modernity. Samuel Butler and Jonathan Swift knew better, at the cost of no little mental comfort.

29 Margaret Duggan first drew my attention to the annotations in this work.

30 He wrote Charles Montague, later Earl of Halifax, that in the passage of the poem to his cousin he states "What an Englishman in Parliament ought to be; & deliver it as a Memorial of my Principles to all Posterity." See Charles E. Ward, *The Letters of John Dryden* (Durham: Duke University Press, 1944), p. 120.

31 Amelot (Abraham-Nicolas Amelot de la Houssaye) had his *Tacite avec les Notes Politiques et Historiques* published twice in Paris in 1690; or Dryden might have used the Hague edition of 1692. See the detailed study by Steven N. Zwicker and David Bywaters, "Politics and Translation: The English Tacitus of 1698," *Huntington Library Quarterly*, 52 (1989), 319–40. They show that, in translating, Dryden worked carefully, comparing the Latin with the French. They do not comment on Dryden's taking over Amelot's political and historical "notes" and reflections or even make anything of their existence.

32 We are now prepared for the most important issues dealt with in this chapter, and unfortunately the evidence is not the clearest or the most abundant. In reaching certain decisions, I shall suggest possible alternatives, and would suggest others if I had not found that readers prefer the assurance of (at least

the appearance of) clarity to the multifariousness of interpretation, and are
disturbed more by harping on the inadequacy of evidence than by positive
assertion. Skepticism is never so welcome as when it applies elsewhere.
33 Steven N. Zwicker has shown the shift in Dryden's typological emphases. The
early use is represented by the title and evidence of his *Dryden's Political Poetry:
The Typology of King and Nation* (Providence: Brown University Press, 1972).
The later (summarized in my main text) is shown in "Politics and Panegyric:
The Figural Mode from Marvell to Pope," in *Literary Uses of Typology*, ed.
Miner (Princeton: Princeton University Press, 1977), pp. 131–41. In the same
book rather similar points are made by Paul J. Korshin, "The Development of
Abstracted Typology in England, 1650–1820," pp. 147–203. The date of
Dryden's conversion cannot be proved, but I have argued that Dryden
implicitly dates it in *The Hind and the Panther*, II: 654–63, to the time of
Monmouth's invasion and his defeat at the Battle of Sedgemoor (6 July 1685).
See "The Significance of Plot in *The Hind and the Panther*," *Bulletin of the New
York Public Library*, 89 (1965), 446–58. This would make the Killigrew ode
(1686) postdate his conversion. But the inclusion in, or exclusion of, that poem
from Dryden's "Catholic" canon is not crucial to the argument.
34 *Works*, XV: 71. There is, in fact, at least one anticipation, in the preface to *All
for Love* (1678), in which Dryden mentions "the excellency of the Moral"
(*Works*, XIII: 10). This remark has not been properly investigated. Most of us
have presumed, rightly or wrongly, that it is of a different class from Dryden's
later emphasis. See the preceding note.
35 Nor are such visions of the king at hazard confined in Dryden's attention to his
own work. He introduces York's "As in a theatre, the eyes of Men" speech
(*Richard II*, 5, 2, lines 28–36) with affecting language, concluding, "refrain
from pitty if you can" (*Works*, XIII: 246; italic usage modernized).
36 "The Grounds of Criticism in Tragedy," *Works*, XIII: 234. On p. 232, he
refers to "*Bossu*, the best of modern Critics" (roman and italic usage reversed).
For other references to Le Bossu, see Watson, II, index.
37 Quotation and diagram from Douglas Lane Patey, *Probability and Literary Form*
(Cambridge: Cambridge University Press, 1984), pp. 110–11.
38 *Ibid.*, p. 110.
39 Alan Roper has carefully defined the conception and practice of "parallels" in
the literature of the late seventeenth century: "Drawing Parallels and Making
Applications in Restoration Literature," *Politics as Reflected in Literature*, introd.
Maximillian E. Novak (Los Angeles: Clark Library, 1989), pp. 31–65. John M.
Wallace has two very thoughtful essays on seventeenth-century ideas of
drawing lessons from history: "Dryden and History: A Problem in Allegorical
Reading," *ELH*, 36 (1969), 265–90, and "'Examples Are Best Precepts':
Readers and Meanings in Seventeenth-Century Poetry," *Critical Inquiry*, 1
(1974), 273–90.
40 In her book that appeared after these remarks were written, *Fables of Power:
Aesopian Writings and Political History* (Durham: Duke University Press, 1991),
Annabel Patterson is the first critic in years to take the animal fable and its
morals seriously. For Dryden she deals chiefly, and understandably, with *The*

Hind and the Panther. If one could impose publicly on a friend, it would be to seek her address not only to matters raised here, but also to a good deal of mid-century poetry. Besides Lovelace's poems, "The Snayl" and "The Ant," there is also "The Falcon," which I have never been able to understand. And one might proceed from Lovelace to interpretation of the fabulistic and emblematic in Waller, Denham, and Marvell, to name but three writers of the moralizing "micrography" of seventeenth-century poetry.

41 The passage cited does not contain the only political allusion in *The Cock and the Fox*. See lines 659–60: "Ye Princes ... Alexander'd up in lying Odes," referring to the standard comparison of the warlike William III to Alexander the Great. Again, political *allusion* gives point, furnishes contemporary details to spice the fable, but it is local, and so not the *moral* of the poem.

42 See *Dryden's Poetry* (Bloomington: Indiana University Press, 1967), pp. 292–94. As Roper (see n. 39) rightly points out, however, "application" to individuals is the least certain feature of "parallels," and it should be emphasized that the linkage of the first two poems in *Fables* is effected by Theseus *qua* Theseus and by subject matter, with or without "application" to William. My connection is founded on a reading of other poets as well as of various poems by Dryden after 1688.

43 *Works*, XIII: 232, italic usage modernized. Dryden makes the same point in *A Parallel Betwixt Poetry and Painting* (*Works*, XX: 50), again referring to Bossu. The two passages date from 1679 and 1695. Does Dryden not seem more consistent on "moral" and "fable" throughout his criticism than we have been in interpreting his poetry and plays? And is it not significant that he should include Homer and Sophocles as writers whose works should be interpreted in terms he applies to his own?

44 Concern with morality or good works is as Catholic in emphasis as emphasis on faith is Protestant. It is also clear that Dryden attributes a Homeric moral to *The Conquest of Granada* (a pre-conversion, pre-Le Bossu double heroic play). Is that attribution merely *ex post facto*, or is Dryden speaking late in life about presumptions he held earlier and in common with his predecessors? The simplicity of the morals suggests one kind of answer, the whole tradition of interpreting Ovid another.

45 The problems I refer to can be characterized more readily than described. One feature is Dryden's innovation: *Annus Mirabilis* is the first poem directed to a city; his linguistic innovations are extraordinary, including those for criticism: a literary age, for example. On the other hand, there are the St. Cecilia's Day odes that go back to sixteenth-century models and the seemingly medieval nature of materials in *The Hind and the Panther*. Some things may be explicable by Dryden's conversion (e.g., change in the nature of use of religious typology), and others by his bleak situation after 1688 (e.g., his shift from a faith in possible historical progress to historical uniformity and even at times historical "decay"). But these are examples, not explanations.

46 *Works*, XVII: 15.

47 Although in what follows I suggest that Dryden and others held a more complex view, I know of no evidence that flatly contradicts the simpler view.

48 *Boswell's Life of Johnson*, ed. Edmond Malone, introd. Chauncey Brewster Tinker, 2 vols. in 1 (New York: Oxford University Press, 1948), II: 27.

49 *The Critical Works of Thomas Rymer*, ed. Curt A. Zimansky (New Haven: Yale University Press, 1956), pp. 132, 134.

50 *Works*, V: 327–28. The characterizations, especially of the first two kinds, go into detail.

51 In addition to the pronoun pointed to in the passage, there are several significant uses of the first-person pronoun in clauses preceding the excerpt. The concern with ancestors here is the counterpart of that concern with "sons" treated by Jennifer Brady in the first chapter, and is not without correspondence to Johnson's self-placement *vis-à-vis* Dryden recounted by Greg Clingham in the next chapter.

52 Some of my reasons for not postulating here a theory of anxiety, repression, and misreading among what Harold Bloom terms "strong poets" will be found in "The Poetics of the Critical Act: Dryden's Dealings with Rivals and Predecessors," *Evidence in Literary Scholarship*, ed. René Wellek and Alvaro Ribeiro, pp. 45–62. I argue there (among other things) that contemporaries are far more dangerous as rivals to a writer's feelings than are predecessors. More than enough confirmation is found in the Preface to *Fables* in the one feature that darkens the golden glow of that essay: his grumbles over Jeremy Collier, Sir Richard Blackmore, and Luke Milbourne. See Introduction, above.

53 With Dryden's "pale Primrose" and its context we may compare, in the lines Milton added to "Lycidas," "the rathe Primrose that forsaken dies," the other flowers, and the final dismissal of such consolations as "frail thoughts" that "dally with false surmise" (lines 142 ... 153).

54 The words are taken with some duress from the opening and closing lines of the fifteen-book poem.

55 Such are the unprompted responses of my students, recalling my own "discovery" of this perpetual poem when I was a student.

56 See, however, Jennifer Brady's chapter and its account of Congreve's response to Dryden. See also n. 52.

4

Another and the same:
Johnson's Dryden

GREG CLINGHAM

Among the achievements of eighteenth-century scholarship has been the revaluation of the works of Dryden and Johnson. Yet surprisingly little thought has been given to the relationship between these two writers who might be said to represent some of the finest things, respectively, in late-seventeenth and late eighteenth-century English culture.[1] A predisposition to historicize, categorize, and theorize has led to scholars and critics saying a great deal about Johnson and Dryden in their respective cultural and literary milieus, but neither the broad continuity between the two writers, nor Johnson's specific criticism of Dryden have been illuminatingly discussed. My proposition is the simple, yet untested, one that Johnson's criticism of Dryden illuminates both Dryden and Johnson significantly. Leading critics of Johnson over the last twenty to thirty years have not believed that Johnson could teach us anything directly about literature. Of his criticism in general it has been assumed that it is either historically determined, and therefore limited or irrelevant critically; or that it is only good common sense, and therefore assimilated into the body of much more sophisticated modern critical thinking.[2] A brilliant exception to this rule is G. F. Parker's *Johnson's Shakespeare* (Clarendon Press, 1989). But critics have generally had great difficulty in explaining why the modern reader should bother with the *Lives of the Poets* as criticism. They have tended to work within the terms of the early attacks on Johnson by Wellek and Leavis, and the most suggestive work on Johnson's criticism – such as that by Keast, Bate, and Fussell – has treated it theoretically, allegorically, or as moral philosophy, but not as practically illuminating criticism.[3] Despite the expressed admiration for Johnson by such scholars as James Clifford and William Wimsatt, and the widespread lip-service paid to Johnson's greatness as a critic, equally ubiquitous is the belief that, as a critic, he is decidedly limited.

Of the "Life of Dryden" in particular commentators have agreed on its excellence as critical biography, but have been indecisive on the nature of its excellence. For example, Leopold Damrosch and Lawrence Lipking agree that Johnson's purpose in the "Life of Dryden" is to trace the establishment of the heroic couplet as a major verse form, and to associate it with the particular unity of life and work in Dryden, but they find nothing new or challenging in Johnson's work.[4] These works give us little idea as to the experiential content of the "Life," or its manner and tone. Likewise, nothing Johnson says is really entertained as potentially illuminating about Dryden's mind or poetry. Indeed, Damrosch says that Johnson's criticism ought to be taken in the context of the poetry with which he deals, and remarks of Johnson's prose that it defines "the essential qualities of each poet's verse ..., is a concise statement that the reader should then expand by reflecting on his own experience of the poems,"[5] but he does not do this himself. There is little conviction that we would find in Johnson anything we had not thought ourselves, or anything of which we had not already taken the measure.

Dryden scholars evidently feel this way too. Very few find occasion to consult Johnson, and among those who do Johnson tends to be used as a respectable historical repository of quotation in order to support, and not to modify, the view taken.[6] James Winn's substantial *John Dryden and His World* (1987) disappointingly fails to alter this state of affairs, and the very success of his contextual and biographical labors – constituting virtually the first critical biography of Dryden since Scott – effectively strengthens the reasons for ignoring Johnson as a serious critic of Dryden.[7]

In this essay I wish to discuss some ways that Johnson's "Life of Dryden" constitutes eloquent and profound criticism of Dryden's poetry and life.[8] As often with Johnson the "Life" offers no single, neatly worked out, and coherent critical system or interpretation: he has nothing to prove or argue about Dryden, whose status as a modern classic and great poet was accepted throughout the eighteenth century.[9] Yet the fullness of experience and the accumulated literary wisdom which Johnson brought to the reading of Dryden in the 1770s, and the great pleasure he exhibits in writing about Dryden's poetry, make for a work of peculiar richness worth reading with attentiveness. Johnson admired Dryden most obviously for the civilizing of English thought effected through both his prose and poetry, for teaching the English "'sapere et fari', to think naturally and express forcibly," and for transforming the English language from brick into marble (para. 356).[10] This civilizing process was one, I shall argue, which Johnson saw as inseparable from the articulation of a certain kind of poetic genius in Dryden. Simultaneously Dryden's self- and cultural articulation entailed the actualization of "nature," a tapping of experience that Johnson understood as having implications for knowledge of the human soul, and for the late seventeenth- and the late eighteenth-century's interest in the relationship between past and present. These phenomena are defined by Johnson, however, both in terms of ideas and critical and cultural precepts, *and* artistically, especially in the creative manner in which he engages with Dryden. For, as Boswell perhaps recognized, when Johnson described Dryden's criticism as being that of a poet, "where the author proves his right of judgement by his power of performance" (para. 199), he was describing his own.[11]

The relationship between critical judgment and creative performance in Johnson's thought suggests the importance of reciprocity and structure. Decontextualizing his particular observations, which become fully meaningful only in the context of the whole Life, makes the criticism less accessible. Reciprocity and serendipity are major ingredients in Johnson's thought: the *Lives of the Poets* are "prefaces" to collections of poetry, consciously written in relation to the poetry, and the cutting edge of Johnson's literary biography is his imaginative participation in the life and work with which he is dealing. As a necessary first step, therefore, to examining what Johnson's particular observations might tell us about Dryden's poetry, I wish to suggest how the structure of the "Life of Dryden" provides evidence for constructing Johnson's imaginative response to particular poems by Dryden, and also how the "Life's" structure traces the revelation of the essential characteristics of Dryden's genius operating in his life and work.

Structure in the "Life of Dryden" and the realization of genius

The "Life" comprises five sections: the biographical and critical sections (paras. 1–156 and 234–320); the two parts of a central portrait (paras. 157–92 and 193–233) balance each other and correspond roughly to the same biographical–critical form of the whole "Life." A final section (paras. 321–56) on Dryden's poetic character sums up many of the motifs of the "Life," but also makes a judgment about Dryden's mind not explicit in the earlier parts.

While the opening biographical section of the "Life" contains a chronology of Dryden's main works and events in his life, and the final critical section offers brief critical comments on individual works, the central portrait is where Johnson creates an image, or a series of images, for the unity of life and work he finds peculiar to Dryden. This unity Johnson discovers to be grounded in general nature, an experiential and structural principle that the biographer reflects in his prose even as he discovers it in Dryden's life and work. Johnson's artistic apprehension of Dryden's poetic character in the central section of the "Life" is a focus for the various aspects of Dryden's life and work dealt with, so that the deeper structure of the "Life" is not linear, but circular, radiating and taking meaning from the center. Just as the whole "Life" traces the transformation of the historical, circumstantial, and contingent Dryden into a more permanent, poetic presence, so the central portrait – in its two balancing sections – first takes a reflective, judicial view of Dryden's personal encounters with the world, and then imaginatively describes how that experience is transformed in the prose and poetry to reveal an artistic character or genius which unifies the "Life," and for which Johnson's whole work is a fictional representation embodying nature.[12]

The first part of the portrait consists of a series of embodied paradoxes which Johnson finds to be integral to Dryden's character – aspects which are both dignifying and degrading, attractive and disgusting, but which Johnson's vision does not allow to become disjunct. Included here would be Johnson's treatment of Dryden's manners and relationship with his friends and contemporaries, the profanity of his drama, his religious immorality, his literary controversies, his straitened financial circumstances – in short, all the aspects of Dryden's life which some commentators believe Johnson used simply to condemn the poet.[13] The tone of Johnson's treatment of these facets of Dryden's life is one of moral severity and sharp skepticism. For example:

His tendency to profaneness is the effect of levity, negligence, and loose conversation, with a desire of accommodating himself to the corruption of the times, by venturing to be wicked as far as he durst.   (para. 181)

Johnson has many observations of this kind, and he spares vice, pride, and self-righteousness in Dryden as little as he does in Milton, Pope, and Swift. Yet, when taken in context, these observations on Dryden do not detract from his character. Johnson is not ironic at Dryden's expense, for he has no desire or need to elevate himself above the poet whose failings arise from a real encounter with the world of politics, money, and daily events. The scrupulosity and temporality of Johnson's attention at this stage of the "Life" is informed by his sense of Dryden's immediate contact with his historical moment, which, therefore, becomes the proper object of Johnson's moral scrutiny.

Perhaps Johnson permits himself such clear moral condemnation of Dryden because it stands as a foil to Congreve's portrayal (quoted in para. 159) of Dryden's generosity and friendship. But that too serves to highlight

the contrast between Dryden-the-man (according to Johnson) bereft of
the good-humored powers of conversation and Dryden-the-poet who had
the gifts to create an intimate connection with his audience. The capacity
to stimulate and to receive love and affection – often distinct from the
realms of virtue and knowledge – is what Johnson finds characteristic of
the man of good conversation:

Many find their way to the tables and the parties of those who never consider them
as of the least importance in any other place; we have all, at one time or other,
been content to love those whom we could not esteem, and been persuaded to try
the dangerous experiment of admitting him for a companion whom we knew to be
too ignorant for a counsellor, and too treacherous for a friend.[14]

But Johnson emphasizes Dryden's lack of this good humor (in this sense he
is the antithesis of Savage and Falstaff):

He probably did not offer his conversation, because he expected it to be solicited;
and he retired from a cold reception, not submissive but indignant, with such
reverence of his own greatness as made him unwilling to expose it to neglect or
violation.   (para. 161)

There is no irony in the mention of Dryden's greatness in this passage,
because it becomes clear in due course that it constitutes a kind of
redemption of the baseness that Johnson has delineated. This redeeming
quality does not supersede Dryden's moral limitations, which are quite
real, but arises straight out of them and, in the way Johnson handles this
issue, suggests a self-knowledge and humanity in Dryden that flourishes in
the poetry. This may be seen in Johnson's description of Dryden's tendency to flattery, and especially those from whom he hopes to receive
financial reward. Johnson says:

in the meanness and servility of hyperbolical adulation I know not whether, since
the days in which the Roman emperors were deified, he has been ever equalled . . .
When once he has undertaken the task of praise he no longer retains shame in
himself, nor supposes it in his patron. As many odoriferous bodies are observed to
diffuse perfumes from year to year without sensible diminution of bulk or weight,
he appears never to have impoverished his mint of flattery by his expenses,
however lavish. He had all the forms of excellence, intellectual and moral,
combined in his mind, with endless variation; and when he had scattered on the
hero of the day the golden shower of wit and virtue, he had ready for him, whom
he wished to court on the morrow, new wit and virtue with another stamp.
                                                                (para. 172)

As with many of Johnson's remarks on Dryden's moral sensibility, this
passage strikes a note of moral disapproval even while affirming the
fertility of Dryden's poetic imagination, and locates something essential

about Dryden's mind in the simultaeneity of the baseness and the beauty. In this passage there *is* some irony, focused around Johnson's attempt to hold together such contrary notions as Dryden's creative capacity and his shamelessness, and it is expressed in Johnson's diction – "As many odoriferous bodies are observed to diffuse perfumes." Although Johnson well understood the generic conditions of the Dedication, Dryden's attitude would have been particularly repugnant to him because of his general hostility towards patronage of the kind Dryden invokes, and because of his personal experience of Lord Chesterfield's "patronage."[15] But Johnson's diction is not only ironic; it also mirrors some of the creativity, some of the same vigor and suppleness, that Dryden is envisaged as having exercised on his patrons: "He had all forms of excellence, intellectual and moral, combined in his mind, with endless variation." Even the extreme zest of Johnson's moral indignation – "in the meanness and servility of hyperbolical adulation I know not whether" – even this revels in Dryden's energy and pays him the compliment of echoing the emotional trajectory of his own hyperbolical efforts. Indeed, Johnson's overall attitude to Dryden at moments such as this is as nicely balanced – as skeptical and sympathetic – as his response to the heroic plays:

the scenes are, for the most part, delightful; they exhibit a kind of illustrious depravity and majestick madness: such as, if it is sometimes despised, is often reverenced, and in which the ridiculous is mingled with the astonishing.

(para. 48 – on *The Conquest of Granada*)

Johnson is too honest and his responsiveness too complete not to respond to the art which, though lying, seems to bestow the qualities it offers: Dryden "scattered on the hero of the day the golden shower of wit and virtue." From one point of view Johnson remarks that "[s]uch degradation of the dignity of genius, such abuse of superlative abilities, cannot be contemplated but with grief and indignation" (para. 171). From another he cannot but respond to that genius and those superlative abilities, which seemed to keep Dryden's mind inviolate. Dryden's integrity, I suggest, is most obvious in the freedom with which Johnson feels able to give his whole weight to his own literary formulation, knowing that Dryden is substantial enough not to crumble under his gaze. Likewise, Johnson's willingness to enter so far into the different sides of Dryden's situation betokens a love – not necessarily a liking, but an impersonal love – which mitigates the finality of his moral judgment, and anticipates the imaginative sympathy and penetration which Dryden's poetry commands in him. The Falstaffian good humor that Johnson could not find in Dryden's conversation seems to be more present in these embodied paradoxes, and draws from Johnson the attitude that "we have all, at one time or other, been content to love those whom we could not esteem."

Johnson's position becomes clearer in the second part of the portrait of the "Life." Here he deals more directly with Dryden's literature, and records how Dryden's poetic character is shaped by his specific poetic apprehension of experience. It is in and through this poetic process that the poet moves towards the nature that Johnson sees as the result of his labors. For example, Johnson notices the compromised, sometimes eccentric, nature of Dryden's particular critical judgments – such as his statement, in the Preface to *Fables*, that Chaucer's Knight's Tale "is of the epic kind, and perhaps not much inferior to the *Ilias*, or the *Aeneis*."[16] And part of Dryden's manifest fallibility is the fact that he was not as well-read and learned as Milton or Cowley (or Johnson for that matter), that he contributed nothing original to scholarship, and made elementary errors when talking about books (paras. 208–10). Yet Johnson sees these "failings" as being redeemed by Dryden's art, the abundance of his imagination, and the actualizing power of his mind. So if his scholarship is scanty

it cannot be said that his genius is ever unprovided of matter, or that his fancy languishes in penury of ideas. His works abound with knowledge, and sparkle with illustrations. There is scarcely any science or faculty that does not supply him with occasional images and lucky similitudes; every page discovers a mind very widely acquainted both with art and nature, and in full possession of great stores of intellectual wealth.   (para. 211)

This is one of the many occasions in the "Life of Dryden" where Johnson's suppleness seems to be directly conditioned by Dryden's give-and-take attitude towards a fellow poet, here Anne Killigrew. The Killigrew ode demonstrates, among other things, how the poet is able to participate in the grace of poetry despite her limitations. What she lacked in art was supplied by nature; her ignorance of the English literary tradition ("our boasted Stores") is redeemed by her being "rich in Treasures of her own" (lines 74, 73). Just so does Dryden, in Johnson's treatment, go from relative critical ignorance to being in "full possession of great stores of intellectual wealth."

While Johnson clearly values scholarship, he feels about Dryden the way Dryden feels about Shakespeare – that no amount of book-learning could have replaced the knowledge of the human heart that Dryden exhibits in his writing: "A mind like Dryden's, always curious, always active ... had a more pleasant, perhaps a nearer, way to knowledge than by the silent progress of solitary reading" (para. 211).[17] Just as Shakespeare finds nature within his "comprehensive soul," and not necessarily

in books, so does Dryden. Thus, while Dryden's critical ideas are sometimes wayward, Johnson perceives something essential and disinterested in
his thought, for he says that "[i]n Dryden's general precepts, which
depend upon the nature of things and the structure of the human mind, he
may doubtless be safely recommended to the confidence of the reader"
(para. 202). Johnson's distinction between Dryden's temporary opinions
and his "general precepts" reiterates a distinction he frequently makes
between custom and nature, and it also illustrates his view that "the task of
criticism [is] to establish principles [and] to improve opinion into knowledge" (*Rambler* 92; *Yale Works*, 4:122).

   In short, despite the compromises of personality – the inevitable egotis-
tic demand to be special and individual – Johnson finds that Dryden's art
bodies forth a deeper poetic character often only dimly visible, but clearly
detectable when seen in nature. Johnson's passages on Dryden's prose
style point to his indivisibility:

none of his prefaces were ever thought tedious. They have not the formality of a
settled style, in which the first half of the sentence betrays the other. The clauses
are never balanced, nor the periods modelled; every word seems to drop by
chance, though it falls into its proper place. Nothing is cold or languid; the whole
is airy, animated, and vigorous; what is little, is gay; what is great, is splendid. He
may be thought to mention himself too frequently; but while he forces himself
upon our esteem, we cannot refuse him to stand high in his own. Every thing is
excused by the play of images and the spriteliness of expression. Though all is easy,
nothing is feeble; though all seems careless, there is nothing harsh; and though
since his earlier works more than a century has passed they have nothing yet
uncouth or obsolete.

   He who writes much will not easily escape a manner, such a recurrence of
particular modes as may be easily noted. Dryden is always "another and the
same"; he does not exhibit a second time the same elegances in the same form, nor
appears to have any art other than that of expressing with clearness what he thinks
with vigour.   (paras. 214–15)

   These passages give a vivid sense of how Dryden's prose is a very
personal medium of expression, and at the same time so deeply rooted in
reality that the random and capricious movements of Dryden's mind seem
to reflect the change and permanence of life itself. All the formal qualities
which come to mind to describe what Johnson sees in Dryden's prose –
such as ease, spontaneity, freedom, animation, clarity, capaciousness,
pleasure – are at the same time qualities of mind. Rather, they are not
qualities of mind but of experience, of the continuity of mind with world
resulting from artistic thinking, of the experience of Dryden being at home
in himself, and also at home in the spiritual and material worlds. These are

the qualities of general nature. This is Dryden being "always 'another and the same'." The continuity of self and world is important because it suggests the phenomenal quality of Dryden's thought, in which the combination of his inward and outward perspectives makes for a substantiality and an imaginative recognition of the materiality of reality otherwise impossible. It is important also because the self-knowledge it posits is that of one having circumvented the demands of the mind and the ego, of one playfully encountering whatever there might be, and so radiating great trust in, and love of, experience, and of the self.

In this passage Johnson suggests that Dryden's artistic integrity is one with his confidence ("we cannot refuse him to stand high in his own [esteem]"), and with the ease which is at once the profound and the obvious manifestation of his love of experience. It is Dryden's ability to stand, as it were, with one foot in the historical world and the other in the eternal, that generates the obvious reciprocity of Johnson's descriptive prose. The pleasure that Dryden feels, Johnson reflects.

Perhaps the finest stroke of this reciprocity goes to the heart of Dryden. By way of differentiating Dryden from the polite, decorous, and (by the 1770s) normative prose of Addison, Johnson concludes by describing Dryden's harmony in the following metaphor:

His style could not easily be imitated, either seriously or ludicrously; for, being always equable and always varied, it has no prominent or discriminative characters. The beauty who is totally free from disproportion cannot be ridiculed by an overcharged resemblance.   (para. 215)[18]

Johnson compares Dryden's genius to a beautiful *woman*,[19] (the "beauty") so, while reinforcing his sense of Dryden's inviolability, he also suggests that there is something feminine in Dryden's genius, in Dryden's apprehension of experience, his capacity to be "always 'another and the same'." This psychic femininity is then elaborated through Johnson's association of Dryden's attractiveness with natural, feminine, and sexual imagery, culminating in the powerful, quasi-seductive description of Dryden's Virgil:

Works of imagination excell by their allurement and delight; by their power of attracting and detaining the attention. That book is good in vain which the reader throws away. He only is the master who keeps the mind in pleasing captivity; whose pages are perused with eagerness, and in hope of new pleasure are perused again.   (para. 312)[20]

At this point it becomes clear that the feminine seductiveness of Dryden's verse and energy to which Johnson responds connects with a more clearly masculine principle, one suggested by the notion of "master." However, dominance and pleasure are not severed in Johnson's experience of Dryden's verse. He does not break Dryden's energy down into more conventionally conceived, mutually exclusive feminine and masculine principles, for his response to the pleasure of the verse is at one with the response to the androgynous nature of Dryden's mind. Earlier in the same central portion of the "Life" Johnson introduces a new idea by describing the success of the *Essay of Dramatick Poesie* by saying of Dryden that "[a] writer who obtains his full purpose loses himself in his own lustre" (para. 196). This "loss" of self is then equated with a particular poetic apprehension of experience, and with a process of artistic articulation. The paradoxical movement from "loss" of self to articulation of character through art is Johnson's way of indicating the movement *through* Dryden's mind of something *other* than Dryden himself – something transcending theological dogma, philosophical argument, and normal gender differences – in short, of the realization of general nature *in* Dryden's thought. This description is not one of Dryden transcending himself, but of his character enlarging to embody an experience of general nature. What I mean by this will become clearer below.

Having established the nature of Dryden's genius by discussing his prose, Johnson then explicitly moves on to the poetry in such a way as to indicate that the qualities in Dryden just delineated are taken up and continued in the poetry:

> From his prose however Dryden derives only his accidental and secondary praise; the veneration with which his name is pronounced by every cultivator of English literature is paid to him as he refined the language, improved the sentiments, and tuned the numbers of English poetry.   (para. 216)

Johnson next (paras. 217–22) places Dryden's poetry in the context of literary history, by giving a brief sketch of versification and poetic diction as English poetry in the seventeenth century moved towards "nature and harmony," and by taking it down to a point where Dryden confers these qualities on language. Johnson then identifies this poetic maturity with translation:

> The affluence and comprehension of our language is very illustriously displayed in our poetical translations of ancient writers.   (para. 223)

And this tradition culminates not only in Dryden's principles, but also in his practice of translation: "It was reserved for Dryden to fix the limits of poetical liberty, and give us just rules *and examples* of translation" (para. 223, my emphasis). The structure of the "Life of Dryden," therefore, directly associates the discovery and articulation of Dryden's poetic genius with nature, with his "refinement" of the English language, and with his poetic translations.

One might then sum up, and make some propositions: the central section of the "Life" traces Dryden's move towards nature, and in so doing deliberately mirrors qualities which Johnson found in Dryden's translations in general and, as I will argue, in *Fables* in particular. While Johnson believes that certain qualities of mind are present in all Dryden's poetry, in tracing Dryden's move toward nature – away from the pseudo-metaphysical wit of the works of the 1660s and '70s (and the heroic plays in particular) to greater "harmony" – Johnson's prose jettisons particular commentary on the poems in which nature is most clearly expressed.[21] Nowhere in the "Life" does Johnson discuss the translations other than in historical or bibliographical terms (except for brief comments on the poetic qualities of the Juvenal and Virgil translations [paras. 299–313]). This may be one reason why modern scholarship has overlooked a judgment in the "Life of Dryden" which directly challenges our conception of seventeenth- and eighteenth-century literary history – namely, Johnson's view that Dryden is a great poet most especially in his translations, and that this is where Dryden's genius is most manifest. The genius of the translations is (as Johnson says in the "Life of Pope," when comparing Dryden with Pope) an "energy which collects, combines, amplifies, and animates" (*Lives*, III: 222, para. 310). At the same time the absence of particular, interpretive comment on the translations makes a certain sense, in addition to the fact that it is integral to Johnson's critical method. For the eighteenth century (such writers as Congreve, Dennis, Pope, Joseph Warton, Churchill, Keats, Wordsworth, and Scott) regarded the translations, and especially the *Fables*, as the epitome of Dryden's poetic genius. Johnson shares with Dryden and Congreve a common interest in England's cultural heritage, its conscious relation to history, by admiring works which establish a vital relationship with the past. More particularly, if the epitome of Dryden's poetic achievement is in the translations, and if – as Johnson says – Dryden loses himself in his own lustre, there isn't going to be much for Johnson to talk about, except either the language or the general experience of being part of that imaginative world. This is what Johnson does talk about.

What seem like circumstantial misfortune and temperamental weakness in Dryden when considered theoretically – his commitment to occasional verse (in which "no height of excellence can be expected from any mind" [para. 230]), and his aversion to "an unwearied pursuit of unattainable perfection" (para. 201) – turn out to be, in practice, the perfect conditions for successful translation. For, as I have suggested, all Johnson's general

description of Dryden's genius is most aptly applicable to the paradoxical
simultaneity of different qualities, essential to the metamorphoses of
experience which could be said to characterize his translations. But this
situation still leaves the reader in doubt as to *what* Johnson says about
Dryden's translations, and how those works and their qualities of mind
stimulated a critical acuteness in Johnson unmatched by any, except,
perhaps, Shakespeare, Milton, and Pope. In the following section, therefore, I find it necessary to turn to Dryden's translations in more detail,
temporarily switching the focus from Johnson to Dryden while I elaborate
on the paradigmatic experience Johnson discovered in Dryden's translations, and that is the subject of the general thoughts of Johnson I have so
far discussed. The dialectical relationship between critic and poet forms
the core of Johnson's experience as a reader of, and writer about, poetry,
for it forms the subject of Johnson's general thoughts about Dryden and
constitutes the structure of the "Life."

Nature and Dryden's translations

Dryden's most complete statement about translation is in the Preface to
Sylvae (1685). For Dryden, the translator must maintain "a character of an
author, which distinguishes him from all others, and makes him that
individual poet whom you would interpret"; he must consider the "genius
and distinguishing character" of the author, and needs to be a master in
both his author's language and his own in order to recreate the "spirit
which animates the whole," without which real translation cannot take
place (Watson, II: 20–21). What makes a poet translatable for Dryden is
his possession of a general experience which can find different form in
other times and other places: for example, it is Chaucer's "most wonderful
comprehensive nature" which convinces Dryden that "mankind is ever
the same, and nothing lost out of nature, though every thing is altered."
This is no *a priori* judgment, but a truth Dryden discovers in the process of
reimagining Chaucer. As a result of Dryden's entering into that experience, he discovered that Chaucer "had a soul congenial to his, and that
[he] had been conversant in the same studies,"[22] so he was able to
translate and alter Chaucer, and make him shine.

Dryden's concretizing description of encountering character in the
Preface to *Sylvae* (and other prefaces dealing with translation, such as the
prefaces to Ovid [1680], *Examen Poeticum* [1693], and *Fables* [1700], the
"Life of Plutarch" [1683], and the "Life of Lucian" [posthumously
published, 1711]) suggests two things: one is how he sees the poet's style
and tone as manifesting an inner quality of mind. The other is that Dryden

recognizes that the purpose of translation is to realize his own poetic character through meeting and articulating the Other, the character being translated. This notion is closely related to Dryden's idea of poetic influence and poetic descent, such as informs "Mac Flecknoe" and the poems addressed to Roscommon, Congreve, and Kneller. But in translation he stresses the physical and spiritual intimacy:

Milton was the poetical son of Spenser, and Mr. Waller of Fairfax; for we have our lineal descents and clans as well as other families: Spenser more than once insinuates that the soul of Chaucer was transfused into his body; and that he was begotten by him two hundred years after his decease.

(Preface to *Fables*; Watson, II: 270)[23]

Not only is the idea of poetic translation (transfusion, as he calls it in the Preface to *Fables*) akin to poetic inspiration –

We, who are priests of Apollo, have not the inspiration when we please; but must wait till the god comes rushing on us, and invades us with a fury which we are not able to resist. (Preface to "Eleonora"; Watson, II: 261)

– but he also conceived of the process by which a poet was translated as a meeting *and* a containing of that godlike inspiration:

A translator that would write with any force or spirit of an original must never dwell on the words of his author. He ought to possess himself entirely and perfectly *comprehend the genius* and sense of his author, the nature of the subject, and the terms of the art or subject treated of.

("Life of Lucian"; Watson, II: 215 – my emphasis)

Johnson presents Dryden's mind as comprehensive – in his re-enactment of the imaginative effect of Dryden's writing, and also in the opening statement of the final section of the "Life," in which the general, fundamental qualities of Dryden's mind are once again set out: "In a general survey of Dryden's labours he appears to have had a mind very comprehensive by nature, and much enriched with acquired knowledge. His compositions are the effects of a vigorous genius operating upon large materials" (para. 321). In the *Dictionary* Johnson defines "comprehensive" as "[h]aving the power to comprehend or understand many things at once," and uses Dryden's description of Chaucer's "most wonderful comprehensive nature" as illustration.[24] The only other writers to whom Johnson ascribed the quality of comprehensiveness were Shakespeare and Homer.

What Johnson understood by Dryden's comprehensiveness is essential, and may be seen in more detail by bringing his general thoughts into contact with some of the salient poetic and experiential features of *Sylvae*. Tom Mason has described *Sylvae* as a Montaigne volume,[25] since Dryden translates passages from Horace, Virgil, and Lucretius that figure repeatedly in the *Essais,* and also because of Dryden's similar preoccupations in the collection. Montaigne offers a powerful and seductive discussion of the limits of human nature and the pleasure which is gained from accepting them; he also stimulates Dryden's thinking on the subject of the interpenetration of mind and body in the composition of human experience. The first time Montaigne is mentioned by Dryden is in the Dedication to *Aureng-Zebe* (1676):

As I am a man, I must be changeable ... I have observed, says Montaigne, that when the body is out of order, its companion is seldom at his ease. An ill dream, or a cloudy day, has power to change this wretched creature, who is so proud of a reasonable soul, and make him think what he thought not yesterday.[26]

Dryden's interest in the basis of the soul in the mind–body nexus is expressed with a profound and pleasurable freedom in the *Sylvae,* and arises out of his direct experience of the world; it entails a comic realization of the writer's changing relations with the world of both past and present.

In a variety of forms and styles, and from different related points of view, the *Sylvae* explores the question of what it is to live happily and fully, with openness both to the end of things and to the particulars of domestic life. As with Montaigne's *Essais,* Johnson's *Rambler,* and *Fables, Sylvae* presents its ideals by exploring the realities which impinge upon them, in negotiation with which the ideal has to be wrested and life to be lived. For example, *Horat. Ode 3. Lib. I* asks how one ought to venture out onto the seas of life without bringing the vengeance of the gods down on one's head for overreaching. Of the five passages from Lucretius, the first presents the power of Venus moving through human kind and through nature; the second presents the ideal of "A Soul serene, a body void of pain" achieved in opposition to the demands and temptations of the world; the excerpts from Books 3 and 4 depict two experiences – fear of death and sexual passion – which threaten integrity from within the soul; and the fragment from Book 5 provides an image of humanity's essential homelessness in nature.

The ease of *Sylvae* is, therefore, no quiescent quality: its surface is directly in touch with its depths. The poems are dominated by the energy of Venus, even when she does not figure explicitly. The tone of the volume is epitomized by an energetic, sensuous rendering of the powers of Venus – taking her out of the mythological and incarnating her in the material through poetry – in whom nature's creativity is concentrated, and through whose power humanity, nature, and the gods meet:

Delight of Humane kind, and Gods above;
Parent of *Rome*; Propitious Queen of Love;
Whose vital pow'r, Air, Earth, and Sea supplies;
And breeds what e'er is born beneath the rowling Skies:
For every kind, by thy prolifique might,
Springs, and beholds the Regions of the light:
Thee, Goddess thee, the clouds and tempests fear,
And at thy pleasing presence disappear:
For thee the Land in fragrant Flow'rs is drest,
For thee the Ocean smiles, and smooths her wavy breast;
And Heav'n it self with more serene, and purer light is blest.
      ("Lucretius, The beginning of the First Book," lines 1–11)[27]

The sensuousness of Dryden's language, in excess of the Latin, inculcates an abundance, and it explicitly identifies the verse's energy with Venus' movement through nature:[28]

Be thou my ayd: My tuneful Song inspire,
And kindle with thy own productive fire;   (lines 32–33)

At the same time, Dryden adds to the Latin (*De Rerum Natura*, I: 21–25) the idea of the infusion of the god into the poet. Dryden's image of a fiery infusion is one for all his efforts in and pronouncements on translation, anticipated by Sir John Denham,[29] and used by Congreve in describing Dryden himself:

Sure Phoebus' self Thy swelling Breast inspires,
The God of Musick, and Poetick Fires:
. . .
So, stubborn Flints their inward Heat conceal,
'Till Art and Force th' unwilling Sparks reveal;
But thro' your Skill, from those small Seeds of Fire,
Bright Flames arise, which never can Expire.[30]

Dryden's relationship with natural energy encouraged him to translate parts of Lucretius and Horace when there was a conventional moral and philosophical opposition to both poets.[31] Dryden shared some of those values – for example, he mentions the falsity of Lucretius' atheism and knew that Horace "used" his gods as literary fictions (Preface to *Sylvae*; Watson, II: 25–26, 30–31). But out of the realm of dogmatics Dryden responded to the poetic representations of these poets, and found that he was deeply struck by what they revealed of the human mind and passions: those were the aspects of the poetry to which he responded. According to Emrys Jones "[i]t is unreal to talk of Dryden's Lucretius in isolation from the substance and quality of Lucretius's own poetry. If Dryden's translation is a 'masterpiece,' it is so largely because the *De rerum natura* is itself a very great poem" (p. 50).

However, Dryden's understanding of passion and the irrational is not benign; what comes across most strongly, in such poems as "Concerning the Nature of Love," is the insatiability and uncontrollable amoral force of the passion which utterly transports an individual. Dryden's eloquent and mysterious use of sea-imagery in "Concerning the Nature of Love" –

> Just as the raging foam of full desire,
> When both press on, both murmur, both expire,
> . . .
> In vain; they only cruze about the coast,   (lines 74–75, 78)

– is somatically suggestive of the unknown surrounding the soul at moments of great intensity and reality. They are emblematic of his position in the *Sylvae* as a whole. The sea-imagery may often be present in the originals, but Dryden's rendition is vividly energetic.[32] Although the images by which he focuses his equanimity in the face of tempestuousness and fortune are ones which show him at a distance from life –

> What is't to me,
> Who never sail in her unfaithful Sea,
> If Storms arise, and Clouds grow black;
> ("Horat. Ode 29. Book 3," lines 88–90)

> 'Tis pleasant, safely to behold from shore
> The rowling Ship; and hear the Tempest roar:
> (Lucretius, "The beginning of the Second Book," lines 1–2)

– the experience his poetry actually conveys is not that of controlling the sea itself, but of being himself *in* the sea of life. These are commonplaces in the originals that spark off a profound sense for Dryden of one's existential place in the universe, and this sense is embodied in the *manner* of Dryden's writing, which is the focus of all Johnson's comments.

Johnson's understanding of Dryden's genius begins with Dryden's manner, and is of one at once turbulent and at ease. He focuses on Dryden's poise, on the balance arising from the weight of being in two apparently contradictory positions at once, and thereby making them one.[33] This is essentially what Johnson feels about Shakespeare's "mingled drama," which are "compositions of a distinct kind; exhibiting the real state of sublunary nature, which partakes of good and evil, joy and sorrow, mingled with endless variety of proportion and innumerable modes of combination; and expressing the course of the world" ("Preface," *Yale Works*, VII: 66). Johnson perceives Dryden's comprehensiveness as a poise in which he contains the forces that beat upon him. The pleasure Johnson takes in Dryden's poetry is a paradoxical openness to, and inward experience of, passion and forces Dryden knows to be dangerous and amoral, but which he also knows to be representatives of a larger, deeper natural world in which people live, and therefore necessary to be tapped in the name of civilization. So, while Dryden responds to Lucretius' presentation of the action of love in the very rhythms of the ocean and nature – connecting the power of Venus with sexual energy, as Lucretius does in his First Book – Dryden's poetic expression of that experience effectively distinguishes human happiness and fulfillment from sexual passion and desire. Venus is presented in *Sylvae* as an attractive force, but one that needs in the name of civilization to be contained and transformed. It is significant that the final poem in the collection – *Horace, Epod. 2d* – though by no means a simple summary of all the foregoing interests, nevertheless seems like a natural culmination and conclusion to the *Sylvae*. And Dryden's "Beatus ille" is, of course, about the wisdom and inner contentment arising from balance.[34]

Dryden's containment – comprehension – of the power of Venus is clear in his version of Horace's 9th Ode of the First Book. This poem is remarkable for apparently advocating escape from moral norms and responsibility, while in fact intensifying the enjoyment of feeling and of the present. Its delight and beauty arise out of unified oppositions between mind and body, thought and experience, the human and natural – where both imaginary and real oppositions are harmonized and revealed as one in experience. These are made available to the understanding by being presented as one with Providence. Dryden is good-naturedly aware of his mind encountering the solid world beyond itself ("Behold yon' Mountains hoary height ...," line 1), but he does not dissolve the world in seeking something purer or more ideal. Rather, he recreates it more intensely and vividly, in a language whose sensuousness is a medium in which different levels of experience, and both the Biblical wisdom and the Epicureanism on which Dryden draws, come into harmony with each other. For the poem finds sweet pleasure and freedom in the notion that "[t]o every thing there is a season, and a time to every purpose under the heaven ... " (*Ecclesiastes* 3: 1–2, 11–15); or, as the poem puts it when speaking of the deity, "Let him alone with what he made, / To toss and turn the World below" (lines 13–14).

Dryden's translation of Horace's Ode I.9 portrays the separateness of nature and the mind, and the flow of the one into the other, in a way that makes it of particular interest for the context in which Johnson considers Dryden's poetry. In the following lines Dryden identifies the qualities of the ripe and (by implication) the withering fruit with the pleasures and

pains of life, and places both nature and human feeling within the
historical world of passing time:

> Secure those golden early joyes,
>   That Youth unsow'rd with sorrow bears,
> E're with'ring time the taste destroyes,
>   With sickness and unweildy years!
> For active sports, for pleasing rest,
>   This is the time to be possest;
> The best is but in season best.   (lines 25–30)

This is a pleasing and mysterious unity, but Dryden does something other,
and more significant, than identify the human with nature, and then
subsume them under a notion of Providence. Since by 1699–1700 Dryden
sees his own genius as being most like Homer's, and (as I am arguing)
Johnson takes the *Fables* as paradigmatic of Dryden's poetic experience, a
passage from Homer (rather than Virgil, Horace, or Ovid) may provide a
helpful comparison and contrast as a means of clarifying the point about
Dryden I am making.[35] The following is a famous simile in the *Iliad*, Book
VI, lines 146–49:

Just as in the generation of the leaves, so also of men. It is certain that the wind
scatters the leaves onto the ground, but the woods bloom anew in the coming
spring. So will the generation of men grow and vanish.[36]

Homer seems to offer birth and death not as successive, but as simultaneous within a reality permeated by one power; while we would usually
expect a chronological order of birth preceding death, Homer gives us
falling before blooming. The absence of syntactical logic and chronology
lies behind the absence of emotion in the words describing mortality;
Homer does not describe people changing in front of his eyes: they are
simply no longer there. But this manner of thinking makes way for a more
profound, impersonal feeling, rooted in nature. The manner is not, strictly
speaking, metaphorical; there is rather an *a priori* position where subject
and object, though different, are at one with each other, and connected by
the same flow of energy; an inner coherence exists between the natural
order, of which we are part, and language. The language *is* the reality of
the experience; all the verbs are in the present tense, and, though there are
several actions, they make for a unity in the present impossible to grasp
intellectually. Both Pope and Johnson, in fact, distinguish Homer's
imagination for its capacity to seize and realize experience immediately:

... each Circumstance of art and Individual of Nature summon'd together by the
Extent and Fecundity of his Imagination; to which all things, in their various

Views, presented themselves in an Instant, and had their Impressions taken off to Perfection at a Heat.[37]

... the force of his imagination, which gave him full possession of every object ...[38]

Time, however, is part of Dryden's linguistic habits and historical consciousness, and his manner of achieving a timelessness is different. Yet Homer's example suggests how the relationship between the human and the natural in Dryden yields something greater than the particular forms – arising from *between* the entities presented, and arrested in a sensuous present.[39] The human and nature, though separate, are part of the same pervading reality; it is as if Venus – the pervading energy in *Sylvae*, and more a concentration than a representation of the variety and fertility of nature – is embodied in a harmony of numbers. The harmony *is* the experience and the wisdom of the poem. As Johnson says of Dryden at the end of the "Life": "To him we owe the improvement, perhaps the completion of our metre, the refinement of our language, and much of the correctness of our sentiments" (para. 356).[40]

At the same time Dryden "contains" in his translation not only Venus' energy, but also Horace's poetic character. The poem's peculiar combination of factualness and timelessness, so elusive of definition, arises not only from the interpenetration of spirit and nature, but from the taking of the past into the present. The activity in which these different phenomena harmonize is both good-humored and deeply *comic*. This comedy manifests itself, for example, in Dryden's playfulness – a consciousness in the poem which Johnson described when he spoke of the "pleasing captivity" of Dryden's art in general, and linked it with sexual pleasure (para. 312). This activity is more than linguistic play. It is a profound, expatiating participation in experience, particularly in the process of translation as Dryden meets and "seduces" Horace's character, which then brings Horace into the present, just as it releases Dryden's full creative powers.

Dryden anticipated his creative encounter with Horace and Lucretius in the preface to *Sylvae* by saying, "I have both added and omitted, and even sometimes very boldly made such expositions of my authors, as no Dutch commentator will forgive me. Perhaps, in such passages, I have thought that I discovered some beauty yet undiscovered by those pedants, which none but a poet could have found" (Watson, II: 19). Dryden's confidence that he can see into the soul of the poets he translates also carries the connotation that he *needs* to enter into this union with them – not merely because there are psychic, soul-similarities between Dryden and Horace or Dryden and Lucretius, but, as important, because of Dryden's *unlikeness* to these poets.[41] Of the Lucretius translations Emrys

Jones remarks that "Dryden's under no illusion as to the wrongness of Lucretius's beliefs, but that is not going to deter him from striving, as strenuously as he can, to assume the personality of that same Lucretius" (p. 52). Yet Jones takes Dryden too literally when he says that he lays aside his own "character" to take up that of Lucretius. Dryden and Lucretius or Horace are not consecutive, but simultaneous. Dryden requires the relationship with Horace and Lucretius to complete and fulfill his own genius, detecting in the classical poets something more than a "personality."[42] Like a sexual union, in which two individuals become something larger and other than themselves in becoming one – but at the same time discover their individuality most fully in that experience – so Dryden's poetic relationship with Horace and Lucretius is successful because he is already both clearly defined as a poet, and open to other experiences. "A writer who obtains his full purpose loses himself in his own lustre" (para. 196). In other words, Dryden is able to love Horace and (surprisingly) Lucretius so deeply because he loves himself.

The confidence and the love which comes with such unconditional self-acceptance and acceptance of the world is one of the main thoughts of Johnson's "Life of Dryden." Based on this is Johnson's sense of Dryden's poetry moving effortlessly from particularity to generality, and from self to world, and back again. This is clearest in Johnson's description of the inner movements of Dryden's mind culminating in architectural metaphor. Johnson also echoes the movement of Dryden's mind when, in the "Life of Pope," he describes Dryden's relative self-indulgence (as compared to Pope) by saying that "[h]e wrote ... merely for the people; and when he pleased others, he contented himself ... he poured out what the present moment happened to supply, and, when once it had passed the press, ejected it from his mind ..." (para. 304). Personal self-indulgence becomes poetic ease and beauty.

These "comprehensive" qualities[43] of Dryden's genius also characterize the *Fables*, which perhaps influence the structure of thought of the "Life of Dryden" more strongly than the *Sylvae*. This idea might seem odd since Johnson's particular remarks on the *Fables* are meager, enigmatic, suggesting a contradiction between his critical particular judgments of individual poems, and his great pleasure in the whole collection. It is noticeable, however, that the dismissive tone of Johnson's comments is directed against the original works or the incidental remarks by Dryden associated with these works. For example, the works of Chaucer chosen by Dryden "require little criticism," "[t]he Cock and the Fox" "seems hardly worth revival," and "Palamon and Arcite" is anachronistic and has been praised too highly by Dryden in the Preface to *Fables* (para. 314). The only remotely affirmative remarks Johnson makes on the *Fables* in particular are about the language – viz., Dryden modernizes the language of the ancients, "[w]hatever subjects employed his pen he was still improving our measures and embellishing our language," and all the poems in the *Fables not* mentioned by name, "if he had written nothing else, would have entitled him to praise of excellence in this kind" (para. 317 – Congreve's observation, as Johnson notes). In other words, these affirmative comments are directed at Dryden's poetic language, which, as I have been arguing, Johnson finds the most appropriate way of talking about the peculiar qualities of Dryden's genius and cultural achievements.

Cedric Reverand has cast some light on this situation by writing of the *Fables*:

Dryden relies upon various value systems, Christian, heroic, domestic, sentimental, consistently making appealing and convincing cases for a host of possibilities for civilizable mankind. The possibilities include passionate love, conjugal love, love of principle, love of country, love of God, all of which vie against limitations, failures that Dryden presents persuasively as equal parts of the human scene. All the ideals have their appeal and their temporary successes, but all are constantly under a subversive pressure, so that the ideals are unattainable or inapplicable to life, even as they are precious and necessary.[44]

The skeptical, humane comprehensiveness Reverand describes is something Johnson responded to strongly; when he describes Dryden's comprehensiveness by saying that he is "always 'another and the same'" he echoes Dryden's vision, in "Of the Pythagorean Philosophy," of an ever-changing, interrelated world where "All Things are alter'd, nothing is destroy'd," and "we, that are of Soul/And Body mix'd, are Members of the whole" (lines 388, 672–73). Johnson's echo of Dryden's phrase at the same time draws attention to the *sui generis* self-renewing nature of Dryden's character suggested by Dryden's lines in the "Pythagorean Philosophy," placing the mythical phoenix against nature in its capacity to beget itself:

> All these receive their Birth from other Things;
> But from himself the *Phoenix* only springs:
> Self-born, begotten by the Parent Flame
> In which he burn'd, another and the same.   (lines 578–81)[45]

Dryden himself cited "Of the Pythagorean Philosophy" as central to the spirit and content of the *Fables* by singling it out in the Preface as "the Masterpiece of the whole *Metamorphoses*" (Watson, II: 270). And Reverand has argued that Ovid's Fifteenth Book – although not the only key to Dryden's collection – comments on all the other tales, and sets up an understanding of Dryden's ideas in the last phase of his career.[46]

What Johnson responds to in a poem such as "Of the Pythagorean Philosophy," is the poet's complete acceptance of, and self-generating presence in, the process of constant change, the choicelessness of mind, the freedom of spirit, and flexibility of language which, in fact, characterize Dryden's personal and political attitudes throughout the last ten years of his life and particularly in the *Fables*:

> And since, like *Tiphys* parting from the Shore,
> In ample Seas I sail, and Depths untry'd before,
> This let me further add, that Nature knows
> No stedfast Station, but, or Ebbs, or Flows:
> Ever in motion; she destroys her old,
> And casts new Figures in another Mold.
> Ev'n Times are in perpetual Flux; and run
> Like Rivers from their Fountain rowling on;
> For Time no more than Streams, is at a stay;
> The flying Hour is ever on her way;
> And as the Fountain still supplies her store,
> The Wave behind impels the Wave before;
> Thus in successive Course the Minutes run,
> And urge their Predecessor Minutes on,
> Still moving, ever new: For former Things
> Are set aside, like abdicated Kings:
> And every moment alters what is done,
> And innovates some Act till then unknown.
>
> ("Of the Pythagorean Philosophy," lines 261–77)

The poetic vision of poise and acceptance of change that Johnson responds to also represents a wholeness beyond the self – or beyond the ego and deep in the self – arrived at through the playful union with another poet, and through the containment of the past within the present. These poetic and experiential qualities were arguably what Johnson discovered to be common to *all* the *Fables*. They are at one with that "femininity" Johnson reveals in Dryden through the use of imagery in the "Life," which I have mentioned above. This femininity is not defined by Johnson in social, political, or sentimental terms, but refers, rather, to a layer in Dryden's psyche, a part of his heart, that expresses itself in the fluidity and malleability of mind – the humanly apprehended sensuousness and permanence of constant change. It is special to the *Fables* and the *Sylvae*, but common to all Dryden's poetry, notwithstanding the strength of his language, remarked on by Pope and Johnson:

> Waller was smooth; but Dryden taught to join
> The varying verse, the full-resounding line,
> The long majestick march, and energy divine.[47]

Dryden's divine energy has a sexual connotation encompassing the masculine and the feminine in the idea of making a union with another poet through translation. The mixture of masculine and feminine qualities as I have defined them – a form of androgyny, and expressed, too, in the peculiar combination of political commentary and deep feeling in the *Fables* – is indicative of Johnson's manner of describing the attractiveness of Dryden's poetic genius, and is central to the *Fables'* multifarious presentation of sexuality and love. Johnson puts his finger on Dryden's complex presentation of experience in the *Fables* when, in the eloquent general thoughts beginning the final section of the "Life," he writes:

The power that predominated in his intellectual operations, was rather strong reason than quick sensibility. Upon all occasions that were presented, he studied rather than felt, and produced sentiments not such as Nature enforces, but meditation supplies. With the simple and elemental passions, as they spring separate in the mind, he seems not much acquainted; and seldom describes them but as they are complicated by the various relations of society, and confused in the tumults and agitations of life.

Dryden's was not one of the *gentle bosoms*: Love, as it subsists in itself, with no tendency but to the person loved, and wishing only for correspondent kindness; such love as shuts out all other interest; the Love of the Golden Age, was too soft and subtle to put his faculties in motion. He hardly conceived it but in its turbulent effervescence with some other desires; when it was inflamed by rivalry, or obstructed by difficulties: when it invigorated ambition, or exasperated revenge. He is therefore, with all his variety of excellence, not often pathetick; and had so little sensibility of the power of effusions purely natural, that he did not esteem them in others.   (paras. 322, 324–25)

When Johnson wrote these passages he may have been bringing to bear as touchstones such simple and sublime moments in literature as the love of Adam and Eve in *Paradise Lost* ("Love, as it subsists in itself ... correspondent kindness"), the love of Dido for Aeneas in *Aeneis* Book 4 ("the simple and elemental passions, as they spring separate in the mind"), and the last parting of Hector and Andromache in Book 6 of the *Iliad* ("sentiments ... such as Nature enforces"). Comparisons like these constitute a criticism of Dryden, placing him against great poets of human experience. But Johnson's very eloquence, speaking about love with more obvious heart and feeling than anywhere else in the *Lives of the Poets*, testifies to the challenging attractiveness of the experience in Dryden *against* which (though not necessarily in *opposition* to which) Johnson formulates his thought. And this thought obviously fits the dramatic sexual passion of Dryden's Sigismonda, and Myrrha, and Theodore, and Cymon, and of the gods in the version of *Iliad* Book I. While the passion of the *Fables* may be antithetical to the heroically simple pathos of Homer,

Virgil, and Milton – that is, to literature valued as touchstones of the
natural by Rapin, Bouhours, Boileau, Pope, and Dryden himself –
Johnson sees Dryden's fundamental comprehensiveness as being more like
Shakespeare's.[48] As Johnson points out in the "Preface to Shakespeare,"
Shakespeare, too, does not isolate a single passion for dramatic purposes;
the inner experience of his "mingled drama" is, like Dryden's poetry,
characterized by a harmonious simultaneity of different, sometimes opposite, perspectives, giving a sense of the "real state of sublunary nature"
(*Yale Works*, VII: 66).

Reverand argues that there is no necessary synthesis of these different
perspectives, and that the informing ideal of the *Fables* may be the very
process of doing and undoing. He also discusses the apparent delight
Dryden takes in a world of change, turbulence, and unreconciled opposites, where his long-cherished values are crumbling.[49] Yet I feel that
Johnson has located in this process a value that no modern critic has
expounded; for though there is no deliberate reconciliation of opposites in
Dryden, yet in his very turbulence, confusion, passion, and suffering,
Johnson detects the acceptance, poise, and clear presence of the poet I
have discussed above. Emrys Jones has noticed the detachment with
which Dryden depicts the exaggerated and comically conceived suffering
of Sigismonda's predicament; this insight may be applied to the depiction
of passion throughout the *Fables*.[50] But it is only Johnson who detects, in
the pleasure and responsiveness of his own prose, the divine irresponsibi-
lity, the divine foolishness, of such complete acceptance of humanity
implied in Dryden's comedy and detachment. It is a humanity which is
evident throughout the "Life of Dryden" – in the reciprocity, imaginative-
ness, and the intimacy which distinguishes it from the *Lives* of Milton,
Swift, and Pope. It is as if Johnson's own prose reflects the friendship and
the love he feels for Dryden's genius, so clearly and attractively articulated
in his writing.

The "Life of Dryden" and Dryden's Catholicism

Johnson's delineation of Dryden's poetic character touches on his Catholicism in several illuminating ways.

The movement towards nature and articulation of character, which I
have argued Johnson saw as taking place in Dryden's translations, entails
an increasing consciousness of the distinction between language, experience, and truth, and also a conviction of the capacity of language to recall
and re-create significant values and experience from the past. Dryden's
mature poetry conveys an increasingly serious understanding of the preca-

riousness of human institutions and the limits of the human will; and these attitudes have been associated by Earl Miner with Dryden's "discovery of history in the modern sense of actual, even nearly contemporaneous, events with mortal actors."[51] At the same time, this historical sense is not purely secular. The greater fullness of character arising from his acceptance of impermanence is spiritual, and finds expression not only in the explicitly religious poems and the Pindaric Odes, but in a wide range of poetry, including the translations commencing with *Sylvae*.

In charting Dryden's move towards nature (in the 1680s) in the central portrait of the "Life," Johnson does not mention his conversion. Johnson's view is that "when [Dryden] professed himself a convert to Popery he did not pretend to have received any new conviction of the fundamental doctrines of Christianity" (para. 181). Johnson, indeed, suggests that Dryden was sympathetic to Catholicism before his conversion in 1685–86, even though he might not have then been a practicing Catholic:

> It is some proof of Dryden's sincerity in his second religion, that he taught it to his sons. A man conscious of hypocritical profession in himself is not likely to convert others; and as his sons were qualified in 1693 to appear among the translators of Juvenal, they must have been taught some religion before their father's change.
>
> (para. 158)

Charles was born in 1668, Erasmus-Henry in 1669, and John junior in 1670. It seems, therefore, that Johnson thinks Dryden was permitting his children to be instructed in Catholicism from the 1670s, even if there is no certainty as to how active Dryden himself was in this process.[52]

Johnson's question, however, is, What kind of mind does Dryden have? His attitude to Dryden's actual conversion is nicely balanced, keeping in play his own preference for Anglicanism, as well as his desire to establish the truth about Dryden. Johnson first mentions the widely assumed possibility that Dryden's conversion is not honest: "[t]hat conversion will always be suspected that apparently concurs with interest" (para. 119). But Johnson is unconvinced by this, because of Dryden's subsequent steadfastness, and because the whole tenor of Dryden's thought contradicts it.

Johnson's reasoning on this issue goes in two directions. He first notices: "Dryden, having employed his mind, active as it was, upon different studies, and filled it, capacious as it was, with other materials, came unprovided to the controversy" (para. 120). That is, although Dryden's was a reasoning mind ("The favourite exercise of his mind was ratiocination ... " [para. 327]), he thought most effectively in poetry. In comparing Dryden's theological prose – *A Defence of the Papers Written by the*

Late King (1686) – with *The Hind and the Panther* (1687), Johnson distinguishes two very different kinds of knowledge:

Having probably felt his own inferiority in the theological controversy [with Stillingfleet and Burnet] he was desirous of trying whether, by bringing poetry to aid his arguments, he might become a more efficacious defender of his new profession. To reason *in verse* was, indeed, one of his powers.

(para. 125, my emphasis)

Despite the hint of irony in Johnson's voice, the point he makes about Dryden is penetrating. The experience with which Dryden's mind was full when his vulnerability in theological controversy laid him open to the persuasive powers of the papists is that peculiarly associated with his poetic activities. Johnson's observation may be seen from two points of view: it may convey the implicit criticism that Dryden was preoccupied and wantonly unprepared to meet a challenge of the most important kind (one on which Johnson, anyway, would never have been caught napping); or it may simply be recording the fact that Dryden's poetic mind is what is peculiarly sympathetic to Catholicism.

Johnson substantiates the latter point by a characteristic act of skeptical affirmation: he raises the question of Dryden's "honesty" ("It is natural to hope that a comprehensive is likewise an elevated soul, and that whoever is wise is also honest" [para. 120]), only to transcend judgment by acknowledging that complete knowledge of Dryden's "soul" was open only to God ("enquiries into the heart are not for men" [*ibid.*]). Having removed the issue of absolute knowledge as being humanly impossible, Johnson proceeds to write with conviction of Dryden's profound integrity *vis-à-vis* his new religion and its relation to his poetry. For the "Life of Dryden" is structured so as to trace the articulation of Dryden's genius or character, which draws life and work together. Johnson reasons from what he knows of Dryden – i.e., his poetic genius – which, for Johnson, is full of the knowledge of the heart that is the only ground on which Dryden's "honesty" can be fully known, and his "comprehensive soul" discovered to be "elevated." It is in the "heart," too, that Johnson discovers the continuity between "soul" and poetic genius that might otherwise seem to be kept apart by the clearly Christian identity of "soul." Everything I have argued suggests that Dryden's comprehensiveness includes spiritual elevation in the knowledge of the heart it conveys – although not necessarily a conventional Christian (either Anglican *or* Catholic) spirituality, and certainly not a conventional poetic sentimentality ("Dryden's was not one of the *gentle bosoms* … "; see above, p. 143). In the *Dictionary* Johnson's definition of "soul" includes both the Christian, and what might be called the more philosophical–poetic, understanding: it is both "the immaterial and immortal spirit of man," and "spirit, essence, quintessence, principal part"; he associates it, in other definitions, with the mind, active power, fire, grandeur, and being human.[53]

Johnson's treatment of Dryden's conversion suggests that evidence for Dryden's thought was not exhausted by the doctrinal statements, but that the poetry which most fully articulated his genius was essential in understanding this crucial aspect of his life.[54] In being most true to himself, and expressing himself most fully and with humanity, Dryden reveals the nature of his soul. It was not that he changed his opinions to suit Catholic doctrine, but that the changing state of his mind and soul, and his deepening experience of himself and the world, were most fully expressed by Catholic, rather than Anglican, theology, just as they were most fully created through the poetry he wrote. Johnson's train of thought, surprisingly, leads one to the realization that under certain circumstances theology and religious dogma may be less important and reliable in revealing a person's spirituality than poetry. Johnson's understanding at this point is akin to D. H. Lawrence's when he writes of the essentially religious nature of the material and substantial world:

The reality of substantial bodies can only be perceived by the imagination, and the imagination is a kindled state of consciousness in which intuitive awareness predominates ... In the flow of true imagination we know in full, mentally and physically at once, in a greater, enkindled awareness. At the maximum of our imagination we are religious.[55]

Therefore, the poise, integrity of character, and comprehensiveness that I have described above – as being recognized by Johnson as coming to fruition in the translations, especially in *Sylvae* and *Fables* – are equally important for understanding how Johnson responds to Dryden's Catholicism, and its place in the humanity of his poetry. This situation also entails the recognition that in facilitating the larger consciousness of translation, its very process is, for Dryden, not only a comic, but also a sacrificial, one.

As so often in Dryden's poetry, what is "sacrificial" in translation is the other side of what is material and self-affirming. For example: in *Rambler* 41 Johnson turns to Dryden's version of the 29th Ode of Horace's Third Book (rather than the versions of Francis Elphinston or Philip Francis, from whose Horatian translations he usually quotes in the *Rambler*) for an example of memory at its finest:

> Happy the Man, and happy he alone,
> He, who can call to day his own:
> He, who secure within, can say

> To morrow do thy worst, for I have liv'd to day.
>   Be fair, or foul, or rain, or shine,
> The joys I have possest, in spight of fate are mine.
>   Not Heav'n it self upon the past has pow'r;
> But what has been has been, and I have had my hour.
>
>   (lines 65–72)[56]

The quality of Dryden's realization in this passage may be felt more clearly by comparing what Thomas Creech, Dryden's contemporary, made of these lines:

> He lives that can distinctly say
> It is enough, for I have liv'd to day:
> Let *Jove* to morrow smiling rise,
> Or let dark clouds spread o're the Skys:
> He cannot make the pleasures void
> Nor sower the sweets I have enjoy'd,
> Nor call that back which winged hours have born away.[57]

Creech translates literally, his verse exhibiting none of the inner energy and tautness characterizing a real contact with the original, and he renders the poet's immunity from fortune passively: the reason the gods have no control over the past is because it has gone. Dryden, however, emphasizes the personally empowering nature of the experience and activity of translating: the gods have no control over the past because Dryden the poet possesses it. An apparently passive, subservient relation to the past is transformed into a triumph over the acknowledged limiting facts of life. The past is irretrievably past ("what has been has been"), yet it is vitally present in the way Dryden takes hold of the factor of difference in translating from one language and culture into another. The discontinuity between the past and present is accepted, and then erased; also the sameness in difference and the larger emergent consciousness are presented joyfully and are focused in Dryden's articulated character. The utterance is both impersonal and a manifestation of a deep personal self-possession and self-knowledge on the poet's part.

"Possessing" the past in translation – and the associated sentiment in this ode of containing implacable natural forces associated with providence and fortune (e.g., lines 50–64) – bodies forth a vital and individual power over experience, even while the individual is in the midst of life, that is not open to the "gods." The capacity to undo what by all human logic appears to be finally done, to redeem the time, is at one with the self-acceptance, acceptance of the world, and the implicit forgiveness which marks Dryden's poetry and which I have already discussed. Just as the forgiveness advocated in the New Testament (e.g. Luke 5: 21–24, 17: 3–4) is capable of breaking the concatenation of the historical process, in which the individual feels victimized by fortune, and, just as it is capable of revealing character and establishing relationship, so does Dryden's encounter with Horace (and other poets) in translation. Johnson responds to this simple but complexly rich experience of Dryden's translations, at the level of tone and style – that is, at the place where the spiritual and the material, the mind and the body, and different levels and attitudes to rational and irrational experience are mysteriously but naturally blended.

The same paradoxical combination of mind and body informs Dryden's treatment of the issue of transubstantiation in the *Hind and the Panther*.[58] Dryden's lines on transubstantiation in *The Hind* (I: lines 134–40, 417–29) are disarmingly simple and honest: "literal sense is hard to flesh and blood" (I: lines 428). Yet he argues that if people can accept the mysterious truth that God became human, then we ought to be able to accept the same mysterious conjunction of physical and spiritual in the Eucharist without construing the "clearest words" with "frantick pain" (I: lines 138–39). His lines themselves eschew all temptation to be mystical or lyrical; they remain clearly focused on the empirical facts. Yet, seen in the context of his perception of the comprehensive relationship between human kind and nature in *Sylvae*, this suggests a consciousness of the spiritual mysteries in the material, sensible world.[59] Such a sacramental vision of nature accepts an infinite gap between an individual and divinity which human faculties by themselves cannot bridge, even while the faith which is the subject of *Religio Laici*, and permeates *The Hind and the Panther*, carries the conviction that divinity reveals itself to souls through – not in defiance of – their limits and their humanity. *Sylvae* reveals that mysteriousness abundantly, and at the same time demonstrates, as Johnson knows, that Dryden is often most religious when not talking directly about religion.[60]

The "Life of Dryden" may be free of explicit philosophical or theological apparatus, yet it goes to the heart of the matter by virtue of Johnson's capacity to establish a relationship with Dryden's poetic character in much the way Dryden approaches the poets he translates. It is with Johnson's insights, therefore, that I suggest that the transference and bodily presence that Catholicism stresses in the Eucharist, is close to both the spirit and the letter of Dryden's procedure as a translator. Dryden emphasizes the physicality of the meeting of "original" poet and translator, the possession of the translator by the genius of the poet, and the translator's containment of that power akin to a god and to the irrational forces of fortune (and the past). Dryden's understanding of cultural continuity is fundamentally related to his essential subject matter of the mutability of human experience and human institutions. Both of these general propositions suggest a closer link with a more ritualistic, Catholic understanding of the Eucharist, whose teleology is action, rather than with the more symbolically commemorative understanding of the Christian mystery in the Anglican communion, which might be said to appeal more to the mind. Metonymically, the presence of the Holy Spirit (the fire essential in the process of translation) in the Eucharist, linking the celebrant with the universal church back to Christ (the Logos), is acknowledged and recreated in the translator's containment of the genius of the Other, opening up the past, and revealing most fully the humanity of both. As Dryden says of Chaucer: " . . . for mankind is ever the same, and nothing lost out of nature, though every thing is altered" (Preface to *Fables*; Watson, II: 285).

Conclusion

Howard Erskine-Hill has argued that one of the "defining characteristics of Jacobite writing is that it inherited the full authority of what had been only recently most central and orthodox doctrine, but, with the sudden revolution of power, could not express such doctrine with the old openness."[61] But, whereas Pope wrote political satire in response to this state of affairs, Dryden translated. Most of Dryden's major post-1688 works are translations, or, like the poems to John Driden, Kneller, the Duchess of Ormond, and Congreve, "Alexander's Feast," and some of the plays (such as *Don Sebastian* and *Amphitryon*), are works directly concerned with historicity, the translatability of the past, and political authority in a world in which the individual is open to forces more powerful than the self. I have tried to suggest how Johnson provides us with a basis on which to appreciate the peculiar importance in Dryden's poetic career of the very process of translation. While it is clear that after 1688 Dryden uses the authority of the Catholic church, and the spiritual confidence it sustained, as a basis from which to reflect on the illegality (as he saw it) of William III's rule, Johnson shows us how integral to that issue is the integrity and quality of Dryden's poetry as poetry.

The translations of Dryden's last fifteen years, and especially the *Fables*, dramatize the central paradox of Dryden's poetic character, the main subject of Johnson's "Life of Dryden." That is, that now standing on the outside of the political establishment, and witnessing the collapse of his political and cultural ideals of the 1680s, his grasp of experience becomes more inclusive and more accepting as he deals explicitly with the temporality of the political process, and feels the individual's powerlessness and smallness in history.[62] By the late 1690s the whole issue of political authority was up for discussion. If, as William Myers argues, *The Hind and the Panther* reveals a belief that the indifference of parochial English political life to the more humane European philosophy of Catholicism threatened an extinction of civilization, then Dryden felt it morally incumbent upon himself to find alternatives in the poets he translated.[63] The very act of translating, for Dryden, becomes one of political defiance and self-definition, because it locates in the experience of the classical authors an authority other than that of the political and social present. Their authority is now possessed by Dryden. Dryden acts as a kind of sacrificial medium, becoming both sacred and profane in bringing into being a new knowledge of the heart transforming political and historical understanding.[64] The character Johnson sees is one in which feminine and masculine are finely integrated, and the integrity of that mind – combining strength of language and suppleness of feeling – testifies to Dryden's acceptance of his situation and to a great love of life. Johnson clearly detects that love of life, and – in the very tone and contours of his own prose – reflects its deeply comic nature. The comedy is Dryden's complete acceptance of the foolishness and variousness of human nature, and of the historical nature of experience. As with Chaucer, Erasmus, Montaigne, and Johnson himself, Dryden's response to human-kind's vulnerability to the indifference and material independence of the world, is to embrace these things more fully, to see suffering and change in a long, comic perspective, mysteriously depriving them of their threats and anxiety, because of their place in the flow of time and experience.

> Thus are their Figures never at a stand,
> But chang'd by Nature's innovating Hand;
> All Things are alter'd, nothing is destroy'd,
> The shifted scene, for some new show employ'd.
>
> *Mycene, Sparta, Thebes* of mighty Fame,
> Are vanish'd out of Substance into Name.
>
> All suffer change, and we, that are of Soul
> And Body mix'd, are Members of the whole.
>   ("Of the Pythagorean Philosophy," lines 386–89,
>   635–36, 672–73)

Dryden's translations, and especially *Fables*, are in fact perfect Johnson material: like the *Rambler* they deal with problems of human consciousness, with the nature and the limits of experience, and with the roots of civilization in the irrational; like the *Lives of the Poets* they deal with the nature and the limits of human artifice and memory, and affirm the historical nature, and the infinite repetitiveness, of all reality. The *Lives*, too, embody a structure similar to the *Fables*; not only are different sections of individual lives played off against each other in a process by which the character of the poet is articulated, but different "Lives" are brought together in an ever-changing, ever-present apprehension of reality – " . . . for mankind is ever the same, and nothing lost out of nature, though every thing is altered." Johnson responds so well to Dryden because he is as clearly in possession of that nature as Dryden is. However, neither *Fables* nor the *Lives* proposes a final meaning for history, nor, indeed, any meaning at all, other than that of the experience embodied in, and recalled by, the various artifacts. The *Lives* also stand on the outside, conscious of the absence in English culture of the late eighteenth century of anything comparable to Dryden's *Fables* and translations, which operate in the *Lives* as a touchstone of the natural. Only now, in the 1770s and '80s, there is a sense that the translation of nature from the past into the present is less possible, and that – almost in opposition to Johnson's religiousness – the grace that Dryden was simply able to accept, has to be labored for by Johnson. None the less both writers derive a similar empowerment and express a similar love by creating works that demonstrate that all history and all experience are nowhere if not in the present moment.

Notes

1 Part of this essay is based on a paper ("What *Did* Johnson Think of Dryden's *Fables?*") given at the ASECS conference, New Orleans, 1989. I wish to thank the section chairman, Cedric D. Reverand, for suggesting how the paper might be improved. I particularly wish to thank Professor Reverand, in his capacity as Cambridge University Press manuscript reader, for his careful and sympathetic reading of my work, and for his suggestions for improvement. Of course the work as it now stands is my responsibility. I am grateful as well to the National Endowment for the Humanities for financial support by way of a summer fellowship, which gave me time to write this essay. I should also like to take this opportunity of remembering my friend, the late Dr. Christopher Macgregor, who first taught me to read and to love Dryden.

2 E.g., see Jean Hagstrum, *Samuel Johnson's Literary Criticism* (Minneapolis: University of Minnesota Press, 1952), and Leopold Damrosch, Jun., *The Uses of Johnson's Criticism* (Charlottesville: University of Virginia Press, 1976).

3 René Wellek, *A History of Modern Criticism 1750–1950. I: The Later Eighteenth Century* (London: Jonathan Cape, 1955), pp. 79–104; F. R. Leavis, "Johnson as Critic," *"Anna Karenina" and Other Essays* (London: Chatto and Windus, 1967), pp. 197–218, and "Johnson and Augustanism," *The Common Pursuit*

(London: Chatto and Windus, 1952), pp. 97–115; W. R. Keast, "The Theoretical Foundations of Johnson's Criticism," *Critics and Criticism*, ed. R. S. Crane (Chicago: Chicago University Press, 1952), pp. 389–407; W. J. Bate, *The Achievement of Samuel Johnson* (New York: Oxford University Press, 1955); and Paul Fussell, *Samuel Johnson and the Life of Writing* (London: Chatto and Windus, 1972).

4 Damrosch, *Uses*, pp. 168–190; Lipking, *The Ordering of the Arts in Eighteenth-Century England* (Princeton: Princeton University Press, 1970), pp. 443–48. I am told that James Winn read a paper entitled "The Intuitive Accuracy of Johnson's 'Life of Dryden,'" at the 1984 MWASECS conference, but I have not seen a copy of it.

5 Damrosch, *Uses*, p. 149.

6 David Hopkins' *John Dryden* (Cambridge: Cambridge University Press, 1986) is an exception. Johnson is integral to his understanding of Dryden, but the brevity and the "introductory" nature of his book curtail a thorough critical use of Johnson.

7 See my review of *John Dryden and His World*, *Eighteenth-Century Studies*, 22 (1989), 602–06.

8 The "Life of Pope" should ideally be taken into consideration in a discussion of Johnson's thinking about Dryden, but wider treatment of the *Lives of the Poets* lies beyond the scope of this essay, and I reserve it for my forthcoming *Writing Memory: The Integrity and Paradox of Johnson's "Lives of the Poets."*

9 E.g., see the extracts on Dryden from Dennis, Congreve, Pope, Gray, Joseph Warton, Malone, and Scott in *Dryden: The Critical Heritage*, ed. James and Helen Kinsley (London: Routledge and Kegan Paul, 1971); Mark Van Doren, *John Dryden: A Study of His Poetry* (Bloomington: Indiana University Press, 1920 and 1967), pp. 233–66 ("Reputation: Conclusion").

10 Quoted from *Lives of the English Poets*, ed. G. B. Hill, 3 vols. (Oxford: Clarendon Press, 1905), I: 469, from which all subsequent quotations from the *Lives* will come, and be identified in the text by paragraph number.

11 Boswell thought that "in drawing Dryden's character, Johnson has given, though I suppose unintentionally, some touches of his own" (*Life of Johnson*, ed. G. B. Hill, revised L. F. Powell, 6 vols. [Oxford: Clarendon Press, 1934–64], IV: 45). See Greg Clingham, "'Himself That Great Sublime': Johnson's Critical Thinking," *Etudes Anglaises*, 41 (1988), 165–78.

12 I discuss the art and general nature of Johnson's literary biography in the forthcoming *Writing Memory: The Integrity and Paradox of Johnson's "Lives of the Poets."* James Osborn (*John Dryden: Some Biographical Facts and Problems* [New York: Columbia University Press, 1940], pp. 25, 28) and Lipking (*Ordering of the Arts*, p. 443) feel that Johnson did not make every effort to find new material on Dryden, and this is implicit in Winn's *John Dryden and His World*. Damrosch (*Uses of Johnson's Criticism*, pp. 168–69) and Maximillian E. Novak ("Johnson, Dryden, and the Wild Vicissitudes of Taste," *The Unknown Samuel Johnson*, eds. John J. Burke, Jun. and Donald Kay [Madison: University of Wisconsin Press, 1983], p. 72) point out that Johnson's response to the paucity of biographical information on Dryden was to emphasize what Dryden's writing revealed of

his mind. The question, however, is what *kind* of mind or genius did Johnson find in Dryden's work and how does he do this? My extended answer to this question entails the realization that Johnson would have shaped his "Life" as he did, and emphasized the relationship between Dryden's mind and work, no matter how much new biographical information he had.

13 E.g., see K. J. H. Berland, "Johnson's Life-Writing and the *Life of Dryden*," *The Eighteenth-Century*, 23 (1982), 197–218.

14 *Rambler* 188 (*Yale Edition of the Works of Samuel Johnson*, vols. III–V, ed. W. J. Bate and Albrecht B. Strauss [New Haven: Yale University Press, 1958], V: 220–21.) The echoes of Johnson on Falstaff are noticeable; see *Rambler* 72 (*Yale Works*, IV: 15).

15 While in the Hebrides, Boswell reports Johnson as saying:

"I do not myself think that a man should say in a dedication what he could not say in a history. However, allowance should be made; for there is a great difference. The known style of a dedication is flattery: it professes to flatter. There is the same difference between what a man says in a dedication, and what he says in a history, as between a lawyer's pleading a cause, and reporting it."   (*Life*, V: 285–86)

16 John Dryden, *Of Dramatic Poesy and Other Critical Essays*, ed. George Watson, 2 vols. (London: Everyman, 1962), II: 290. (This work cited subsequently as Watson.) Johnson quotes Joseph Trapp (*Lectures on English Poetry* [1742], p. 348) on the wrongness of Dryden's comparison (para. 202). Yet even Trapp's point conveys a sense of Dryden's empathic connection with his material ("What was in hand was generally most in esteem.").

17 In "Of Dramatick Poesy: An Essay" (1668) Dryden writes of Shakespeare:

... he was the man who of all modern, and perhaps ancient poets, had the largest and most comprehensive soul. All the images of nature were still present to him, and he drew them not laboriously, but luckily; when he describes any thing, you more than see it, you feel it too. Those who accuse him to have wanted learning give him the greater commendation: he was naturally learned; he needed not the spectacles of books to read nature; he looked inwards, and found her there.   (Watson, I: 67)

Johnson emphasized this essay, and particularly Dryden's portrait of Shakespeare, when he wrote that "the criticism of Dryden is the criticism of a poet ... where the author proves his right to judgement, by his power of performance" (paras. 198–99).

18 Addison's prose is described as "always equable, and always easy" ("Life of Addison," *Lives*, II: 149, para. 167). A significant critical and historical valuation lies behind Johnson's subtle differentiation between Dryden and Addison ("variety" versus "ease"), representatives in their prose style of two substantially different orders of civilization; see Greg Clingham, "Johnson and the Past," *Essays in Criticism*, 36 (1986), 255–63, and "Johnson on Dryden and Pope," Cambridge University Doctoral Dissertation (1987), pp. 86–89. "Ease," of course, is a key concept for Johnson, and describing Dryden as "equable and varied" as opposed to "equable and easy" does not mean that Dryden was without ease; see Clingham, "Johnson's Critical Thinking," *passim*.

19 Johnson echoes Dryden's own image of himself expressed in the Dedication to the *Aeneis*; see Clingham, "Johnson's Critical Thinking," 176. Could Johnson also have been responding to Kneller's famous portrait of Dryden, with his soft and gentle features? He would have seen it at the home of the Tonsons, for whom it was painted, and Samuel Derrick's edition of Dryden's *Miscellaneous Works* (1760) carried an engraving as frontispiece. See David Piper, *Catalogue of the Seventeenth-Century Portraits in the National Portrait Gallery, 1625–1714* (The National Gallery, 1963), p. 113, and Margaret Whinney and Oliver Millar, *English Art, 1625–1714* (Oxford: Clarendon Press, 1957), pp. 197–98.

20 For further examples of this kind of imagery to describe Dryden's genius, see paras. 196, 200, 221, 227, 334, and "Life of Pope" (*Lives*, III), para. 309.

21 As early as the poem addressed to Clarendon, "To My Lord Chancellor" (1662), Johnson identifies Dryden's mind as "at once subtle and comprehensive," and as containing "those penetrating remarks on human nature, for which he seems to have been peculiarly formed" (paras. 242, 245). In the light of Johnson's eventual association of Dryden's particular poetic character with developing and deepening religious experience associated (if not completely identified) with Catholicism, it is significant (as James Winn points out) that Dryden praises Clarendon, and designates his importance as a patron to the poets, by comparing him to the Pope and the poets to the various Roman Catholic orders (such as Dominicans and Franciscans) – "To My Lord Chancellor," lines 13–16. See Winn, pp. 126–27, and pp. 123–28 for Clarendon's political activities in 1662–63 and their connection with Dryden and the Howard family, into which the poet married.

22 Watson, II: 284, 285, 286.

23 See also the imaginative stroke by which Dryden compliments Anne Killigrew by specifying that "Thy Father was transfus'd into thy Blood" (line 25). My thanks go to Cedric Reverand for pointing this out.

24 To illustrate "comprehend" Johnson quotes the first two lines of Waller's "Upon the Earl of Roscommon's Translation of Horace, De Arte Poetica": "Rome was not better by her Horace taught,/Than we are here, to comprehend his thought." Quotation taken from *A Dictionary of the English Language*, 2 vols., 4th edn. (1773).

25 "Dryden's Chaucer," Cambridge University Doctoral Dissertation (1979).

26 *The Works of John Dryden*, by Walter Scott, 18 vols. (London, 1808), V: 186. In the light of the importance Johnson places on the revelatory powers of language, it is interesting that he mentions that Dryden "settled his principles of versification in 1676, when he produced the play *Aureng-Zebe*" (para. 264).

27 All quotations from *Sylvae* are from *The Works of John Dryden*, III, *Poems 1685–1692*, ed. H. T. Swedenberg, Jr., et al. (Berkeley and Los Angeles: University of California Press, 1969).

28 The similar sensuousness of the Virgilian episodes in *Sylvae* – especially "Venus and Vulcan" – were toned down when these were inserted into the full *Aeneid* in 1697. For an analysis of Dryden's Lucretian style see Emrys Jones, "A 'Perpetual Torrent': Dryden's Lucretian Style," *Augustan Studies: Essays in Honour of Irvin Ehrenpreis*, eds. Douglas Lane Patey and Timothy Keegan

(Newark: University of Delaware Press, 1985), pp. 47–63. On the sensuousness of Dryden's style see also Anne Middleton, "The Modern Art of Fortifying: *Palamon and Arcite* as Epicurean Epic," *Chaucer Review*, 3 (1968), 124–43.

29 Sir John Denham, "To Sir Richard Fanshaw Upon His Translation of Pastor Fido" (written 1643–64, ptd. 1648, pub. 1650), esp. lines 23–24, and The Preface to "The Destruction of Troy" (1656) (*The Poetical Works of Sir John Denham*, ed. T. H. Banks, Jr. [New Haven: Yale University Press, 1928], pp. 144–45, 159–60).

30 "To Mr. Dryden, on his Translation of Persius," quoted from *The Satyrs of Decimus Junius Juvenalis: and of Aulus Persius Flaccus*, Translated ... by Mr. Dryden (London, 1726), pp. 233–34.

31 See Paul Hammond, "The Integrity of Dryden's Lucretius," *MLR*, 78 (1983), 1–23, who convincingly argues against the formerly commonly held view, expressed by Norman Austin ("Translation as Baptism: Dryden's Lucretius," *Arion*, 7 [1968], 576–602), and echoed by Miner in the California edition, III (pp. 276–81), that the heightened sensuousness of Dryden's version is a rhetorical means of damning Lucretius' atheism in order to assert a Christian perspective. Both Hammond and Jones ("Dryden's Lucretian Style," pp. 48–50) demonstrate that the seriousness and imaginative sympathy of Dryden's Lucretius is integral to the success of the translation as poetry. (The California editors, Miner and Austin, see Dryden's attitude to Horace in similar terms to the way they see his attitude to Lucretius [pp. 293–94], but, in fact, Dryden discovers as much of himself in Horace as he does in Lucretius, by entering into Horace's imaginative world.) For Lucretius' reception in seventeenth-century England, see W. B. Fleischmann, *Lucretius and English Literature 1680–1740* (Paris: Nizet, 1964), esp. pp. 138–41, 227. Fleischmann suggests that "Dryden's view of Lucretius coincided with the traditional humanistic acceptance of Lucretius the poet and rejection of the Epicurean metaphysics" (p. 227).

32 While Dryden adds the imagery to Lucretius IV: lines 1101–20, in the quotation immediately above, in the version of Books 2 (lines 1–61) and 5 (lines 222–34) he echoes what he finds in Lucretius, as he does with Horace's imagery of the same kind – in *Odes* I: 3 (lines 11, 19, 24) and III: 29 (lines 53–4, 61).

33 Hammond uses "equanimity" to describe Dryden's position ("The Integrity of Dryden's Lucretius," 8), defined by the *OED* as a "quality of being undisturbed by good or ill fortune, an evenness of mind and temper." Cf. also H. A. Mason, "Living in the Present: Is Dryden's 'Horat. Ode 29. Book 3' an Example of 'creative translation?'" *The Cambridge Quarterly*, 10 (1981), 91–129 (this journal subsequently cited as *CQ*).

34 E.g., see H. A. Mason, "Dryden's Dream of Happiness," *CQ*, 8 (1978–79), 11–55, and *CQ*, 9 (1979–80), 218–71.

35 Dryden's experience in translating many classical authors led him to say that:

> I have found, by trial, Homer a more pleasing task than Virgil ... For the Grecian is more according to my genius than the Latin poet. In the works of the two authors we may read their manners and natural inclinations, which are wholly different.
> (Preface to *Fables*, Watson, 2: 274)

36 I am indebted to Jo Ann Warren for helping me with the translation from Greek.

37 "Preface to Homer," *Twickenham Edition of the Works of Alexander Pope*, VII–VIII; *The Iliad*, ed. Maynard Mack (London: Methuen, 1967), VII: 9.

38 *Rambler* 92, *Yale Works*, IV: 124–25. In the "Life of Dryden" Johnson talks of Homer's "discriminative excellence" as being "elevation and comprehension of thought," and invokes the ancient poet's "solidity" and "massy trunk of sentiment" (para. 304).

39 Ruskin points out that that "thing" arising from between the separate, identifiable forms is by Homer called a god (*The Literary Criticism of John Ruskin*, sel. and ed. Harold Bloom [New York: Doubleday, 1965], pp. 77–78). Cf. George Steiner's remarks on Dryden's poem in *After Babel: Aspects of Language and Translation* (Oxford: Oxford University Press, 1975), pp. 64–65. For a full discussion of the literary and moral experience which went into making the "wisdom" of this poem "neither Hebrew nor Greek but simply human," see H. A. Mason, "The Hallowed Hearth: Some Reflections on Dryden's Version of the Ninth Ode in Horace's First Book," *CQ*, 14 (1985), 205–39.

40 Cf. Greg Clingham, "Johnson's Criticism of Dryden's Odes in Praise of St. Cecilia," *MLS*, 18 (1988), 165–80; and "Johnson, Homeric Scholarship, and the 'Passes of the Mind,'" *The Age of Johnson*, ed. Paul J. Korshin, III (New York: AMS Press, 1990), pp. 113–70.

41 The basic idea is Mason's, "The Hallowed Hearth," 208, and "Living in the Present," 98.

42 "Personality" is used by Jones (p. 52); it is implied by Winn in the psychological emphasis he gives to Dryden's activity of translating (pp. 395–97).

43 Many modern commentators speak of the *Fables* as "comprehensive," though they might not understand what Johnson does by the term. For a survey of modern criticism see Cedric Reverand's *Dryden's Final Poetic Mode: The Fables* (Philadelphia: University of Pennsylvania Press, 1988), pp. 1–10. Recent doctoral dissertations in Britain, not mentioned by Reverand, have also discussed the *Fables* illuminatingly: see Robin Sowerby, "Dryden's Homer" (Cambridge University, 1975); T. A. Mason, "Dryden's Chaucer" (Cambridge University, 1978); David Hopkins, "Dryden's Translations from Ovid" (Leicester University, 1979); and Richard Bates, "Dryden's Translations from *The Decameron*" (Cambridge University, 1983). A little of this excellent work has been published in Hopkins' *John Dryden*, pp. 168–200; "Dryden and Ovid's 'Wit Out of Season,'" *Ovid Renewed: Ovidian Influences on Literature and Art from the Middle Ages to the Twentieth Century*, ed. Charles Martindale (Cambridge: Cambridge University Press, 1988), pp. 167–90; and "Nature's Laws and Man's: The Story of Cinyras and Myrrha in Ovid and Dryden," *MLR*, 80 (1985), 766–80; and Tom Mason's "Dryden's Version of the *Wife of Bath's Tale*," *CQ*, 6 (1975), 240–56.

44 Reverand, *Dryden's Final Poetic Mode*, p. 126.

45 The phoenix imagery was drawn to my attention by Cedric Reverand.

46 Reverand, *Dryden's Final Poetic Mode*, pp. 164–84 ("Of the Pythagorean Philosophy") and pp. 203–19 ("Dryden's Final Poetic Mode"), esp. pp. 217–19.

47 Quoted by Johnson in para. 342 from Pope's Horatian Imitation, 2nd Epistle of the First Book, lines 267–69.

48 René Rapin, "A Comparison of Homer and Virgil," in *The Whole Critical Works, Translated by Several Hands*, 2 vols. (London, 1706), I: 116–210; Dominique Bouhours, *La Manière de Bien Penser dans les Ouvrages d'Esprit*, 3rd edn. (Amsterdam, 1703), p. 85; Nicolas Boileau, "A Treatise on the Sublime," *The Works, Made English by Several Hands*, 2 vols. (London, 1712), II: esp. 1–9; Alexander Pope, Preface to Homer (pp. 3–25) and notes to the Hector and Andromache episode of *Iliad* Book 6 (pp. 349, 355–56), in *Twickenham Works*, VII; Joseph Addison, *Spectator* 62, ed. D. F. Bond, 5 vols. (Oxford: Clarendon Press, 1965), I: 268. See also H. A. Mason, "The Founding of Modern European Literary Criticism," *CQ*, 11 (1982), 281–97; "The Founding of Modern European Literary Criticism. Part II: A Bundle of Letters," *CQ*, 12 (1983), 26–55; and "Rapin's Critical Reflections on Modern Poetry," *CQ*, 13 (1984), 93–128.

49 Reverand, *Dryden's Final Poetic Mode*, pp. 183–84 and 190–219.

50 Jones, "Dryden's Sigismonda," *English Renaissance Studies*, ed. John Carey (Oxford: Clarendon Press, 1980), p. 282.

51 Miner, *Dryden's Poetry* (Bloomington: Indiana University Press, 1967), p. 202. See also Greg Clingham, "Dryden's New Poem," *Essays in Criticism*, 35 (1985), 281–93, and Carl Niemeyer, "The Earl of Roscommon's Academy," *MLN*, 49 (1934), 432–37.

52 Louis L. Bredvold (*The Intellectual Milieu of John Dryden* [Ann Arbor: Michigan University Press, 1934]) and Philip Harth (*Contexts of Dryden's Thought* [Chicago: University of Chicago Press, 1968]) differ on the nature of Dryden's thought at this point in his career. Bredvold stresses its skeptical and fideistic side, and, on the basis of the philosophical similarity of the two main religious poems, argues that Dryden "was already in 1682 far along the road to the Roman communion" (p. 121). Harth minimizes Dryden's skepticism and argues that he maintains, throughout the 1680s, the same belief in reason as he did in his early career (p. 229). There is no evidence, he concludes, in the works immediately preceding Dryden's conversion, of the change to come (p. 230). Like Harth, Charles E. Ward assumes that Dryden was converted soon after the accession of James II (*The Life of John Dryden* [Chapel Hill: University of North Carolina Press, 1968], p. 215). James Winn has demonstrated the complex influences on Dryden in his conversion from Anglicanism to Catholicism, including the possible influence of the Howards, Elizabeth Dryden's family, in the 1660s and '70s (pp. 121–24, 563–64), and, later, that of Dryden's own sons (pp. 415–16).

53 For all Johnson's commitment to Anglicanism he thought Roman Catholicism "a religion of external appearance sufficiently attractive" (para. 119), and appreciated the spiritual claim of its ritual and liturgy, and the religious experience they facilitated:

> A man who is converted from Protestantism to Popery may be sincere: he parts with nothing: he is only super-adding to what he already had. But a convert from Popery to Protestantism gives up so much of what he has held as sacred as anything that he retains:

there is so much *laceration of mind* in such a conversion that it can hardly be sincere and
lasting.   (Boswell, *Life*, II: 105–06)

In 1784 Johnson told Boswell that "an obstinate rationality" had prevented
him from becoming a Catholic (*Life*, IV: 289). For Johnson's further defence
of Catholicism see *Life*, II: 104, 255; and IV: 289–91.

54 The testimony of the repentance Johnson refers to in remarking on Dryden's
   move away from the vulgarity of the early dramas is in Dryden's poetry:
   "What consolation can be had Dryden has afforded, by living to repent, and to
   testify his repentance" (para. 171), perhaps in such a poem as the Killigrew
   ode.

55 "Introduction to His Paintings," *Selected Essays* (Harmondsworth: Penguin,
   1972), p. 317.

56 *Yale Works*, III: 225 (Johnson quotes only lines 69–72).

57 *The Odes, Satyrs, and Epistles of Horace* (London, 1684), p. 124.

58 See Donald R. Benson, "Dryden's *The Hind and the Panther*: Transubstantiation
   and Figurative Language," *Journal of the History of Ideas*, 43 (1982), 195–208,
   who argues that the issue of transubstantiation in seventeenth-century religious debate implied an interest in the nature of substance itself (196), and,
   furthermore, that Dryden's acceptance of transubstantiation entailed a skepticism about the independence and ontological status of language (203–04). The
   paradoxical nature of transubstantiation – "the realm of material substance in
   space is independent and self-ordering, subject only to miraculous intervention
   by divine power" (206) – testifies to a faith that frees Dryden to accept the
   simple materiality of the world, such as is evident in *Sylvae*.

59 Hammond speaks of Dryden's "mystery of consciousness in a material universe," in "Dryden's Lucretius," 11.

60 Emrys Jones notes that the translations of Lucretius come midway between
   Dryden's two main religious poems: "Lucretius was notoriously the great poet
   of doctrinaire materialism and atheism, so that, poetically speaking, in passing
   from his Anglican poem (November 1682) to his Catholic poem (April 1687),
   Dryden chose to travel via the most coherently argued, most intransigent, and
   greatest anti-religious poetry of the Western tradition" ("Dryden's Lucretian
   Style," p. 47). That Dryden was prepared and able to give himself so fully to
   Lucretius in his poetry emphasizes how completely his whole religious experience was under scrutiny and revision.

61 Erskine-Hill, "Literature and the Jacobite Cause," *MLS*, 9 (1979), 17.

62 Cf. Reverand, *Dryden's Final Poetic Mode*, pp. 203–19, and Winn, *Dryden and
   His World*, pp. 500–13.

63 Myers, *Dryden* (London: Hutchinson, 1973), p. 127.

64 See Emile Benveniste, *Indo-European Language and Society*, translated by Elizabeth Palmer (London: Faber and Faber, 1973), who writes of the ambiguous
   character of the sacred as expressed in the relationship between the Latin
   terms "sacer" and "sanctus": "There is no sanction for the man who by
   touching the *sacer* himself becomes *sacer*. He is banished from the com-
   munity ... " (p. 455; and see p. 452).

Index